Eight Symphonic Masterworks of the Twentieth Century

Eight Symphonic Masterworks of the Twentieth Century

A Study Guide for Conductors

Leonard Slatkin

ROWMAN & LITTLEFIELD
Lanham • Boulder • New York • London

Published by Rowman & Littlefield
An imprint of The Rowman & Littlefield Publishing Group, Inc.
4501 Forbes Boulevard, Suite 200, Lanham, Maryland 20706
www.rowman.com

86-90 Paul Street, London EC2A 4NE

Copyright © 2024 by The Rowman & Littlefield Publishing Group, Inc.

All rights reserved. No part of this book may be reproduced in any form or by any electronic or mechanical means, including information storage and retrieval systems, without written permission from the publisher, except by a reviewer who may quote passages in a review.

British Library Cataloguing in Publication Information Available

Library of Congress Cataloging-in-Publication Data
Names: Slatkin, Leonard, author.
Title: Eight symphonic masterworks of the twentieth century : a study guide for conductors / Leonard Slatkin.
Description: Lanham : Rowman & Littlefield, 2024. | Series: Scores to settle ; volume I | Includes bibliographical references.
Identifiers: LCCN 2023047839 (print) | LCCN 2023047840 (ebook) | ISBN 9781538186794 (cloth) | ISBN 9781538186800 (paperback) | ISBN 9781538186817 (ebook)
Subjects: LCSH: Orchestral music—20th century—Analysis, appreciation. | Conducting. | Debussy, Claude, 1862-1918. Mer. | Shostakovich, Dmitriĭ Dmitrievich, 1906-1975. Symphonies, no. 5, op. 47, D minor. | Bartók, Béla, 1881-1945. Concertos, orchestra. | Stravinsky, Igor, 1882-1971. Vesna svi͡ashchennai͡a. | Gershwin, George, 1898-1937. American in Paris. | Copland, Aaron, 1900-1990. Appalachian spring. Suite. | Barber, Samuel, 1910-1981. Quartets, violins (2), viola, cello, no. 1, op. 11, B minor. Adagio; arranged. | Britten, Benjamin, 1913-1976. Young person's guide to the orchestra.
Classification: LCC MT125 .S57 2024 (print) | LCC MT125 (ebook) | DDC 784.2/0904—dc23/eng/20231020
LC record available at https://lccn.loc.gov/2023047839
LC ebook record available at https://lccn.loc.gov/2023047840

To the memory of my inspirational conducting teachers,
Jean Morel and Walter Susskind

"Leadership and learning are indispensable to each other."

—John F. Kennedy

"Music is a moral law. It gives soul to the universe, wings to the mind, flight to the imagination, and charm and gaiety to life and to everything."

—Plato

"You are always a student, never a master. You have to keep moving forward."

—Conrad Hall

"One ought, every day at least, to hear a little song, read a good poem, see a fine picture, and, if it were possible, to speak a few reasonable words."

—Johann Wolfgang von Goethe

"Conducting! A subject, truly, concerning which much might be written, yet scarcely anything of real importance is to be found in books."

—Anton Seidl

Contents

Preface	ix
Introduction	1
Claude Debussy: *La Mer*	3
Dmitri Shostakovich: Symphony No. 5	29
Béla Bartók: *Concerto for Orchestra*	53
Igor Stravinsky: *Le Sacre du Printemps* (*The Rite of Spring*)	81
George Gershwin: *An American in Paris*	117
Aaron Copland: *Appalachian Spring* Suite	141
Samuel Barber: *Adagio for Strings*	165
Benjamin Britten: *The Young Person's Guide to the Orchestra*	175
Bibliography	187
About the Author	191

Preface

> The real art of conducting consists in transitions.
>
> —Gustav Mahler

Conducting doesn't look all that hard, does it? We all do it, perhaps when a recording is playing on our phone, or when the radio emits a piece of music that we love, or even when we hear the rhythm of the construction equipment repairing the road. The infectious desire to be part of the world of sound is so strong that to some extent, we would all like to lead the band.

I do a little experiment every so often, one that can be performed with just one person or an auditorium of two thousand. Contending that the basic elements of conducting can be taught to most people in about ten minutes, I proceed to demonstrate the fundamentals as I interact with the audience. They stand up, learn a four-beat pattern, how to use the left hand, and how to put the right and left hands together. If there is an orchestra onstage, the dramatic conclusion of this activity has all the audience members leading the ensemble at the same time. The piece of music I select is either in two or in four, and I always choose something familiar to most everybody. Marches are particularly suitable for this exercise. By the time the excerpt concludes, we have produced many mini-Karajans.

Of course, conducting is not that simple. In fact, it is the final step for most musicians who venture out of their role as instrumentalists or vocalists. A score contains details on every page, in every bar, and in every note. The conductor must be prepared for any situation that may occur in rehearsal as well as in concert. The only way to accomplish that is to know the score inside and out.

I have written previously about what it is that the conductor does. How do we get into the profession? How do we study? What is the role of the music director, opera conductor, guest on the podium? I have also made a series of videos, available on YouTube (@leonard_slatkin) and at leonardslatkin.com, in which I demonstrate the basics, concluding with an examination of Beethoven's Seventh Symphony from the conductor's point of view.

In this series of essays, I take on the role of the devil, working out all the details. Short of having an orchestra in your living room—something I do not recommend—learning a score is one of the loneliest activities that exists. It is just you and the composer, and the only communication between the two of you is the music that sits on the desk. The person who wrote the piece has left you this last will and testament, and it is up to you to decipher who gets what.

Depending on your score-reading skills, this can be a laborious and time-consuming ordeal. Just as directors of plays must envision how the script will come to life onstage, so conductors must try to hear the music in their heads. No amount of score study at the piano can prepare you for the sonic world of an orchestra.

Each piece has its own profile and, as such, presents a new challenge every time you open the score. Sometimes the conductor adds copious notes and scribblings ranging from whether a note should be played long or short to essay-like musings on the meaning of a particular phrase.

The essays in this book are intended for those who are considering entering the conducting profession or are already on that path. At the same time, I hope that my insights into how a maestro learns the score and the techniques used to get the desired results might also be of interest to the general music lover or orchestral musician. If you have a little musical knowledge, most of what is contained in these pages will be understandable.

At first, I thought that trying to discuss interpretive matters would be counterproductive. I believed it might be more straightforward to present a universal set of rules for any given passage. But of course, music is all about what we feel and thus does not always lend itself to a one-size-fits-all approach. Therefore, I have tried to show several interpretive possibilities and solutions for corresponding problems, as each subjective decision will have a direct impact on how to conduct at a given moment.

Selecting pieces to examine for this series was not as difficult as I expected. I revisited the early days of my conducting education, when I pored over countless texts devoted to the oeuvres of single composers. I have chosen to focus on pieces that might come up in the first five years of a conductor's studies.

Moreover, I have purposely selected compositions that I have continued to conduct throughout my career. For more than half a century, I have lived with these works, first just as abstract dots and lines on a page and then as living, breathing organisms that have developed over the course of my life. Indeed, I have seen each of these pieces at the podium at least one hundred times, as a conservative estimate.

The reader should have the full score on hand, or at least on a computer screen, to understand the musical references in context and to annotate as desired. I am specific about the editions I use, and they are all readily available. Reference points are by bar numbers, or the rehearsal numbers/letters used in those editions. The International Music Score Library Project (IMSLP) is a particularly useful resource for downloading scores in the public domain, and the publishers' websites offer score previews of those works under copyright.

The pieces I have chosen are works that all conductors need to have in their repertoire. Some of them will come up very early in their career, and others only after several years of experience. The solutions for dilemmas posed by the seemingly easier pieces can also be applied to more complex works.

Always keep in mind that there is no one solution for any enigmatic spot. Each conductor is built differently and must never try to imitate anyone else. You may have to adjust your technique a bit, but if a gesture runs counter to your natural physiognomy, then you must reject the idea.

One final thought: The twenty-first century has given us equal footing when it comes to the opportunity to watch and listen to performance material from earlier times. It can be instructive to observe the great and not-so-great conductors to find out how they achieved their results. But under no circumstances are you to mimic them. You must find your own way, and to do that, one pertinent question needs to be in the front of your mind: "Why?"

Every solution should be the result of not only a thorough examination of how the orchestra sounds but also an analysis of why conductor X approached a passage one way and conductor Y another. A logical, musical reason must underpin every decision. Saying "I feel it that way" has no place in the conductor's—or any musician's—lexicon.

Each chapter concludes with a bit of housekeeping. When we finish conducting an exhausting work, it can be difficult to remember whom to acknowledge for solo bows. I have taken the first step in removing that hurdle by pointing out which musicians to recognize.

Let's dive in and begin our journey together.

Introduction

The development of orchestral music during the twentieth century required new conducting techniques to accommodate the ever-increasing technical difficulties presented to musicians. The addition of American music into the orchestral canon introduced a whole new set of musical idioms. As more composers incorporated multiple meters, numerous tempo shifts, and greater dynamic contrasts, the clarity of the conductor's beats and gestures became increasingly important.

The eight works selected for this volume all make some reference to music that came before the twentieth century. For example, *The Rite of Spring* looks back to Russian folk heritage, *La Mer* sees similarities to the works of César Franck, and even *An American in Paris* finds some of its roots in Jewish culture. Some of the pieces are abstract, such as Bartók's Concerto for Orchestra, while others are descriptive, like Britten's *Young Person's Guide to the Orchestra*.

Within this volume, I present guidelines for how to physically conduct the pieces, share tricks of the trade, and discuss interpretive possibilities that can be considered matters of opinion. Conductors have the unenviable task of making decisions bar by bar. In many cases, this means trying to decipher the composer's intentions when it comes to dynamics or a written instruction. I have tried to look at various solutions for certain spots that conductors have found troublesome ever since the pieces were penned.

Sometimes, especially when multiple solutions are possible, I explain what I do and, more importantly, why I do it that way. Ultimately, it will be up to the reader to determine the best formula to achieve the desired result.

I would like to thank Andrew Litton, David Loebel, Cindy McTee, Michelle Merrill, and Yaniv Segal for their help in editing the musical matters of each piece, and Leslie Karr for copyediting.

I hope you will find the information contained within these pages helpful. With good study habits, a strong work ethic, and ample time on the podium, you might just come up with better ideas and solutions than those presented here.

Claude Debussy: *La Mer*

Art is the most beautiful deception of all. And although people try to incorporate the everyday events of life in it, we must hope that it will remain a deception lest it become a utilitarian thing, sad as a factory.

—Claude Debussy

Nadar (6 April 1820–20 March 1910), Public domain, via Wikimedia Commons

Bridging the centuries, Claude Debussy is probably the composer who led the charge into the 1900s. Although written several years before *La Mer*, his *Prelude to the Afternoon of a Faun* (*Prélude à l'après-midi d'un faune*) presaged a new style of composition. This suggestive piece anticipated the harmonic language of Stravinsky while presenting a much wider palette of colors than had been heard before.

In general, most artistic movements begin with poetry and painting, and music tends to lag by at least twenty years. This was certainly the case with impressionism. By the time *La Mer* was first performed in 1905, Monet, Renoir, Sisley, and Bazille had been sharing their landscapes and scenes from contemporary life with the public for three decades. Those artists used quick, loose brush strokes and complementary colors to convey the fleeting nature of light in their paintings. Composers, on the other hand, had to find a different way to express the hues and contrasts captured in the visual art of their inspired colleagues.

In addition to the French impressionists, Debussy was also influenced by artists on the other side of the world. Japanese watercolors became a passion for him, in particular Hokusai's *Under the Wave off Kanagawa*, also known as *The Great Wave*. What does any of this have to do with how we conduct *La Mer*? Probably not much, but any information we can glean about the composer becomes useful at some point.

France did not have a tradition of composers writing works with "Symphony" in the title, with Bizet, Saint-Saëns, and Gounod being notable exceptions. Debussy also resisted that formal structure, subtitling *La Mer* "Three Symphonic Sketches for Orchestra." At one time, he did refer to it as a symphony, but the work really did not follow in the traditional path of pieces with that designation. Perhaps the Moderato—Scherzo—Finale design made it appear similar to Franck's D-Minor Symphony. It is also worth remembering that in his two books of preludes for piano, the titles Debussy gave to each piece only appear after the final bar, as the composer wanted the music to be descriptive in itself.

La Mer is all about the sound world, and therefore it is important to study the visual art of this era that influenced Debussy's aesthetic. It can help us understand the canvas of sonority Debussy creates and convey this to the orchestra. Initially, the work received a cool critical reception, but that may have been due to a poorly prepared performance by a conductor who was reportedly—shall we say—under the influence. It fared much better in London when the composer, who initially did not want to lead the piece, conducted it there in 1908. From that point on, the work has remained in the repertoire.

Two editions of *La Mer* were published during the composer's lifetime, the original in 1905 and another four years later. Most of the revisions are minor, but I will note a couple of them as we go along. At least one of these revisions has influenced my own interpretation enormously. For this discussion, I will use the 1909 Dover edition[1] with occasional references to the 2014 Bärenreiter.[2] In addition, you may wish to consult the 1997 Durand, edited by Marie Rolf, which can probably lay claim to being the most authentic.[3] You might also seek out the versions available on the International Music Score Library Project (IMSLP).[4]

La Mer is scored for two flutes, piccolo, two oboes, English horn, two clarinets (in A for the first two movements and B♭ for the third), three bassoons, contrabassoon, four French horns in F, three trumpets in F, two cornets in C, three trombones, tuba, timpani, bass drum, cymbals, triangle, tam-tam, glockenspiel, two harps, and strings. The cornets only appear in the last movement. We will discuss the glockenspiel a bit later.

The minimum string size for the piece is probably fourteen first violins, twelve second violins, ten violas, eight cellos, and six basses, although a bit more weight on the lower end cannot hurt. My recommended string size is based on a passage that comes up in the first movement. Debussy is kind enough to show us, four bars before **reh. 9**, that at least eight cellos are needed to play this passage. But look two bars later—sixteen of them! Let's discuss later.

Performance times generally fall near twenty-five minutes.

First Movement: De l'aube à midi sur la mer (From Dawn to Noon on the Sea)

It certainly looks clear enough to begin. The time signature is 6/4, and the tempo indication is *très lent*. However, the metronome marking of ♩ = 116 is hardly slow, much less very slow. Not for the first time do we find that what would normally be a tempo is actually more of a mood. This should be conducted, at least to start, with six beats in the bar. Nevertheless, I recommend that you try to get the feeling of two beats instead, even though Debussy does not say so.

A clear and precise downbeat is necessary to coordinate the double basses' pizzicatos. The timpani roll is misleading. Debussy certainly would not want each bar to be reattacked, so we can add ties. It is worth noting that the timpani's dynamic is *pianississimo* as opposed to the basses' *pianissimo*; the softest possible mallet should be used. Since Berlioz was probably the first composer to give specific instructions on this matter, I would have expected Debussy to follow suit, but he did not.

The physical placement of the harps depends on the acoustics of the venue. We usually see them somewhere in the back of the violin section. Photographs going back to the early part of the twentieth century often show these instruments at the front of the stage. Over time, as harps became more closely associated with music played by mallet percussion instruments, they moved back to be near that group.

I think the location of the harps is really a matter of taste, but the visual component is also important. Watching the harpists' fingers flying and hands wafting over the harp strings while their feet dance among the pedals can add something to a performance for the audience.

Being able to hear the bass pizzicatos equally with the second harp gives some extra harmonic meaning to these seemingly isolated notes; the pizzicato has a dot over it, so it should be played very dryly. We can see that Debussy put lines over the second harp but not the first. Many interpret this to mean that the principal harpist is shadowing their colleague and therefore playing just a slight bit softer. Hopefully you are getting the idea that what at first appears very simple on the page is not as it seems.

I suggest dividing the cellos by the stand, with the first stand playing the upper line, the second stand the lower line, and so on, so that the octaves sound equal. The same holds true for the violas. Try to avoid the natural tendency to crescendo as the line ascends. Do observe the subtle differences between the third bar in the cellos and the following two bars.

At the 4/4, the violins must enter with absolutely no accent. As with almost every composer, Debussy often leaves us in the lurch when it comes to dynamics at the beginning and end of a crescendo. We can see an issue already in the seventh bar. The violins clearly go to single *piano*, but what about the woodwinds? In the next measure, there is another crescendo, for one beat. Are we supposed to start at the dynamic from the earlier measure, or is it a continuation of what is already taking place?

As you can already tell, this piece requires a lot of unraveling. At the *piano* dynamic in the eighth bar, there is a line over the first note in the violin parts. What does that mean? Debussy uses this indication constantly but not consistently. In the ninth bar, we see it appear in the English horn and trumpet. The use of this line tells us many things. Here, it serves as a gentle accent, as there is a slur over the passage. In the next measure, the lines inform us that these notes are reattacked in some way, but the slur must mean that they remain legato and sustained.

If we jump to **reh. 1**, the same instruments are doing roughly similar phrasing, but this time we have dots instead of lines, as well as the instruction *expressif et soutenu*. This last word is different from the frequently used sostenuto, which means "sustained"; here it means "supported," a very unusual, somewhat vague choice. How these two passages are played, and if they are different, is something you may ponder for the rest of your conducting life.

If you wish to confound the musicians involved, ask them if they feel a difference should be made. All of a sudden, at least two players will have a little more respect for the conductor's job, assuming that you have come up with an answer.

Back to the line issue, the double bass part contains another one in the eighth measure that gives us a possible clue as to how Debussy wants us to interpret the stroke. He does not indicate this two bars earlier, which certainly signals that there is no accent or even stress on the note. When he elects to utilize it, it is almost like a very quiet sigh.

One last point about this small but important marking: It can be interpreted, in some cases where a tremolo is involved, to be a very slight lengthening of the attack, with the strings leaning in before starting to move the bow quickly. In any event, all the shivering sounds, especially when soft, need to be devoid of any hint of rhythm—fast but not nervous.

At **reh. 1**, we face another decision regarding the timpani. Is this note attacked separately, or is it a release from the lengthy roll that has been with us from the beginning of the work? I prefer the latter but have heard it with an individual stroke.

The question of mutes often comes up when dealing with the trumpets. I could spend the whole essay discussing this, but at least for this first passage, I recommend something that blends with the English horn. It should create a sound that makes us believe there is a new instrument, the English trumpet. A straight metal mute usually works, but you might also try a couple of alternatives.

Even though it is *più pianissimo*, the descending line in the cellos and basses should be clearly heard. Just when you thought we were through with the line issue, here it is again in the sixth bar after **reh. 1**, only this time, an accent is involved. Aha! We have learned something. The line is not played in the same way as the accent, because they appear together. My feeling is that we must add a slight stress on this note—but very discreetly—to give the attack just a bit of weight before commencing the tremolo. Will this hold up for both markings as the piece progresses? We shall see.

As noted earlier, Debussy gives us many detailed instructions but also seems to forget to supply information that we have to fill in. Six measures before **reh. 2**, we have a crescendo in most of the instruments but no indication as to what dynamic it reaches. This is further complicated by the woodwinds, who do not have the *subito pianissimo* in the next measure.

8 Claude Debussy: *La Mer*

Context is everything here. Until the 6/8 almost half a minute later, the dynamic does not increase beyond single *piano*. Yes, clearly the music will get louder than that, but this occurs later, so exaggerated dynamics would seem out of place at this point. Just a slight crescendo will suffice.

We have a true dichotomy at **reh. 2**. Conductors have struggled with the buildup to the 6/8 ever since the piece was written. Let's start with the two meters that occur at the same time, something still unusual at the turn of the twentieth century, although it was found in music by Wagner, Rimsky-Korsakov, and Berlioz, among others.

The harps will pick up the pattern established by the strings. But the first harp plays the notes as syncopations, which, when put together with the second harp, establish a series of eighth notes. This harp line must be thought of in four, just as was conducted previously; asking the first harp to try to play these notes against a six-beat pattern is fruitless.

I remember my teacher, Jean Morel, telling the first harpist not to watch him in this place but just to listen to her colleague, doing it by ear rather than sight. I can recommend a better way, but first I would like to draw your attention to what else is happening at this point.

The time signature for the winds is 6/4, just as we saw at the start of the piece. Your first decision is whether to return to the original tempo, thereby causing the harps and strings to play the figure slower than before, or to maintain the tempo dictated by the quarter notes in the four pattern. Debussy does not help us out here.

Common sense suggests that the tempo does not change because the harps are taking over for the cellos and basses. The 6/4, by default, is now quicker than it was at the start of the piece. In other words, the 4/4 tempo is ♩ = 116, but the 6/4 is ♩ = 172. How do we reconcile these two tempos in terms of our beat?

After what appears to be a few paragraphs of higher mathematics, and contrary to what my own teacher did, I go into two the bar before **reh. 2**. The beat is now ♩ = 58. The harp picks up the rhythm from the lower strings, and the clarinets have a full bar to feel how their notes fit in.

Whew! Glad that is out of the way so that the remainder of the movement can flow easily. Not so fast.

The instruction at this point says, *Animez peu à peu jusqu'à l'entrée du 6/8*, which in my French 101 class meant to gradually get faster until you arrive at the 6/8. But at this landing point, we discover that ♪ = 116, the same number of beats per minute specified at the start of the piece! In other words, ♩ = ♪ here. I believe, in this case, that *animez* is a feeling of restlessness rather than a speeding up of the tempo. Almost every conductor I have heard stays in the same tempo throughout or only moves ahead slightly. But perhaps a few think of this as a sudden return to the opening tempo rather than one that is derived from the *animez*.

Although you are conducting in two at **reh. 2**, the underlying quarter notes of the instruments playing in four must be in your head. The transition should be smooth and not feel at all like a tempo change but rather a shift to a new sound color. Please note that some of the musicians make a long crescendo and others return to *piano* in each bar.

As if this were not enough, look at the timpani part. It looks like a trill from an A to B. Although I have never heard this done, perhaps it is possible that one of the percussionists, none of whom have played anything yet, could play the A, and then we would have two rolls occurring at the same time. Just thinking out loud here.

There are two ways to get into the 6/8: You can either just go from two to six directly, or you can subdivide the last two quarter notes of the 4/4 grouping. The latter option shows everyone the tempo that is coming up. The majority of the musicians playing are only looking for the downbeat. Debussy does not want us to drag and says that the rhythm should be supple and smooth.

Divisi passages are a critical part of almost every score by this composer, and you must be prepared to tell the strings how you would like to split the various lines. Sometimes the composer will specify how to divide the players, and other times he does not. Marking the parts in advance is always a good idea.

Six measures before the double bar, Debussy starts building his crescendo by adding more strings bar by bar. I ask the players to divide on the stand, inside players on the lower line and outside on the upper line. This should change at the *Modéré*, but not for all the sections. Second violins continue as they have, but the violas are best served with the pizzicatos played by the last two or three stands, depending on how many you have at your disposal. The cellos' lower line is very important, as it continues the pattern established during the triplet of the second beat. To hear those rich low notes, I usually tell those musicians not to make much diminuendo, and I divide the cello line by alternating stands.

Two measures before **reh. 3**, the woodwinds play an octave apart, and often the upper register of the flute is too loud for the clarinets. In the next bar, the second harp takes the lead, probably starting out *forte* and with just a slight diminuendo.

At **reh. 3**, the horns take over, expressive and sustained. The fourth bar finds them coming up to a *subito mezzo forte* but still muted. Debussy allows for this by having the strings play *pianissimo*. The sheer number of sixteenth notes in the accompaniment can often cause those playing them to increase the volume; do not let this happen. The oboe and cello soloists should not need to force to be heard, and the bassoonist will also appreciate not being covered.

At the start of the flute solo, all the strings are divided into four parts, with the first violins and cellos playing pizzicato. Do this passage once with just the strings and second harp to ensure that their lines are equally balanced. The actual divisi is up to you, although I recommend that those playing the syncopated rhythm be seated together.

Two bars before **reh. 5**, the winds go back to single *piano* in the middle of the bar, but the next bar is a crescendo leading to the *au Mouvt*. The early editions surmise that the two measures should be alike in terms of dynamics. At **reh. 5**, the violins and violas play the thirty-second notes on the string at the tip of the bow. The cellos do the same but are also instructed to play over the fingerboard. Even though they are marked *pianissimo*, the two flutes have a rhythm that is different from anyone else.

The motion winds down a bit at **reh. 6** and we see *Cédez un peu* without a metronome indication; in this case, hold back a little. The inflections in the oboe and flute are clear, but the second harp line has another of those anomalies that can be frustrating—a slur over the bar but also dots on each note. Are we supposed to stop each note or let all six of them ring? I interpret these as pizzicatos with vibrato, and the slur is just to show that this is one phrase. With no dynamic to guide us, you can choose how loud the crescendo should be in the second and fourth bars.

A solo violin has the tough job of getting to the high C♭ in both the fourth and fifth bars of **reh. 6**. Some will play it as written, even with an expressive vibrato; others choose the safer and more reliable natural harmonic. I prefer the latter, as it adds a nice color that we have not encountered yet. These five bars are under the spell of the *Cédez un peu*, which can be a slight problem when placing the final pizzicato before **reh. 7**. Both a line and a dot appear over this note, perhaps indicating that some vibrato is needed.

I assume that every time the words *au Mouvt.* are written, the metronome marks of ♩ = 116 or ♪ = 116 are in play. Clearly, Debussy wanted to give some formal structure to a freeform work. Including the opening, we either start or return to this tempo seven times. Looking at the *au Mouvt.* spots individually, however, without referencing any of the others, leads to the understanding that some of these passages should be a little slower and others quicker. **Rehearsal 7** provides us with the understanding of this concept, as it echoes a similar flute passage heard previously. Nevertheless, the music at this point is just a bit livelier than the opening tempo.

When you follow the printed dynamics, the flute solo should cut through the orchestral texture without a problem. It has become common practice to add a little ritard to end the phrase during the 9/8. Make eye contact with the tuba player for the entrance on that low note five measures after **reh. 7**, especially since it is marked solo.

The violin entrances six bars after **reh. 7** are usually played *forte-piano*, but it is certainly possible to play them more gently and accomplish the one-beat diminuendo indicated. The woodwinds can perform the thirty-second-note figurations with some exaggeration to the hairpins. The next few measures are often done with an *agitato* feeling to them as the tempo increases just a little.

At **reh. 8**, the big question here is whether to stay in six. While the muted trumpets can easily place their duplets against your beat, it is a different matter for the harps and cellos. My advice is to do the same as at **reh. 2**, going into two halfway through the first bar of **reh. 8**. Each of these measures has most of the instruments making a crescendo for the full length. The *mezzo forte* just lets you know where you are at that point; it is not a *subito* dynamic.

There is a very interesting difference between the manuscript and printed editions at the *Retenu*. In Debussy's handwriting, the woodwinds have eighth notes followed by eighth rests rather than quarters. This is certainly worth trying at rehearsal if you have time. Debussy's original rendering makes it clear that the strings' notes are played with a very strong attack followed by a diminuendo each time. This is not a *forte-piano*, as is often heard. We do not know, but can surmise, that the grace note is played on the beat.

At the *a tempo*, you can exaggerate the accent in the second violins and violas, and then add another light accent in the next bar. This can continue for those groups who have the syncopation against the tremolos. The suspended cymbal should be played with the softest mallet possible. Just before the 4/4, Debussy writes eighth notes for the cymbal as opposed to the previous quarters. Most conductors let the sound ring a bit, but you could also make the case that these last strokes should be shorter.

We now come to one of the most unusual requests from any composer of any piece of music. Two bars before **reh. 9**, the manuscript clearly says that sixteen cellos should play this passage. Debussy even goes to the trouble to say who plays on what line; I wonder if this has ever been observed. Earlier in the movement, passages are divided into four parts, but Debussy gives no indication of the number of players he requires for this piece. At most, orchestras today might have twelve cellists, but more than likely, that number is either ten or eight. Before we delve into the complexities of what else is going on, we must figure out who plays what. And this, like all the divisions in the piece, needs to be determined well in advance, lest most of the rehearsal time be spent assigning individuals to specific parts.

If your orchestra has eight cellos, it is probably best to have each stand take one of the lines. With ten cellos, it becomes more complicated to divide the four parts in a way that balances the voices. This is not an easy passage in terms of intonation, so I ask the first three players to take the top line and assign the second line to cellists four and five, the third line to cellists six and seven, and the bottom line to the remaining three players. The cellists playing the two middle lines might need to play out a bit more than their colleagues.

If approached carefully, the two bars before **reh. 9** can be truly magical. Several layers of sound are going on simultaneously, and you must pay attention to each. The cellos start *piano* before making a strong crescendo to *sforzando-piano*, which must occur quickly to let the other instruments take over. On the second beat, the timpani and double basses enter. The timpanist will be the only one making a crescendo while the others reduce the dynamic.

Unmuted horns give a sharp entry and come down quickly to allow room for the timpani crescendo. Although the score indicates a top dynamic of *piano*, I think you can allow the timpani roll to be a bit louder than that. Meanwhile, the cellos fade out, and the horns have a hairpin, meaning that they get stronger as the timpani gets softer. You can be very free with the tempo for these two bars, giving the effect of no meter at all.

At **reh. 9**, I recommend encouraging the cello ensemble to rehearse on their own to establish consensus about how to phrase this passage, although you should certainly be present when they do. There are many alternatives, especially regarding where to insert some space. Because the horns are usually quite far away, they can get behind, so you really lead them more than the cellos. As far as the phrasings are concerned, even though Debussy writes *Très rythmé*, I think you can exercise some flexibility in terms of moving forward and holding back over these measures.

In one edition, the cellos play until the pizzicato, but Debussy's manuscript, as well as the 1909 edition, have the horns taking the last few notes, which is the only feasible way to perform this. Everything is straightforward until the *au Mouvt.* at **reh. 10**, where the tempo should be a little livelier, but not much.

Three bars after **reh. 10**, you must judge the crescendos in the first violins and cellos based on the dynamic that results when the second violins and violas enter. Often, we hear a huge, virtuoso display, which seems jarring. If you need to, for the sake of clarity, you can pull back slightly at **reh. 11**. From here, a very extended ritard takes place, so be careful not to get too slow too soon. As the tempo continues to relax, another important decision confronts us. Should the string figuration, particularly the sixteenth note at the end of each three-note group, be played more slowly as the passage progresses? Most conductors keep the quicker pace but just for this single note.

The violin line at **reh. 12** needs to be considered in the context of what will occur at **reh. 13**. Both sections will go into a four-part divisi, but you have to divide this earlier for continuity throughout the whole passage. In my experience, it makes sense to split it up by stand, with the first two players taking the top line and the next two the bottom line. The same is true for the violas at **reh. 13**.

One measure before the *Très Modéré*, I recommend conducting the first half of the bar with two beats and then subdividing the second half to indicate the note changes. These notes have dots as well as slurs, which helps justify that choice. However, some literalists believe that Debussy would have wanted the off-balance feeling of two against three—your call.

Another stroke of genius occurs in the orchestration at the *Très Modéré*, which must be conducted in six. I think that the metronome mark of ♩ = 104 is a bit too fast, but that is purely based on instinct. A general rule of thumb dictates that when a passage is marked for two string players to play the same notes, it should instead be played by either one musician or three musicians for intonation reasons. Here, however, the duo coupled with the English horn creates a truly remarkable sonority. As with the earlier trumpet/English horn passage near the beginning, aim to create a new sound. I ask the other string players to play with vibrato. The grace notes in the flutes are usually played on the beat, but slowly.

While we are on the subject, let's talk about these ornaments. It is very important to remember something you might have learned earlier in your musical training. There are two types, the acciaccatura, played before the beat, and the appoggiatura, played on the beat. In French music of the impressionist school, the distinction can make all the difference in the world, so go through the score and examine each one carefully.

How can you tell the difference? The one with the slash on the stem is the acciaccatura, falling before the beat. Simple? Not really, because in many instances the slash could mean that the ornament is played very quickly with no reference to where it is placed. Be forewarned that Debussy is not always consistent; sometimes, we just have to use our best musical instincts.

The *très lent* at **reh. 14**, with a tempo of ♪ = 80, is conducted in eight and can be drawn out so that all the harp notes are audible; this also means bringing up their dynamic a little. Three bars later, even though it says *cresc. molto*, most conductors will peak at the single *forte* that begins the next measure. Please look at the horn dynamic in the second and third bars. They have a hairpin, which lends itself to a question that will have a tremendous impact when this music returns near the end of the third movement. Is the *piano* marking in the third measure a result of the diminuendo or is it a *subito* dynamic? I will get to this later.

I highly recommend you explore the New York Philharmonic's digital archive, which includes hundreds of scores marked by conductors.[5] You can glean a lot of very interesting information from this resource, and I bring it up at this point for a specific reason.

At what was once called Avery Fisher Hall, the conductor's dressing room housed a framed page of the score we are discussing here. It documented a substantial orchestration change made by Toscanini, in his hand, starting one measure before **reh. 15**. What makes this change particularly interesting is that Toscanini was thought to be a literal interpreter prone to sticking to the text. Rather than detail his amendments in these pages, I will allow you to find this passage yourself, and along the way, you can also see a few other conductors' thoughts about *La Mer*.

The 2/4 bar is conducted in four and is followed by a 3/4 bar in six but beat as if there were fermatas on each note. When the trumpets, trombones, timpani, and cymbal enter, many conductors have changed this *fortissimo* to a *forte-piano* to create a huge wave of sound. Once again, the grace notes are on the beat. The final note of the timpani is a release from the roll and not a reattack. Take plenty of time before moving on to the next sketch.

Second Movement: Jeux de vagues (Play of the Waves)

Earlier in this essay, when I gave the instrumentation list, I said that we would be discussing the glockenspiel later; that time is now.

The score lists the glockenspiel above the harps, accompanied by an asterisk to indicate an alternative option, the celeste. When this work was written, the glockenspiel was common in many orchestral works.

I mention this because the glockenspiel that you know and love is not the one for which Debussy wrote. Rather, he composed for the *Jeu de timbres*, a box-like instrument containing a keyboard with hammers that strike metal bars to produce the pitches, kind of like a piano. This instrument, at least back in the day, was handy for playing fast passages, like those in *The Sorcerer's Apprentice*, for example.

However, very few of these keyboard glockenspiels still exist in the world today. One thing we can do to emulate the sound is to have the percussionist play virtually all the passages with a metal mallet, which requires great skill.

It would be helpful if the score told us that the cymbal part is played with a mallet throughout the movement. But if that is true, why does Debussy use the plural, *cymbales*, in the instrumentation list at the start of this movement?

Much of what I had to say about the first movement will also apply here as well as in the Finale. So, if there is a tremolo and a line is above the note, as in the violins' and violas' opening bars, the attack is played a little longer before moving to the faster stroke. Try to have the glockenspiel placed near the harps, even if it means separating that instrument from the other percussion. When you look at the second bar, you will see why I suggest that.

The metronome mark of ♩ = 116 is interesting, as this was the same that governed the beginning of the first movement. Divide one beat in half to arrive at the eighth-note value for the 3/8, which is conducted in three and not in one, as the composer's metronome mark suggests. If you subdivide the last beat of the 3/4, you will be right where you need to be for **reh. 16**. The trumpet triplets are the clue. But for you mathematicians, the numbers don't really add up.

Those pesky tenuto lines that keep appearing continue to be a necessary nuisance. Look at the sixth bar of **reh. 16**. What are these dashes under the harp notes? And how are those musicians supposed to crescendo over their two-note groups? The only way I have found to interpret this is to think of these notes as accents.

The markings at **reh. 17** only add to the confusion. Now there is an accent as well as the line over the tremolo. (My head is starting to hurt.) The principal motif is in the oboes, and this is a difficult passage for them. Your tempo is determined by the ability of these two musicians to clearly delineate all their notes. All the other instruments have to get out of the way.

The second bar of **reh. 18** brings to our attention the benefits of the keyboard glockenspiel. Mallet instruments were just coming into general usage when *La Mer* was written, and passages like this would have been difficult for the percussionists of the day. The use of the keyboard glockenspiel certainly explains the slur over the first two notes; even though the instrument did not have a pedal, it could distinguish between long and short notes.

Most conductors slow down a bit during the cello trills before **reh. 19**, at which point we return to 3/4 with a different speed indication, *Assez anima*. At first this seems confusing, but we have been conducting eighth notes in three and will now lead quarter notes in the same tempo. It might have been clearer if the composer had written ♪ = ♩ here. The physical appearance of smaller denominations makes us believe that those notes are faster, but in this case, they are not. Debussy could have stayed in 3/8, but I suspect he did not want the page to look quite so crowded. His metronome mark of ♩ = 138 is doable.

The word *léger* appears in the violins and indeed, they must play lightly, with subtle off-the-string strokes as appropriate. This is another place where rehearsing slightly under tempo can work well to clear up intonation difficulties. Earlier in this essay, I wrote about the placement of the harps and its visual impact on the audience. The glissandos at **reh. 20** perfectly illustrate that point. They always sound wonderful, especially if the second player can pick up the *mezzo forte* dynamic, so it seems as though just one instrument were playing. But they also present an opportunity for a lovely visual effect that can get lost if the harps are not placed on risers or located in front of the violins.

While we are on the subject, unless you play the harp or compose for it, learning and understanding the pedaling indications is difficult. Unlike the other orchestral players, the harpists, at least in chromatic music, cannot sight-read. If the composer has not specified how a passage is to be played, the harpist must determine the pedaling in advance. The closest parallel is the layout of the percussion instruments and the planning the principal of the section does to decide who plays what.

Sometimes the little things are just that: little. But they can be annoying when we are studying and then trying to explain to the musicians what we want. Look at the triangle in the second bar of **reh. 20**. Until now, almost all the grace notes have been on the beat, and as before, Debussy gives us no indication as to where to place it. But here, he also includes a slur.

We all know that a slur is impossible on the triangle. Plus, there is a dot on the main note that follows. Most conductors play the grace note before the beat and then stop the instrument from ringing as soon as possible after the reattack. But the dynamic is *forte*, so the color is very important. I suggest a medium-sized instrument with a slightly larger-than-usual metal stick.

The dynamics six measures before **reh. 21** present some confusion. The simple solution is to have the horns follow the dynamics of the cellos. So, they are at *mezzo forte* four measures before **reh. 21**, continuing the crescendo all the way until the third beat three measures before **reh. 21**. Then they make a diminuendo for the next two bars.

Some conductors perform **reh. 21** exactly as written, but the majority tend to slow down slightly before the *Cédez un peu* that appears two bars later. Note that the eighth notes in the flutes and clarinets are not played short.

At **reh. 22**, Debussy wants us to get back to the *au Mouvt.* gradually, over four measures, as we approach the double bar. Again, we have *Cédez*, this time taking us down to around ♩ = 112. It always sounds faster than it is because of the flurry of thirty-second notes. Some, including me, let the horns and trumpets continue the crescendo right until the cutoffs.

I wonder why the run two measures before **reh. 24** is divided between the two flutes and then the two clarinets. It could be worth a try with just one musician if the players can do it.

The *au Mouvt.* at **reh. 25** is *subito*, a sudden speed shift of ♩ = 112 following the *Animez*. Once again, we can see from the two-note phrasing that Debussy intended to use the keyboard glockenspiel.

For a lovely, expressive touch in the cello line six measures after **reh. 25**, ask them to do a portamento between the last note of the bar and the A. I also fondly remember another portamento that we used to hear all the time, five measures before **reh. 26** between the G and B in the first violin line. Some conductors also hold back this bar just a smidge.

A ritenuto does not need to precede **reh. 26**, but something like a *subito poco più mosso* might be helpful. If the horn and trumpet triplets do not sound light, even at *forte*, the character of this section will feel out of place. Even though lines are present over the eighth notes, most conductors play them on the short side.

En serrant means pressing forward, so **reh. 27** marks a very slight accelerando for six bars. A few conductors barely move, which makes the transition into the *au Mouvt.* seem like a continuation of the tempo at **reh. 25**. Or, you can increase the tempo a little and then hold back. Let the second horn have a moment of sunshine by bringing out the grace note five bars before **reh. 28**.

After playing them so many times, the strings might automatically assume that these tremolos also have a line above them; they do not, and the fast stroke should commence right away. Meanwhile, be sure to bring out the harps. We then move ahead aggressively for four bars, only to hold back again at **reh. 29**. The octaves in the harps are played arpeggiated, but the arpeggio indication stops after three bars; we can assume that it continues. These octaves need to be played quite loudly at first and should never disappear.

This is a rather dramatic section with all kinds of marvelous nuances. Take, for example, the violin pizzicatos, accompanied by the words *à vide*, an unusual instruction that means open string. Debussy also adds a *sforzando* on the notes, which are doubled in the stopped horns. Then, the lower strings answer by playing a dotted half with a line over it on the downbeat. You can put a bit of an accent here, but it cannot be as strong as its predecessors.

As an aside, but perhaps a needed one: You will likely encounter words in other languages that are not clear, and this can be particularly problematic when they have a different definition in everyday life than in music. The Boosey & Hawkes website has a helpful glossary of musical terms in Italian, French, and German.[6]

There is a discrepancy in the articulation between what the violins have two bars before **reh. 31** and the similar phrase in the clarinet two measures before **reh. 30**. In addition, the violin divisi are inconsistent in that the two lower lines have slurred trills, but the upper line does not. I think the slithery sound is effective and recommend adding the trill indication in all three parts.

For a change, Debussy tells us exactly how to achieve the *animé* at **reh. 32**. We have six bars to get from ♩ = 112 to ♩ = 138. We also must figure out what he wants from the horns. Each of their entries is marked *piano*, but their lines contain overlapping hairpins. You can consider having the second horn take over the dynamic from the first. The grace notes should be played before the beat.

The climactic section of this movement begins at **reh. 33**. We must always be aware of the tempo, because it becomes a blurry mess if the accelerando occurs early. If you are confident in your orchestra's abilities, you can slip into a one-beat-to-a-bar pattern in the fourth measure of this phrase to convey the almost waltz-like nature of this moment. Since we have not started moving forward yet, the steady tempo should provide the security to do this. You will have to resume conducting in three by **reh. 35**.

Sometimes it is difficult to know whether the violins should play on or off the string. You just have to follow what seems either practical or musical, and that might go against what you see on the page. From **reh. 35** onward, your brain will be on overdrive trying to figure out what the upper strings should do. You might see a line on the first of a group of three notes followed by dots on the others, or the score might not provide any indication at all.

I could spend hours—and have—going through each phrase in this way. We must come to some sort of conclusion as to how they are played, not only because this is the right thing to do but also because we must have an answer should a musician ask about it. Occasionally, you can get away with saying, "Whatever you prefer," but only if it does not affect the overall character of the moment.

Four bars before **reh. 37**, we experience a true wave of sound coming from the harp. The score says *glissando sur les 2 mesures en croisant*, but surprisingly, at least to me, only one player does this. Basically, it is a series of cascading chords performed several times in each bar, with the hands literally crossing each other. Opinions are divided on whether the second harp should also join in, but the manuscript does not specify that the glissandos are played by a single player. I have asked several harpists about this, and all of them have indicated that they double it.

All this bustle leads to the only *fortississimo* in the movement at **reh. 38**. As the ritard commences, the first two sets of pizzicatos can be quite violent, especially since the composer indicates a crescendo. Depending on how agitated your tempo has become, you must get back to the ♩ = 138 by the time you reach **reh. 39**. Aside from the harps, the orchestration is quite different from when this material first appeared at **reh. 20**. I cheat just a little for the second set of glissandos and play them a bit softer than the first time, as if the waves were slightly subsiding.

Balance all the little details so that the various moving notes sound equally soft. Debussy makes it clear who is to play which notes for the solo violins at **reh. 41**. Some conductors slow down for this entire last section, but Debussy writes out the tempo relaxation, so I see very little reason to hold back. The suspended cymbal can ring for just a little while, and you can delay the final cutoff until the sound has sufficiently died away.

Third Movement: Dialogue du vent et de la mer (Dialogue of the Wind and the Sea)

Two cornets enhance the orchestral forces for this movement. Debussy does not add them for volume but rather to present some contrasting material. While rarely utilized these days, cornets impart a markedly different sound from their cousins.

Since they never duplicate the musical material of the three trumpets, I place the two additional players in a position away from their colleagues. If you choose to do this, you will need to know where the trumpets are seated and whether enough space can be found to separate them. (By the way, the same can hold true for the five players in Strauss's *Ein Heldenleben*.)

The instruction *Animé et tumultueux* conveys that this will be something dramatic. The meter is 2/2 and the ♩ = 96. Starting in the distance, the timpani and bass drum should have a similar quality. Personally, I want these first cello and bass entries in duple time to sound ominous.

The tam-tam should be of large size but played here with a medium mallet. With this instrument, often you do not hear the attack right away. But since the tam-tam dynamic is not *pianissimo* like the other instruments, we can consider its notes as tiny syncopations. A diminuendo will occur naturally after the tam-tam is struck, so I wonder why Debussy bothered to put that in.

Also new to the orchestral proceedings is the contrabassoon, which makes an entrance that should be audible to the listener. The third bar of **reh. 43** contains several markings to observe carefully. The double basses have the instruction *sur le chevalet*, the French equivalent of *sul ponticello*, which can be interpreted in various ways. If the bow is almost on top of the bridge, the pitch of the note can be obscured; conversely, if it is too far from the bridge, the creepy effect can be lost. The other string groups will have to do this later in the movement, so you might as well establish the sound you want as soon as possible.

The *sforzando* in the oboes and clarinets can be a little aggressive, but you must exaggerate all the swells and relaxations. If the oboes have a problem playing in tempo in the third bar, more than likely they are not thinking about that rhythm in advance. When you get to the eighth bar, ask the woodwinds to crescendo through the whole long note and not cut off on the downbeat. This makes the pizzicatos most effective, as they should sound like the result of that crescendo.

If you need any further proof of whether a grace note comes before or on the beat, consider the oboes five measures before **reh. 44**. Debussy could have written an appoggiatura for the English horn and clarinets in the previous bar but chose a sixteenth instead. I suspect the main reason was to provide a written distinction that could only be interpreted one way. The acciaccatura of the grace note is before the beat.

Several crescendos return to *pianissimo*, and you have to make those big enough to have an impact. The horns have an interesting moment the bar before **reh. 44**. The second and fourth play the grace notes on the beat and have a crescendo, but it is not clear how long these last. When the other two players come in, they pick up the note an octave higher but seemingly do not get louder.

Interestingly, Debussy's manuscript does not show a crescendo for anyone, and I have heard the note played as a straight *forte* in some performances. I prefer to keep the dramatic tension by adding the crescendo in the printed version to the first and third horns as well, with a very strong and abrupt cutoff just after the bar line.

The bar before **reh. 44** is marked *sur la touche*, which is the opposite of *sur le chevalet*. The soft tremolo benefits from the lean sound when the bow is truly on the fingerboard. Five bars later, Debussy employs an ingenious orchestration device, but often it doesn't sound like I imagine the composer conceived it. Basically, the key shifts from what sounds like C minor to major, but the only instruments making a note change are the three bassoons. Be very careful with the dynamics here. Everyone starts *pianissimo* and has the same hairpin, but the trombones tend to sound louder, so ask them to deemphasize this. One subtle nuance is that the timpani has a roll over two notes, F♯ and C♮, rather than just one, à la Stravinsky.

Most conductors let the crescendo before **reh. 45** reach at least *forte* before the very sudden and somewhat frightening ponticello. Debussy does not include a dynamic to guide how loud each crescendo is supposed to be, but probably around *mezzo forte* works best. In the third bar, the horns should take a short breath before reattacking the printed A. It is permissible to change the timpani notes to G♯ here so they fall within the key signature.

As a young music student, I was always surprised by how many conductors sped up during the three bars before **reh. 46**. Maybe it is a natural tendency for the strings to accelerate after playing the sixteenth notes. A loud thwack in the timpani one measure before **reh. 46** precedes a *fortissimo* pizzicato in all the strings.

The next bar is a complete change of mood and color. Debussy provides no indication in his manuscript of any type of pause before commencing. However, as far as I can tell, after listening to at least twenty recordings, every conductor waits before starting **reh. 46**. Most wait for a duration that can be characterized as a grand pause, sometimes amounting to more than a full measure of silence. I suggest you do the same.

We also find what has to be one of the longest descriptive indications in any piece of music: *Cédez très légèrement et retrouvez peu à peu le mouvement initial.* In other words, relax very slightly and return to the opening tempo, which really means start a little slowly and move ahead until **reh. 47**, when you are back up to speed. This amounts to a fifteen-bar accelerando. If you begin with a tempo of ♩ = 84 or so, you will only need to increase the speed by ten to twelve more clicks. Proceed cautiously.

The lower strings should be rhythmically stable, which is worth rehearsing on its own, adding in the accelerando later. The woodwinds can play with very slight rubato but only within an individual measure, or else the coordination with the other instruments gets thrown off. Because of the lengthy time required to get back to the original tempo, conductors often insert a little ritard eight bars before **reh. 47** and recommence the slower speed, making a second accelerando to get back to the *a tempo*.

When we finally arrive at the Tempo I at **reh. 47**, it is wise to have the first three stands of cellos all play the melodic line; it helps ensemble and intonation. As opposed to what the lower strings had at **reh. 46**, the first violins stay in triplets. This changes in the ninth bar and, although not indicated, the first note of the group is played short.

At **reh. 48**, the horns tend to bury the eighth note in the woodwinds; keep the former at single *forte* but exaggerate the crescendos in the second half of this measure and in the third bar. Regarding the violins, you can experiment with the bowing so that the last note of their rhythm is on an up bow. Do keep in mind that the first note of this figure has a line on it and is not short.

The scales at **reh. 49** lead to what seems to be a series of waves crashing on the rocks. The strings' rhythm beginning in the third bar is the same as at **reh. 11** in the first movement, but now it is violent and aggressive, making it more difficult to hear the sixteenth notes clearly. The horns can play with a brassy tone for each of their entries. The three grace notes are played by the English horn and piccolo before the beat. Five bars before **reh. 51**, you can make a huge crescendo prior to the *subito piano*.

Gesture somewhat wildly at **reh. 51**, as this is the high point so far in the movement. All the strings are ponticello, almost on top of the bridge, to produce a coarse sound. Four bars later, their pitches need to be heard clearly, but they still play *près du chevalet*.

About twenty minutes into the piece, the cornets finally get to make an entrance four measures after **reh. 51**. Since this is a new color—remember, a cornet does not sound like a trumpet, or at least it did not back in 1905—it needs to dominate. Should you choose to separate these two musicians from the three trumpets, the sound will come as a slight shock to the audience. The third trumpet player will have to remove their mute sometime before the entrance at the sixth bar of **reh. 51**. After playing just five bars, the cornets get to rest for a couple more minutes before their next entry.

Note that the lower strings change their bow position from ponticello to over the fingerboard at **reh. 52**. Conductors are divided about slowing down over these next eight bars. The argument for staying in tempo is that the composer does not indicate any change, and, to some degree, the motion of the notes makes the music appear more relaxed. However, from my perspective, the clarinet and bassoon notes prior to the *Trés soutenu* seem out of place at a quick pace, and this double bar sounds abrupt as a *subito*.

The real question to ask at the *Très soutenu* is, "Are these notes sixteenths or a slow tremolo?" Given the sustained tempo, and anticipating some rubato in the horns, I think a calmer set of unmeasured notes is appropriate here, as well as a few bars later. Other conductors opt for the printed sixteenths, but this can be difficult if any rubato takes place within these four-bar passages. Since my interpretation is to take this section slower, I go into four at the *Retenu* two before **reh. 53** and continue to conduct in four over the next six bars.

Rehearsal 53 really cannot be *au Mouvt.* in the sense of the tempo established at the start of the movement, as it parallels the passage six bars earlier and must certainly be the same. It is a reprise of the *Très soutenu*. Again, the *a tempo* is calmer than indicated. A rather large diminuendo starts five measures before **reh. 54**, and I usually continue to relax the tempo here. At this point, the basses play a sudden and loud pizzicato, followed by the other strings, who come in after the downbeat.

One of my teachers used to advise that it is more effective not to show this note to the musicians and audience; just give a strong downbeat and make sure that the players watch and listen to each other. He had a good analogy: "If someone hits you, your reaction is not to say, 'Ouch!' at the moment of impact, but rather as a result of the slap." It is quite dramatic if the orchestra can do it, but if they struggle to stay together, you may wish to dictate this note. You have to gauge the cellos' four-bar diminuendo very carefully, but I think that you should only start the fifth bar when the sound is at its most delicate.

Next is a chain of the most wonderous sounds imaginable, starting with the harmonic in the first violins. Debussy is quite specific that he only wants the outside musician of each stand to play, which is, in effect, a divisi with the inside player tacet; he also specifies only four basses but all the cellos. The cello line indicates sixteenth notes, but they may have trouble fitting in that rhythm with the rubato in the flute and oboe line. Notice that the cellos' first two bars begin on A♭ and then on D♭ two measures later; the only reason I can imagine for this is that Debussy wanted to connect the trill without a string crossing.

Even if we do not say anything, the cellos will add extra notes depending on the tempo you choose. If it is a steady undulation, it works. However, the harps cannot do this so easily. You don't want any feeling of rhythm here, so they just have to watch and listen. Debussy provides new instructions every two, four, or six bars. *Retardez* is familiar, but *Reprenez* is new to the *La Mer* vocabulary; it means resume, or in this case, return to the tempo.

The solo flute and oboe must create a sound that blends the two instruments, so that neither stands out; I like to call it the "floboe." Because they are producing the sound and are sitting side by side, it is up to you to let them know when they have achieved this balance. The sixteenth notes in the second violins and violas can be played freely. How you obtain the rubato is really a matter of taste, but technically, it is important to make sure that the second-violin pizzicatos are placed accurately. The woodwinds will need to take a little breath before resuming at **reh. 55**, but the other instruments continue to play with a small ritard.

A gradual *animant* returns us to the *a tempo* at **reh. 56**, but the only metronome marking we have seen so far in the entire movement is the one at the beginning. Most conductors hold back a bit here, sometimes playing this luscious moment *fortissimo* and broadly.

A new word for getting faster appears: *Serrez*. This can be a substantial accelerando, but some will take time before **reh. 57** while others will do the *au Mouvt.* as a *subito* tempo change. Debussy asks the violins to play with vibrato, making us wonder if they have not up to this point; of course, this is just a reminder, especially since both sections are on the G string. The *subito forte* five after **reh. 57** is a sudden reduction in sound. From this point, we have a series of two-bar phrases that diminish in volume each time. At this spot, Debussy's manuscript does not indicate *Retenu*, but all the printed versions do. You can subdivide the last triplet but note that the three quarters are slightly separated.

Beginning at *au Mouvt.*, all the grace notes are before the beat and played quickly. The hairpins can be interpreted in several ways; the problem is that we do not know at which dynamic to begin. There is very little time to start *piano*, crescendo, and come back down again. Consequently, most conductors simply start *forte* and diminuendo over the length of a quarter note. However, the horns have something to say about this four measures before **reh. 58**, as they have the same indication with the addition of a slur connecting two bars; perhaps it really is a quick up-and-down dynamic change after all.

Look who has rejoined the group six bars before **reh. 58**. Yes, the cornets are finally back, and they will be busy for the rest of the movement. As if to say, "Thanks for joining us again," the strings greet them with an aggressive *fortissimo* pizzicato.

The violas have the tune at **reh. 58**, and you will be surprised at how prominent the English horn seems to be, even though it is marked *pianissimo*. Five bars later, a brief exchange occurs among the first clarinet, first bassoon, and glockenspiel. The glockenspiel is answering the clarinet, but because of the timbre and octave differences, this moment never sounds as it looks on the page. Pay attention to the syncopated pizzicatos in the second violins and violas at **reh. 59**.

Now we come to the most hotly debated spot in the entire work, the "fanfares" that occur in the eight bars before **reh. 60**. You can look up the history, but we know that Debussy wrote them in the manuscript and then excised them for reasons unclear. Some speculate that these notes were used in a piece by a different composer, and he did not want to be considered a plagiarist. In the past, most published versions omitted the fanfares, but conductors nevertheless knew that they existed.

Some feel that the interruptions are intrusive. Toscanini, as well as others, managed to infuse these bars with plenty of energy without the additional material, making the passage quite effective. But the fanfares also inject a dramatic charge into a static section of the piece. I listened to twenty recordings, past and present, and found that it was nearly a 50/50 split among the conductors, spanning almost the entire recorded history of the work.

My preference is to keep the brass away for the first two of the original entries. Then I have them come in four before **reh. 60**, allowing the fanfare to be heard twice rather than four times. It feels right as a setup and builds the tension. Debussy might not have condoned this, but since there is no truly conclusive evidence of what he wanted, I feel it is fair game to try something different.

A Brief, Related Diversion

Since this eight-bar passage has been so controversial, I thought it might be interesting to learn who observed the fanfares and who omitted them. It was not feasible to listen to every conductor, but table 1.1 shows the results for several:

Table 1.1.

Conductors Who Included the Fanfare	Conductors Who Omitted the Fanfare
Ansermet	Toscanini
Stokowski	Szell
Munch	Martinon
Reiner	Ormandy
Dutoit	Frühbeck
Haitink (but French horns only)	Boulez
Karajan	Barenboim
Solti	Rattle
Dudamel	Bernstein

This at least gives you the idea that the discussion is ongoing.

The acoustics of the venue will determine if you need a slight pause before commencing the coda. If you do not perform the fanfares, it is possible to go directly into **reh. 60**, but if the brass are inserted, there might be cause for a slight space. From this point, the speed increases gradually, but judge this acceleration carefully, as the strings need to keep a steady rhythmic pulse.

In my long history with this piece, I have found that the double bar ten measures after **reh. 60** presents surprising difficulties. First, the winds and percussion have single *forte*, but the strings are marked *piano*; it can be done, but the strings almost always have to be reminded that they are not to match the same level as the others. The real problem is with the piccolo. Because its notes are in the upper register, they automatically project louder, sometimes to the point of making the piccolo line sound like a solo. You might need to point this out to the player.

Now we come to that glorious brass chorale that the horns played in the first movement. In my opinion, most conductors either misread what Debussy wrote or purposely change it; I am referring to the dynamics and length of the phrase. The text says it is to be played *très sonore, mais sans dureté*, which roughly translates to "very resonant but without harshness," or in other words, noble. The brass are marked single *forte*, and the other instruments are one dynamic less; the swells should be somewhat gentle and certainly not overdone.

Notice that four measures before **reh. 61**, the dynamic is the same single *forte* as when the passage began. Almost all the conductors listed in table 1.1 give it more punch, as if it were not part of the totality of the phrase. It is not for me to condemn all the distinguished maestros from the past, but if you go back to the first movement, you find that the similar passage in the horns is never played with a sudden increase in dynamic in the third bar.

So why do we hear what amounts to a *fortissimo* this time? Probably because it creates a "wow" factor when they let loose, not to mention that the brass need to take a breath. But in my experience, this takes away from the power of the sound at **reh. 61**, where Debussy tells us to be *fortissimo*. One high point here is enough for me.

The *Très animé* is just that, suddenly faster, but be careful not to let it get out of hand. At the second bar of **reh. 61**, the lower strings continue the stream of sixteenth notes, but the diminuendo cannot be so pronounced that the end of the bar is inaudible. Throughout this section, you need a very clear and precise beat, as so many entrances are syncopations.

Debussy introduces a new word in the *La Mer* vocabulary at **reh. 62**: *talon*, meaning that the cellos and basses play at the lower part of the bow, near the frog. You will find that it creates a sound that is both ominous and wonderful at the same time when coupled with the ponticello of the violins and violas.

Additional instruments gradually join to create the illusion of the crescendo, so it is not necessary to add much more volume when you arrive at **reh. 63**. Numerous musical ideas are present here, and you must decide which to bring out. I believe that the brass takes care of itself but should be in balance with the upper strings and woodwinds. Most of the time, it works without needing to be explained as adrenaline kicks in. Still, the second and third trumpets have something different from the others that is worth bringing out a bit. Also, the 1905 version contains different parts for the cornets at **reh. 63** that you may wish to consider.

Remember back at **reh. 54**, when I wrote about not dictating the offbeat pizzicato? The same advice applies to the final note of the piece. Maximum force is on display three bars before the end, with the strings playing a tremolo, not sixteenth notes. They have staccato dots on the two notes, but the winds do not. I suggest cutting off the orchestra directly on the downbeat, giving as strong a gesture as you can, with both arms slightly stretched out to the right and left. Do not move a muscle and let the timpani and strings play the last note on their own, with the timpani's grace note placed just before the beat. If you dictate this final note, it just does not have the same impact. Yes, it will seem a bit confusing to some members of the audience, but it conveys the essence of the dramatic scope of the entire work.

Conductor's Etiquette

This is one of the few major works that does not require any solo bows. You can, however, acknowledge the brass, woodwind, and string sections individually. The percussion will stand when the entire orchestra is up.

> Music is the expression of the movement of the waters, the play of curves described by changing breezes.
>
> —Claude Debussy

Notes

1. Claude Debussy, *Three Great Orchestral Works in Full Score: Prélude à l'après-midi d'un faune, Nocturnes, La Mer* (New York: Dover Publications, 1983).

2. Claude Debussy, *La Mer: Three Symphonic Sketches*, ed. Douglas Woodfull-Harris (Kassel, Germany: Bärenreiter-Verlag Urtext, 2014).

3. Claude Debussy, *La Mer*, ed. Marie Rolf, *Oeuvres complètes*, vol. 5 (Paris: Durand, 1997).

4. International Music Score Library Project (IMSLP)/Petrucci Music Library, https://imslp.org.

5. New York Philharmonic Shelby White & Leon Levy Digital Archives, https://archives.nyphil.org.

6. "Glossary of Musical Terms," Boosey & Hawkes, https://www.boosey.com/cr/musicalterms.

Dmitri Shostakovich: Symphony No. 5

The best way to hold on to something is to pay no attention to it. The things you love too much perish. You have to treat everything with irony, especially the things you hold dear. There's more of a chance then that they'll survive.

—Dmitri Shostakovich

See page for author, Public domain, via Wikimedia Commons

It seems harmless enough. All it says on the title page is Symphony No. 5 and then in smaller letters, "in D Minor"—no programmatic references, just 156 pages of music. For about half of my life, that is all I had to think about when it came to the Opus 47 masterpiece by Dmitri Shostakovich.

Then, in 1979, a book by the Russian musicologist Solomon Volkov called *Testimony* appeared, and all scholarly and interpretive hell broke loose. The supposed interviews with the composer called into question much of what we had taken for granted about his life, his views on politics, and his music. There was no hard evidence that the book was completely legitimate, and scholars have since determined that much of it was fabricated.

Nonetheless, everyone who had conducted, played, or listened to Shostakovich's music could never think about him in the same way. This was particularly true for the work we are about to analyze.

Usually, we do not need to know that much about the compositional history of a given work to produce a satisfactory performance. It is always a good idea to get as much background information as possible, but this does not often tell us how the piece should go. This time, it is different.

Shostakovich wrote the symphony in 1937, and the Leningrad Philharmonic premiered it in November of that year under the direction of Evgeny Mravinsky. The work was an astounding triumph for the still relatively young composer, eliciting an ovation that was said to have lasted for half an hour. But the backstory made the symphony's glowing reception even more impactful.

The year before the first performance, Shostakovich's opera, *Lady Macbeth of Mtsensk*, had not only created a scandal but also raised the hackles of Joseph Stalin, who found the music and subject matter brutal and unworthy of the Soviet people. After this stinging rebuke, Shostakovich withdrew his very adventurous Fourth Symphony, which had to wait twenty-five years for its first performance.

The Fifth Symphony represented "A Soviet Artist's Practical Creative Reply to Just Criticism," according to the anonymous commentator who gave it this informal subtitle, but privately the composer was telling friends that the Finale was a satire of Stalin himself, dressed up in heroic adulation.[1] Considering that *Testimony* was revealed to be—at least partially—fabricated, we really do not know the truth about any hidden meanings in the composer's output.

And this brings us to the interpretive problem of the work. Maybe during the composer's lifetime, the Fifth Symphony could be viewed as deliberately sardonic and unflattering, but at the same time, the work could be performed successfully without knowing anything about its history. That was how conductors saw it, for the most part, until *Testimony* came out. After its publication, all manner of messages were read into it, in particular concerning the tempos. We can experience, through recordings, readings as quick as forty-two minutes by Mravinsky to interpretations almost ten minutes longer by Rostropovich.

Now that we have a bit of background, let's delve into this endlessly fascinating piece and see what is possible as we learn how to conduct it.

I must warn you that currently, the score of this piece is not available on IMSLP due to copyright restrictions. Nonetheless, it is an essential part of any conductor's library, so I encourage you to seek out an inexpensive edition, perhaps from a second-hand music shop or a source such as eBay. It is also possible to view several versions on the New York Philharmonic Archives website.

Although there are several editions, they do not deviate significantly in terms of instruments, tempo indications, or metronome marks. The score I use is a reprint of the first Western version, published by Kalmus, but it has been out of print since the 1990s when Russia rejoined the Universal Copyright Convention. It does not contain measure numbers but has plenty of rehearsal figures to reference when telling an orchestra where to start, as well as what we can assume are the composer's metronome markings. The study score published by Sikorski and currently available through numerous retailers is comparable.[2]

The instrumentation is somewhat conventional for a work of the midtwentieth century. The woodwinds comprise two flutes and a piccolo, two oboes, two B♭ clarinets (the players change to instruments in A for the third movement), an E♭ clarinet, two bassoons, and a contrabassoon. Four horns in F, three trumpets in B♭, three trombones, and a tuba round out the brass section. The timpani part can be accomplished with just three drums, but most musicians have a fourth as well.

The percussion section requires four players performing on triangle, snare drum, cymbals, bass drum, and tam-tam. There are also mallet parts for glockenspiel and xylophone. The instrument listing indicates two harps, but many performances are done with a solo player. In addition, there is a piano part, and that musician also plays the celeste.

Shostakovich does not indicate any particular number of string players, but I think this symphony requires at least twelve first violins and perhaps no less than six double basses to get through the wall of sound produced by the other musicians in the loud passages.

The duration of the work is approximately forty-five minutes.

Movement One (Moderato)

The tempo indication is Moderato, ♪ = 76. This feels about right to me, but some conductors take it quite a bit slower. For the purposes of this discussion, let's assume that all the violins are massed together on your left. With the lower strings on the right, you only need to use your right arm to conduct the opening. Give the first two beats strongly, making sure the musicians understand that no one plays on the downbeat. Then bring your left hand into play for the violins. Keep your eyes on the sections involved but try not to turn your head too much.

This is a vehement introduction, and therefore your beat must carry the weight of the world in it. Throughout the symphony, you will see double-dotted thirty-second notes followed by a slurred single note with a dot over it. In Shostakovich, this always indicates a separation before the one fast note. The slur is just a signal to continue the same bow direction. Sustain as long as possible to maximize tension before making that break.

A crescendo leads into the third bar, but is the landing note long or short? I believe this depends on whether you think the opening is a two-bar phrase or one that continues over the next two measures. Shostakovich tends to write in long lines, so I always play that third-bar downbeat long, making the eighth rest part of the continuing phrase. The diminuendo should continue until **reh. 1**, where the lower strings can play almost *pianissimo*. The thirty-second note and corresponding dots have disappeared, and we are entering legato territory as the violas make their initial appearance.

Conductors who take these first few bars slowly usually speed up a little at **reh. 1**, with good reason. If the opening is appropriately lugubrious, the violins might run out of bow when they begin the tune. Since their marking is *piano*, I ask them to play expressively, putting in the occasional hairpin to keep the feeling flowing. At **reh. 1**, I go into four. It may just be psychological, but if the orchestra sees too many beats, it can distract from the long line you are trying to achieve; try to connect the whole line during this time through dynamic shadings.

Some relaxation can occur during the two thirty-second notes two bars before **reh. 2**; however, the sixteenth must be strictly observed. I go back to beating in eight in that measure.

At **reh. 2**, build the crescendo that leads to the tremolo, but when you arrive, do not come down right away; sustain the *forte* dynamic for one eighth note before starting the diminuendo. You might have to tell the second violins to wait until they have heard the sixteenth in the firsts before starting their own tremolo. A precise and clear beat is necessary for the bassoon entry to ensure tight ensemble with the low strings.

There is some debate as to what happens with the downbeat eighth note three bars before **reh. 3**. The violins certainly appear to have a reattacked note, but I think this goes against what else is occurring. So, I put in a tie, connecting the tremolo to the next bar and just releasing the fast notes rather than reiterating the C. This helps continue the long line by making the second violin passage part of the previous phrase. Stay in eight here for quite a while.

I have often heard conductors take a little time before the moving line one measure before **reh. 3**. Again, I think that it breaks up the line too much, and the first note is a dotted eighth, meant to be played long. At the third bar after **reh. 3**, it is difficult to imagine that Shostakovich wanted the flutes to appear as suddenly as it looks on the page. To that end, I ask the first violins to make a crescendo to *mezzo forte* on the repeated As.

Having written about the need for a long line, I should also acknowledge the importance of taking the occasional breath to impart a song-like quality. This can be accomplished, for example, after the first note of the fifth bar of **reh. 3** and then again following the B♮.

Shostakovich presents many alternatives for interesting phrase groupings, and you should consider all the possibilities. One of the most important of these occurs in the second bar of **reh. 4**. To highlight the dramatic nature of this passage, I ask the first violins to retake the down bow for the high A while allowing the flutes to breathe so their attack on that note can be strong. The Fs three measures before **reh. 5** can be played slightly haltingly so that the first *fortissimo* of the piece has more impact. I remain in eight during this passage and going forward.

The oboe seems to have the tune just before **reh. 6**, but it soon becomes a part of the harmony, supporting the bassoon and cello lines. Melodic material gets handed off from one group of musicians to another in many instances; make sure that they each come out distinctly. It may be instructive to rehearse the first horn, two bassoons, and two oboes alone starting three bars before **reh. 7**.

The trumpets make their first appearance with the pickup to the third bar of **reh. 7**. Their sixteenths should be short and played at the specified single *forte* dynamic. Lower horns and cellos need to dominate here, and marcato should be the order of the day. It is possible to go into four a few bars earlier, but I prefer to stay in eight to instill more tension in the beat.

The second bar of **reh. 8** brings us back to the music of the opening measures. To give it emphasis, I start the upbeat to that second measure on a down bow and then retake it at the bar line. Once again, since there is no dot, the final note in the strings can be sustained.

The horns bring us to the second theme, but there is a minor problem to solve before that tune begins. You will see a dotted line in the middle of the bar before **reh. 9**. There is also a metronome marking, and it is now in terms of quarter notes instead of eighths. Stay in eight for the first half of the bar and then switch over to four, resulting in a total of six beats here. Often, the conductor will simply keep the same tempo, with the eighths and sixteenths staying more or less the same, but the metronome setting tells us that it should be just a bit faster.

The instrumentation list specifies two harps, and at this point in the score, Shostakovich calls for *arpe*, the plural, so he clearly knew what he wanted. However, one harp can suffice to bring out this new color, as both instruments play the same music. Whether you have one harp or two, the line is meant to be played *non arpeggiato*.

The rhythmic figure in the strings shows a slur as well as dots on the eighth notes. This is more for phrasing than an actual bowing, although in this case, the two eighths are clearly on an up bow. The slur tells us that they should not be played particularly short; you could easily take the slur out and put lines on them. You must rehearse this so everyone agrees on the exact length.

There are myriad ways to express this passage, and you should find your own, making sure that the long violin line is not interrupted by any accents. Even though it is difficult, try to sing it, and perhaps the shape will be revealed. Everything proceeds as expected harmonically, except for the change of chord on the second beat, four measures before **reh. 11**; this should not sound like a mistake. A beautiful key change occurs at **reh. 11** itself, best accomplished by having everyone make a diminuendo just before the bar line.

The piccolo note needs to be unobtrusive, even though it is marked at single *piano*. Any musician who takes up this instrument will have a different limit on how softly they can play this B♮, and you need to find out where that is to properly gauge the relaxation just before this entrance. Four measures before **reh. 12**, I find it helpful to have the first violins take a breath after the first beat and then play the A in the next measure as a harmonic.

When confronted with three- or four-note pizzicatos marked *unis*—as occurs three bars before **reh. 12**—the top note almost always falls on the beat unless indicated otherwise by the composer. There is a potential balance problem at **reh. 12**: the lower line of the violas should equal the cellos, which is best achieved by dividing the viola part on the stand and emphasizing that moving line.

At **reh. 13**, I take some expressive liberties for what is one of the darkest moments of the movement. The clarinets and bassoons have three rearticulated notes. I have them take a breath before the last one and then make a little crescendo to the downbeat of the next bar. In addition, I relax the tempo a bit to accomplish the following effect.

I ask the cellos and basses to enter ultra-*pianissimo* and without vibrato so as not to really hear their attack. Instead, they are just there when the woodwinds cut off. The same applies five bars before **reh. 14**. Meanwhile, the flute solo is played *a tempo*. At **reh. 14**, I have the flute take a breath before the low D♭ so it almost sounds like a new phrase when the violins enter.

The repeated B♭s in the upper range can be held back if you wish. Once you have indicated the cutoff in the horns, it is not necessary to conduct the solo clarinet. At **reh. 15**, the string color is different than it was in the corresponding earlier passage; the notes must be the same length, but now they are *pianissimo*. However, the harps dominate slightly, with a dynamic a degree louder.

When I was a student, I played both piano and viola, but not at the same time. The viola passage here was always met with dreaded anticipation. Would I be able to get the high E♭ anything close to being in tune? What kind of sound would I produce? Is there anyone else in the section who can play this? It is just one of *those* places. No amount of rehearsing can fix it if the individuals are not capable of performing it with the correct sound and intonation. As a conductor, you want to be encouraging here, but you will know early in the rehearsal process whether it is worth your while to spend lots of time on this spot.

At **reh. 17**, Shostakovich changes the metronome mark and introduces the piano to play the rhythmic motor along with the cellos and basses. Is this both a *subito forte* and a *subito più mosso*? The difference between the previous indication of ♩ = 84 is not that far from the new one of ♩ = 92. I have gone back and forth about this transition. In the past, I have made a slight accelerando and crescendo in the cellos. More recently, I have favored a *subito* change in tempo and dynamics. After the cellos almost fade away, the new *forte* entrance can come as much more of a shock if it is sudden.

Shostakovich includes an interesting instruction for the pianist: *una corda secco*. He appears to want a slightly muffled sound, and this makes sense to help balance that instrument with the pizzicatos. These should all be played quite vehemently, emphasizing the militaristic nature of what is now commencing.

It is rare for the first and third horn to play in the lowest of their registers, but that is exactly what occurs in the third bar. With all four horns in unison, single *forte* is more than enough power. The same dynamic applies to the trumpets, although I wonder why Shostakovich did not ask the third to join in.

There are four different metronome marks ranging from ♩ = 92 to ♩ = 132 between **reh. 17** and **reh. 27**, as well as a two-bar stringendo before the new tempo marked *poco sostenuto*. Is this actually a written-out accelerando? The same thing will occur on an even larger scale in the Finale. I do not think that I have ever encountered a performance in which the conductor suddenly gets faster with each new metronome mark, and I suggest gradually increasing the speed before an abrupt shift at the *poco sostenuto*.

Remember that piano entrance that is played using the left pedal? The composer does not tell us where to go back to normal, so we must identify a place to do this. I have found that one bar before **reh. 19** works well, and I also add a slight crescendo in that measure. The notes in the treble clef three measures later need to create a different tone color.

A very dry and somewhat aggressive pizzicato from the first violins comes at **reh. 20**. Of utmost importance is making sure that the horns only start the phrase before **reh. 21** at single *forte*. The crescendo that follows should be exaggerated, but the basic dynamic is still just *forte* with the occasional interruption.

I have not touched on discrepancies or errors in the score and parts, but they exist in virtually every edition. **Rehearsal 21** is a good example. Some scores show the upbeat E♮ in the first violins in the same octave as the accented downbeat in the next measure, and in my view the only way to achieve the accent is to play the upbeat an octave lower than printed, so I usually make this change. Other editions resolve the issue by eliminating the accent.

Rehearsal 22 has a very instructive marking: *Allegro non troppo*. This reminds us that however we have chosen to deal with the increasing metronome marks, there is still a long way to go. At this point, the trumpets are marked down to *mezzo piano*, but everyone else has increased their sound level quite dramatically. The string passage starting from the third bar is usually played staccato. The accents on the quarter notes do not necessarily mean that these are to be played marcato. I like the weightier sound of long tones here, as well as at **reh. 24**.

By this time, it is entirely possible that everyone will have forgotten how to phrase the dotted eighth followed by a sixteenth with a dot, and **reh. 23** is a good place to remind them. At **reh. 25**, the upper strings should now play on the string. Again, the horns are only single *forte*, but we can help this passage by putting in a slight diminuendo during the half note, which is then followed by a searing crescendo.

Believe it or not, the trombones and tuba have not yet played one note in this symphony. It is a good idea to get their attention and cue their entrance before **reh. 27**, at least at the first rehearsal. The percussion usually have no problem with this entrance, but getting the tempo right can be tricky. After an initial playthrough of the movement, my usual practice is to start rehearsing directly at **reh. 27**. If everyone knows what the tempo will be, then the transition is much easier to accomplish.

Poco sostenuto at **reh. 27** is not *a tempo*, but at least we have a metronome mark to help us out. Assuming that we have accelerated to somewhere in the ♩ = 140 range, the downshift should be just enough for everyone to realize that not only has the mood changed but the speed has as well. This section has always struck me as being quite sarcastic, so I exaggerate that quality by putting in a slight *forte-piano* in the trumpets two measures before **reh. 28**. I also ask them to make a crescendo and play the third beat very short and loud. I add the same crescendo and *forte-piano* at **reh. 28** and one bar before **reh. 29**. This creates, in my opinion, a more sardonic feel to this section.

Observing the *poco meno forte* indication in the third bar of **reh. 29** is very important, as only a few instruments drop down here. At this point, the motif from the opening of the symphony returns in the low strings and brass. It should all sound like one line, and the violins play on the string throughout. The addition of the xylophone is a wonderful color, but it must not be so loud as to cover up the others who also play this figuration.

Quite often with Shostakovich, it is difficult to understand what some of his indications really mean. One bar before **reh. 31**, he writes *poco stringendo*. The previous metronome mark was ♩ = 126, and we have to arrive at ♩ = 138. Although not indicated, almost everyone makes a slight crescendo going into **reh. 32**. It is also possible, but slightly dangerous, to go into two here.

Basically, this section has everyone playing full out. The rhythmic figure of the strings and woodwinds is quite marcato, while the brass are marked *espressivo*, but with accents. When the trumpets appear at **reh. 34**, they take over the line from the horns; their entrance should be almost inaudible.

A huge ritard begins two measures before the Largamente. We have been racing along at ♩ = 138 and must get to ♩ = 66 in just two bars. The difficulty is not in slowing down but in the lengthening of the sixteenth notes. We do not play them long, but as the tempo slows, these notes are gradually expanded in breadth so that when we arrive at **reh. 36**, the rhythm does not seem abrupt.

Some conductors do this next section in four and others in eight. In my experience, conducting in eight helps establish better ensemble for the thirty-second notes. I start by subdividing the last beat of the measure before **reh. 36**, which emphasizes the upbeat in the timpani. Make sure that those musicians playing the half note tied to an eighth sustain and do not cut off in the middle. I should also add that most conductors take a breath after the quarter note three measures before **reh. 37**; in the strings it is simply a retake of the down bow. In the bar before **reh. 37**—and at **reh. 38**—you might want to drop the brass and timpani down a little on the half note to accommodate what needs to be an exaggerated crescendo.

When you get to the 5/4 bar, which does not contain thirty-second notes, you can slip back into beating quarter notes and then return to conducting in eight in the next measure. The *molto ritenuto* can never be slow enough, but you must sustain the tenuto note in the brass. I try to get broad enough to be able to dictate that last sixteenth note, which is still part of the ritard.

From my perspective, the climax three measures after **reh. 38** is not on the downbeat but on the second quarter; hang on to the first note rather than play it short. Stay in eight to start and give as big an indication to the tam-tam as possible. Once you feel that the tempo of this section has been established, you can go back into four. Some conductors will have the strings do all the notes on a down bow; I prefer normal bowing but quite sustained and, as Shostakovich tells us, *con tutta forza*. Shall we assume that *a tempo* here means the same as at the Largamente?

Although the printed B is not the lowest note for the trumpets, it can sound as if it were. You will need to go back into eight sometime during the rallentando; I do it in the middle of the bar before the *più mosso*, making it seem as if the eighth notes will equal the quarter at **reh. 39**, where it is certainly logical to return to beating in four. There are usually no balance problems between the flute and horn. I have never heard anyone take the alternate, lower-octave notes that appear in some editions in the second and third measures after **reh. 40**, but I am told that some students are advised to do so. Note that the glockenspiel should be played with a relatively soft mallet.

The third bar of **reh. 43** presents a danger because the horns often sound too loud relative to the cellos; you might have to make an adjustment here. Conductors typically make a ritard in the bar before **reh. 44**, and you can choose to be in either four or eight. I prefer the latter.

This magical Coda is enhanced with some interesting dissonances that are often overlooked. You will notice that the violas and cellos no longer have dots over their notes. This sets up a clash between the D♮s and E♭s that can be quite eerie. The glissando before **reh. 46** should not begin until the violas have that indication; I do it on the last eighth note and make a diminuendo as the phrase moves upward. The upper strings all have to agree on the length of the eighth notes at this point.

Pay careful attention to the way the cello and bass lines are notated after **reh. 46**; sometimes Shostakovich indicates a separation, and other times he does not. He also marks them *piano*, which aids the diminuendo over the last five bars. Bringing out the different dynamic levels for those instruments makes this passage particularly intriguing.

The harps should be heard distinctly, and the celeste should sound as even as possible. A slight ritard can be made near the end, and the final bar gives us a somewhat longer note on which to conclude. I do not think I have ever heard anyone play it short, as the dot would suggest. Lower your arms after a few seconds, as the tension of the movement should continue after the last note sounds.

Movement Two

The almost-traditional Scherzo is certainly the drollest of the four movements in the symphony, with lots of humor in a sarcastic vein. As the interpreter, how far you should go in projecting that characteristic?

The fact that it is marked Allegretto only adds to the irony. Shostakovich indicates a quick tempo, ♩ = 138. But that seems to go against the musical content, so I take it down a couple of notches. You can hear straightforward performances of this movement and others that exaggerate, such as mine.

I won't go into every change of nuance, but the opening will give you a good idea of where it is possible to add to the tumult. My preference—and one that I ask the bassoons to repeat later—is to play the first note long. Then I ask for a heavy marcato stroke, slightly off the string, for the next three bars. I drop the dynamic in the fifth bar from *fortissimo* to *mezzo forte* and make a crescendo in the sixth. For the remainder of the passage, I keep the quarter notes marcato, without a diminuendo.

The horns make a forceful entry but only at single *forte*. Try to get the winds at **reh. 49** to sound as desired by the composer: start as shrill as possible and then make a quick diminuendo, as if they realize they should not be playing loudly. The E♭ clarinet is playful, but the high notes come through clearly enough that the phrase does not need to be any louder than *piano*.

At **reh. 50**, it is a nice effect for the woodwinds that enter to come in under the E♭ clarinet's dynamic and then emerge by the second beat. To parallel the opening of the movement, I play the cello and bass downbeat of **reh. 51** a bit longer than the written eighth note, with a slight accent.

When the second violins and violas enter, they can be aggressive, playing near the frog of the bow. Two before **reh. 52**, most conductors slightly separate the groups of two eighth notes, including me. At **reh. 52**, leave enough room to make the crescendo explode by the third bar. Note the hemiola-like accents that begin in the fifth bar and then change in the measure leading into **reh. 53**, where the almost circus-like music should not sound overly elegant. Keep the sixteenths crisp, perhaps playing them a little faster than indicated. The off-kilter 4/4 bar is aided by the timpani's isolated C on the third beat.

At **reh. 54**, we come to an unusual marking that is not repeated when the same phrase reoccurs several times: a comma, which usually represents a halt in the proceedings. It is hard to imagine Shostakovich wanting the beat to stop, and I have never heard anyone do this. However, if you pause, maybe you should at each subsequent appearance of this idea as well.

I used to add a slur for the horns at the pickup to the fourth bar of **reh. 54** for an even-more-raucous feeling, but I find it excessive now. When the violins come in five measures after **reh. 54**, they are marked marcato, but the majority of conductors play it off the string. Because of the glissando, the lower E in the first violins should be played on the open string.

To get the maximum effect of the *subito piano* at **reh. 55**, the brass should play the preceding *sforzando* quite loudly. Often, the strings' crescendo in the fourth bar is fine but the diminuendo is too subtle; be sure they decrease to *piano*. Everything proceeds as before until the buildup four measures before **reh. 57**. To accomplish this crescendo, start these two bars at about *mezzo forte* and then make a huge sweep up.

While it is not specified in the score, I often slow down a bit for the horn notes two measures before **reh. 57** without decreasing their volume. Tradition has it that the Trio section, beginning with the solo violin, is played in a more relaxed tempo. This allows the violinist, and later the flutist, plenty of time for rubato, but for the most part, the underlying accompaniment stays in tempo. Do not impose your own thoughts on how these solos should be played until you hear how the players think of them. After that, you both can make some adjustments.

Shostakovich indicates a *rit.* three measures after **reh. 58**, but the problem lies at the *a tempo* in the next measure. Many conductors observe it at the beginning of the bar rather than on the third beat as printed. Either way works, but I have shifted my thinking to follow the composer's intention in this spot as well as five measures before **reh. 61**. I usually take a little time to allow the harp and string glissandos to be heard clearly at **reh. 60**.

A marcato stroke works well at **reh. 61**, but playing the quarters longer in all instruments four measures before **reh. 62** gives the passage some required heaviness. If this work is new for your orchestra, you will need to practice the first violin line two measures before **reh. 62** slowly, just for intonation. Take care not to overlook the articulation two bars before **reh. 65**: These notes are short, but the previous two measures are not. Enjoy the difference.

The recapitulation of the opening commences, but now the lower strings are replaced by bassoons, playing softly. Some string sections put their bows down on their laps here. That is certainly valid, but holding the bows up imparts a slightly different sound. Getting an accent while playing a pizzicato gently is not easy. The piccolo part needs to be quite discreet and is there because the violins cannot do a pizzicato trill.

Three measures before **reh. 68**, I ask the bassoons to play the first note a bit longer to match the opening of the movement. To highlight another similarity to previous material, I add accents to the fourth measure before **reh. 69**, so that this is the same as four bars before **reh. 53**. Almost everything is equivalent this second time around, except the trumpets replace the horns at **reh. 70**. Don't forget to start the two crescendos after **reh. 73** a little softer.

Usually, I ask the timpani to make a ritard and then conduct the oboe solo more slowly. While nothing in the score tells us to do this, my thought is that we are simply duplicating the speed at which we took the Trio. The low F in the timpani is correct, even if it sounds wrong. One before **reh. 74** has a *subito piano* on the second beat.

If you have slowed for this short phrase, get back to tempo with the upbeat to the second bar of **reh. 74**. Imagine the slow-motion camera at a sporting event. This is how your beat should look right up until the *a tempo* of the final four bars. A strong, angry accent brings the Scherzo to an aggressive close.

Movement Three

One of the most sublime slow movements in all of music, the Largo presents the conductor with an enormous challenge right from the start: the string divisi, specifically the three independent parts designated as Violins 1, 2, and 3. A note at the bottom of the first page in some editions instructs us to divide the section into three equal groups. There are many possibilities for assigning the parts depending on how the violins are positioned on the stage.

Everyone has their own solution for this dilemma, but from my point of view, those playing the same part should be clumped into groups. When the piece starts, all the third violins should be seated near each other; to do otherwise is inviting ensemble disaster. That said, with adequate rehearsal, almost any configuration can work. I just prefer the sound of each group to be unanimous.

More than likely, the first and second violins were on opposite sides of the stage when this work was first performed. A video available on YouTube reveals how Mravinsky handled the divisi in a 1973 performance.[3] Going against the instruction regarding equality in numbers, he begins by having the first four stands of the second violins play the opening Violin 3 line. The remainder of the second violin section takes up the Violin 2 line, and all the firsts play the Violin 1 part. This is a decent solution for several reasons, and some apply even if all the fiddles are massed on the left.

The violas and cellos are split in two, with the first few stands playing the upper line. By having the Violin 3 part played at the front of the section, most of the strings are near each other as the movement opens, making it less difficult for ensemble and richer in sound. Importantly, the second cellos need to be those musicians located nearest the double basses, again for ensemble. Then, at **reh. 77**, Mravinsky brings in the remaining second violins on the right, along with the other strings, leaving only the first violins resting. The full first violin section plays the Violin 1 line at **reh. 78**. It stays this way for the duration of the movement. The same can certainly be done if all the violins are on one side.

Perhaps another clue as to why this division makes sense can be found five measures before **reh. 89**. The second and third violins play in unison, with the first violins patiently waiting. Visualize the dramatic effect with the split violin section and you will see what I mean.

In the old days, I used to get very fancy with how I divided the parts, trying to be faithful to that written instruction. With all the violins seated on my left, I would have the last two desks of the first violins and the first three desks of the second violins play the Violin 3 part. This strategy made it difficult to achieve a sense of ensemble, but I nevertheless persisted. The remainder of the second violin section played the Violin 2 part and the rest of the first violin section took the Violin 1 line. The upper line of the violas was for the first three stands, so they were in proximity to at least some of those playing the Violin 3 part.

Eventually, I tried it the Mravinsky way, and even though the number of players was disproportionate, it worked well. Keep in mind that the sound coming to you on the podium is not the most important thing here but rather the balance as heard by the audience. Some additional tweaks can be made as the movement progresses. The bottom line is that every conductor will have to decide how to divide these passages, communicating this decision to the orchestra as soon as possible.

Let's now look at the whole movement from the beginning. The dynamic is *piano*, not *pianissimo*, so the *espressivo* indication is certainly in order. Try to keep most of this in one singing line. The first real breath I take is not until **reh. 76**, just before the G♯ in the second violins. For the beginning, just a very quiet first beat is needed to show the violins where to come in and, more importantly, the mood you want. I reverse the printed bowing and start on a down bow to make a very subtle diminuendo and slight tenuto on the last note. You will have to decide about the remaining bowings on your own; a few conductors let the musicians play freely with their own individual bowings, but I don't recommend this.

There is a little trick you can use to bring out the Violin 2 entrance at **reh. 77**. Ask those who have been playing the Violin 3 line to switch to Violin 2 at this point, while those in the back stands (originally assigned to Violin 2) enter on the Violin 3 line starting at the *mezzo forte*. This can help increase the tension by making the upper line more prominent to the listener without drawing notice.

As pointed out, all the first violins play Violin 1 at **reh. 78**. Five bars later, the Cello 1 line takes over and may need to be played a bit louder than *mezzo forte*. Keep the vibrato going right through the cutoff.

Two harps might feel like overkill when they come in before **reh. 79**, but it can work if they balance well with the flute. Nevertheless, this can just as easily be accomplished by a single player. The first flute will need to take a breath just before **reh. 80**, but you don't want to shortchange the length of the half note too much. Give the harps just a little time in their last bar so that the four instruments can be together.

It is not entirely clear to me why Shostakovich does not use the whole cello section starting three measures before **reh. 81**. Since all the basses come in at the end of the phrase, I have all the cellos play the entire phrase. Shostakovich builds in the crescendo from **reh. 81** simply by adding instruments as he goes along.

After reaching a *fortissimo*, we see a diminuendo in the bar before **reh. 83** without a dynamic specifying how softly to end. This always feels like an awkward, indefinite moment, keeping us guessing what will happen next. I reduce the volume to *mezzo forte* and hang on to the last note. You can take a little time before giving the second beat at **reh. 83**. I start this on an up bow and follow the phrasing as indicated by the composer. However, after the low instruments arrive at the sustained A♭, they should change freely to a down bow to provide a nice fadeout.

There is always a question as to whether the first violins are supposed to play thirty-second notes or tremolo. I prefer the latter to avoid the feeling of strict rhythm going into the oboe solo. Unless you have a very specific idea for this phrase, let the soloist do as they wish. When the Violin 2 line takes over—remember, we are still in a three-part divisi—the players should enter very quietly so that when one group of violins concludes, the other is simply there, as if there were no change at all.

During these passages, it is not necessary to beat time. Instead, just indicate the measures where something new takes place. You do have to conduct during the clarinet solo because of the two flutes, but keep your beat quite small. Three measures before **reh. 86**, do not place an accent or attack on the first note, which is still connected to the previous tremolo. Those playing Violin 3 enter one measure before **reh. 86** but are not really heard until the third bar.

The cellos' pizzicatos four bars before **reh. 87** must be delicate, as if gently touching the string rather than pulling it. The glockenspiel is played with a soft mallet. Keep in mind that it sounds an octave higher than written. At **reh. 87**, we enter a fairly dark world that reprises the opening of the movement. A transitional moment occurs at **reh. 88** with another of Shostakovich's intense crescendos. At five measures before **reh. 89**, the wisdom of having the Violin 2 and Violin 3 lines played by the second violin section really works; this is especially true with an antiphonal seating arrangement.

A ferocious tremolo sets off the intense section that begins at **reh. 89**. To emphasize the accents of the tune, I ask the xylophone to play in octaves, adding the lower G♭ and continuing for the entire phrase. Ensure that those playing the tremolos do not ease up, as they are responsible for creating the tense atmosphere. The lower instruments should play their lines with as much weight as possible.

To observe the breath mark just before **reh. 90**, it helps to think of the half note as having a fermata on it. Sustain it for the full value and then consider the cutoff the last beat in the bar, as if there were five beats here, the last one being the breath.

The divided double basses are very important at **reh. 90**. Ask them to start at the frog and to pull the bow as fast as possible through the note, playing it with a bit more length than a typical eighth note. Sometimes I take this section just a bit faster to help sustain the long line in the cellos. At **reh. 91**, when the upper woodwinds join, the cellos can make a quick portamento between the two A♮s.

Sustaining the violins at **reh. 91** is simply a matter of bowing decisions. If you want a separation in the sixth bar after **reh. 91**, ask them to retake the down bow, but if you prefer no break, ask them to change direction on the G♯ in the previous bar, so there are two bows for this one note. Then it comes naturally.

To add to the drama of the crescendo one measure before **reh. 92**, I usually wait a little before giving the second beat. To accomplish this, make the cutoff appear to be on the fourth beat of the previous bar. Then wait before giving the downbeat, but only do this with the right arm so it cannot be misconstrued.

There are a couple of ways to phrase the first two bars at **reh. 92** and, once again, they have to do with the bowing. If you want a true sostenuto, just play it as it comes, starting down bow. But if you want to emphasize the accents, as is my preference, play all the notes down bow.

The same principle we employed one measure before **reh. 92** applies to the third bar as well. Wait before giving the cellos their entrance; they continue to play strongly until the diminuendo, which should come down to about *mezzo forte*. I add a little *espressivo* crescendo three before **reh. 93**. Given the key we are in, it is nice to wait just a moment before playing the low C, as it almost seems out of place. The upper line of cellos fades out, leaving only those at the back playing; wait until they are as soft as possible before starting **reh. 93**.

This passage, while marked *pianissimo*, should still be played with slight vibrato. Its counterpart at **reh. 81** contained a crescendo. Here it is the opposite, and you can add a diminuendo in the fourth bar after **reh. 93** to emphasize the difference. Some conductors ask for a portamento from the low instruments, but I think it sounds a little crass and do not do it. The first violins should continue with vibrato right through the passage, so the high notes do not sound pinched.

The harps at **reh. 94** are marked as two eighth notes followed by a quarter note, mirroring their line at **reh. 79**. Even if you let the lower note ring, be sure to maintain the feeling of a four-note group. The second violas and cellos continue this line, so try to make it seem equal in dynamics. Many conductors have all the cellos play the legato line starting at **reh. 95**.

The first violins come in imperceptibly one measure before **reh. 96**, with the celeste entering two bars later along with a single harp. This pickup to the second bar of **reh. 96** can be a little awkward for intonation, but there is nothing you can do about it. Make sure that the two instrumentalists can see each other. Once they start playing, it is more important for them to be in contact with each other than with you.

Four measures before the end of the movement, the first violas have an isolated F♯, which should begin on an up bow. When the other strings enter, they also come in with an up bow, and then, if you wish, you can take a little breath before the final note, played with a down bow. The last note in Violin 1 is not meant to be reattacked; they just cut off with everyone else.

Hold your position to maintain tension during the silence at the end. Since the strings do not play the first six bars of the last movement, they should not move or take off their mutes until the winds play the first note. Of course, if you prefer to separate the two movements and not play them *attacca*, then this is a moot point.

Movement Four

Now we come to one of the most hotly debated symphonic movements in history, controversial not only for the subtext suggested by *Testimony* but also for questions about the tempos. Let's start with those metronome marks.

The piece begins squarely in four, and the indication of ♩ = 88 fits with a stately *Allegro non troppo*. Nevertheless, an awful lot of conductors choose to start it rather quickly. We are really looking at a massive accelerando from this opening all the way to **reh. 111**, about four minutes into the movement, where the metronome mark is ♩ = 92 (equivalent to ♩ = 184). That represents a striking difference.

Very few conductors take all the metronome marks literally, and this has caused a lot of confusion, perhaps because not many of the markings are preceded by the word "accelerando." After arriving at **reh. 98**, some conductors keep the same tempo until **reh. 108**, when the pulse switches from four beats to two.

Considering that we are presented with eight different metronome marks, each increasing in speed, I think this calls for gradually getting faster rather than trying to make sudden changes when the metronome marks appear. I have tried to emphasize this by starting the movement a bit slower than what is marked and making sure that my tempo at **reh. 98** is not too quick, giving me room to make the continued accelerando.

Even Mravinsky strays from the printed score for this opening, but at least he seems to observe the gradual acceleration of the tempo. We can listen to several recordings of his interpretations, including the very first one from 1938 in which he comes the closest to heeding the metronome marks. While its sound quality is very poor, the recording gives us a good idea of how the premiere was performed.

Technically, the main difficulty for the conductor is pacing the accelerando. Orchestras will automatically want to push forward because of the momentum created by all those notes. You need to find the places where the speed can increase without sounding obvious or frantic. The difference between each metronomic indication is not as much as you might think, so Shostakovich clearly knows how he wishes this to proceed.

At **reh. 104**, the metronome mark is ♩ = 132. That is fairly fast, and we must be careful not to let it get out of hand. We get a brief respite from the heavy nature of the music for four bars beginning at **reh. 105** before returning to the serious temperament of the piece. Keep your eyes on the trumpets in the 5/4 bar, as they tend to enter a little late.

The accelerando continues, and we must transition to beating in two at **reh. 108**. Just switching on the downbeat can work, but it is more elegant and clearer if you shift midway through the previous bar by beating two quarter notes and then a half note. This makes it easier for the trumpet to deduce the tempo. Keep all the quarter notes long but still moving forward, observing that the brass play only at single *forte*.

A noble crescendo takes us to what seems like one of the only positive-sounding portions of the movement at **reh. 110**. The trumpets can aid the proceedings by making little crescendos on the triplets. Meanwhile, the strings should use as much bow as possible for each note of the tune. You do not have to continue the accelerando for this section, but five measures before **reh. 111**, start to speed up again to reach the fastest tempo of the movement. Given that **reh. 111** is one of the only times Shostakovich will write quadruple *forte*, the cymbals and tam-tam should ring here, the longer the better.

We can finally relax the tempo at **reh. 112**. But again, the score does not tell us whether we slow down before that point. I used to make a ritard six bars after **reh. 111** and then wait a moment before the upbeat in the brass. Now I just take a little time, start that upbeat six bars before **reh. 112** in the quick tempo, and then use the next five bars to get to a speed of ♩ = 80. If you prefer a ritard on the triple *forte*, it might be best to consider going into four for this and then back into two five measures before **reh. 112**.

This extended transition to the Coda can be quite expressive. For example, you can take some time getting into **reh. 113** and then suddenly move forward. You can also add a diminuendo the bar before **reh. 115** so the entry of the solo flute is clear without sounding forced. When the cellos enter at **reh. 116**, they might need to be reminded of how the bassoon played the same phrase two bars earlier, just for the sake of balance.

The violins need to play with vibrato throughout, lest it seem like a dutiful exercise, especially for the notes on the E string. In the sixth measure after **reh. 119**, you might want to slightly separate the first violins' last note from the downbeat of the next bar so that their A is clearly rearticulated.

The cellos and basses can add a couple of expressive effects at **reh. 120**. For example, the hairpins, which are almost Mahlerian, can be exaggerated. In the fourth bar, a little separation of the two Gs is helpful, and the same holds for the Fs two bars later.

Everyone will need to make a diminuendo starting five measures after **reh. 120**, so the harps will be audible. While the harps are playing, only the low notes change, and you want to bring out the E one measure before **reh. 121**. Almost all conductors make a rather large ritard here, no matter their tempo for the Coda.

We have now come to the crux of the controversy, one that has implications for how conductors perform this grand ending. I think that in the absence of a programmatic narrative, the conductor's job is to realize the musical text as it exists on the page. However, given what we know about Shostakovich's two previous compositions, this piece had some extra-musical meaning, certainly altering the direction of Shostakovich's output into more conservative territory.

Even if the messages are hidden, the ending sounds triumphant, whether played slowly or fast. Let's consider the metronome mark at **reh. 121** first: $\quarternote = 100\text{--}108$, the only time the composer gives us an option. The last speed mentioned was back at **reh. 112** with the indication $\halfnote = 80$.

Perhaps the publisher made an error and instead of $\quarternote = 100\text{--}108$, it was supposed to be $\halfnote = 100\text{--}108$. We could buy that if it were not for the recordings left by the man who conducted the premiere. Mravinsky clearly goes for what is printed and is consistent in his several recordings of the piece. But a surprising number of early versions by other conductors opted for a quicker pace, almost coming close to the above conclusion, including recordings made just a couple of years after Mravinsky's first rendition.

None of this is helped by the composer's enthusiasm for Bernstein's interpretation in 1958, which is the fastest of all. What are we to do today? Is there a "correct" way to deal with this conundrum? Does the political climate of the time affect how we perform the symphony? Is it possible that the tempo can be a hybrid of these two possibilities, or even more?

While I was writing this essay, I had the opportunity to rehearse and perform the work. For that occasion, I wrote the following:

A Conductor's No-Nonsense Response to a Tempo Dilemma[4]

We are all influenced by our first exposure to greatness—whether it is a person, structure, or work of art—which informs our thinking for the rest of our lives. However, once in a while, we are forced to look at certain elements differently, in a way that dramatically alters our original thoughts.

These days, in addition to my conducting activities as well as writing both music and prose, I am engaged in what I hope will be a valuable project for anyone interested in the methodology involved in conducting orchestral masterworks. Among the pieces I examine is the Fifth Symphony by Shostakovich. The essays are intended as a practical guide to how these works should be studied and led.

Readers of *Classical Source* will not need me to tell them about the history behind this specific symphony. However, for the purposes of what I am about to write, we have to throw out the millions of words written regarding ideology and politics.

Perhaps the single most controversial tempo in all of music occurs during the last pages of the Russian master's work. In a recent concert with the Manhattan School of Music Symphony Orchestra, I gave a little demonstration of how the Coda has been performed over the years. To do this, it was necessary to examine, as always, what the composer wrote. What we find is that the last section has a metronome mark of ♩ = 188 beats per minute.

But all you have to do is listen to or watch any recording made by the conductor Evgeny Mravinsky, who gave the world premiere of the work in 1937 and committed it to disc in 1938, to see that he hardly follows this instruction. It is a slow, almost dignified approach, one that he would maintain throughout his career. He can be seen conducting in four but quite contrary to the indicated tempo marking.

Only a few years later, for reasons that are unclear, most conductors during the 1950s, including Eugene Ormandy, one of the composer's strongest advocates, started taking this ending at ♩ = 72 or so. So not only had the tempo changed, but this section was also now conducted with two beats to the bar as opposed to four.

Enter Leonard Bernstein, who took the work to Russia on a tour with the New York Philharmonic in 1958. With the composer present, he dashed off the Coda at ♩ = 104 and even faster in some performances. Shostakovich beamed, praising the performance. It appears that he liked the way everyone interpreted his music. Conductors have varied the tempo over the ensuing years, with Rostropovich leading the way on the slower end of the spectrum.

Why have tempos differed so dramatically, and is the truth out there?

As mentioned, I am not going to get into the social or political subtext, which may or may not have anything to do with this. Instead, I am going to place the blame, as some others have suggested, on the publisher, although mine is not the usual criticism.

The tempo marking of ♩ =188 is ridiculously fast, and it is almost impossible to move your arms at this speed. Some argue that the marking was misread and should indicate the eighth note at this tempo. That really doesn't make sense either, at least for conducting purposes, but it equates to ♩ = 94, which is reasonable but still quite a bit faster than Mravinsky.

Bernstein must have thought that there were actually two misprints, marking in his score held by the New York Philharmonic Archives that the ♩ = 96 (not the ♪).⁵

I have another thought. What if the number "1" before the "88" was the misprint? If we eliminate that, then we have the quarter note at two digits, not three, which is certainly logical. It places the tempo much closer to Mravinsky and still allows Bernstein his belief that there is a second error with the note value.

The icing on the cake is that the designation of 88 then makes the Coda the same tempo as the opening of the movement, giving a true cyclical feeling to the piece.

Can it really be that simple—a mistake on the part of the publisher, consisting of an added digit, as well as an oversight by the composer?

Yes. And it still affords others the opportunity to come up with their own solutions.

It was fairly easy at one time. All you had to do was follow your instincts. There was no "meaning," and if it existed, most did not know about it. With at least two very different ways to play the Coda, both apparently given their blessing by the composer, it is a matter of taste, tempered by a bit of knowledge.

If you choose the indicated metronome mark of ♩ = 100–108 at **reh. 121**, everything is in quarter notes, beat in four with a few other patterns thrown in as well. If you decide on a quicker tempo, then stay in two and beat quarters for the 3/4 bars. The timpani should be played with somewhat hard sticks for rhythmic clarity. When the horns enter four measures after **reh. 121**, the sound might wobble because this is a very low note. Try to get the tuba to take over so that it does not sound like a new entrance but rather a continuation of that horn note.

At the speedier tempo, some conductors opt for playing the tune marcato. When slower, legato seems preferable. At **reh. 123**, the eighth notes should be long, which is not so simple when the tempo is fast. Shostakovich reinforces that idea at **reh. 126** by asking the strings to play tenuto, although they usually retake the down bow after each quarter note.

Depending on how you view it, the entrance of the piano can either be prominent or part of the texture as it builds. The trumpets have the same option as the others who play the theme: marcato or legato. I add a crescendo to the bar before **reh. 128**, where we also see a slightly faster metronome mark of ♩ = 116.

Even at a slower speed, the trumpets at **reh. 130** usually play with a slightly separated upbeat in each bar. During the eight measures preceding **reh. 131**, each of the three trumpets plays the top note, in turn. It must sound as if just one musician were playing it, so make sure the players try to match their colleagues' sound.

Don't start getting too slow too soon when you approach the enormous six-bar ritard; this takes longer than you might think. It is possible to subdivide the last few eighth notes. Just when you thought that the question of tempo might be resolved, we are confronted, in some editions, with the indication at **reh. 131** of ♩ = 188! Other editions put the eighth note at that tempo (♪ = 184), but no one would actually conduct this in eight.

If you have been conducting in quarter notes on the slower side, this is a big problem. Suddenly, what has been a very deliberate set of tempo relationships is shattered with a furious presto, although not indicated as such. And conducting in four at that speed is just not viable. If you follow the metronome, the only solution is to do this in two, meaning ♩ = 92, which is still fast.

And what does Mravinsky do? He deviates from the score for one of the only times in the entire symphony, staying in four at ♩ = 112 or so. This does not impart a feeling of triumph but, at the same time, it is still heroic. I must mention that if you stay with the slower tempos, the trumpets can have difficulty sustaining the dynamic.

There is one final matter that has nothing to do with the cultural or political drama that appears to be contained in the symphony. Should we make a ritard somewhere near the end? No matter the tempo, almost every conductor starts slowing down for the last five bars, and some play the timpani and bass drum strokes quite deliberately, including Mravinsky and Bernstein, the two opposites. It might be interesting someday to hear this ending without a ritard, especially at a quick tempo.

The debates will undoubtedly continue. But when coming to this great work, it is no longer possible to ignore the discrepancies contained in the score. You must come to your own decisions and stick by them, at least for the performance you are about to lead.

Conductor's Etiquette

Solo bows are fairly clear in this symphony, but their order is really up to you. I usually have the horn, flute, oboe, clarinet, and concertmaster rise separately. But since this is a showpiece for the whole orchestra, you can also have the percussion, brass, woodwinds, and strings (including harp and piano) stand as sections.

> Real music is always revolutionary, for it cements the ranks of the people; it arouses them and leads them onward.
>
> —Dmitri Shostakovich

Notes

1. "A Soviet Artist's Practical Creative Reply to Just Criticism," Oxford Reference, https://www.oxfordreference.com/view/10.1093/oi/authority.20110803100520427.

2. Dimitri Shostakovich, *Symphony No. 5 in D Minor, Op. 47* (Berlin: Sikorski, 2002).

3. "Evgeny Mravinsky Conducts Shostakovich Symphony no. 5—video 1973," YouTube video, https://youtu.be/eQOMsLmzJ8c.

4. "A Conductor's No-Nonsense Response to a Tempo Dilemma," *Classical Source*, February 10, 2023, https://www.classicalsource.com/article/a-conductors-no-nonsense-response-to-a-tempo-dilemma/.

5. "Shostakovich, Dmitri / Symphony No. 5, D Minor, op. 47 (ID: 1590)," New York Philharmonic Shelby White & Leon Levy Digital Archives, https://archives.nyphil.org/index.php/artifact/8e3fcd6c-4881-4794-9e6e-1501e7da7036-0.1/fullview#page/160/mode/2up.

Béla Bartók: *Concerto for Orchestra*

I cannot conceive of music that expresses absolutely nothing.

—Béla Bartók

See page for author, Public domain, via Wikimedia Commons

Sometimes misfortune can yield a masterpiece. In early 1943, the fifty-four-year-old Hungarian was in a hospital in New York, having suffered several health setbacks over the previous two years. He was almost destitute and, even though his doctors did not tell him, had developed leukemia.

His importance on the musical scene abroad, as well as in the United States, was of such great value that three musicians came to see him with information they hoped would give him enough strength to carry on writing. The Russian conductor Serge Koussevitzky and Bartók's compatriots, violinist Joseph Szigeti and conductor Fritz Reiner, visited the composer with the news that funds had been raised for him to write a new orchestral composition in memory of Koussevitzky's wife, who had recently passed away.

Not knowing about the disease that would eventually afflict him, the composer found himself buoyed and left the hospital, spending the next two months at the Koussevitzky residence at Seranak, near Tanglewood in Lenox, Massachusetts. In that brief period, he completed his final work for full orchestra, the *Concerto for Orchestra*.

The first performance was given on December 1, 1944, just a year after the commission. It was an enormous success, entering the repertoire of virtually every major orchestra within a couple of years. It is universally regarded as one of the great works of the twentieth, and indeed any, century.

Bartók's compositional world was centered on Hungarian folk music. There are very few pieces of his that do not reference some part of his heritage, even if some of them are thorny for the listener. He wore his Hungarian roots on his sleeve, as evidenced in such pieces as the Third String Quartet and Sonata for Two Pianos and Percussion as well as several of the solo piano works. Although he was grateful to have escaped Nazi occupation in 1940, he found it difficult to feel entirely comfortable in his new home.

When Bartók arrived in America, the musical public knew him much better as a pianist, but this concerto would change that. Unfortunately, he did not survive long enough to accept all the accolades that would follow his passing in 1945.

Almost every major conductor embraced the *Concerto for Orchestra* immediately, with one major exception: Toscanini. Although the work has many technical hurdles, it is not nearly as complicated to conduct as many of Bartók's previous scores. Harmonically and rhythmically, the work is on the conservative side, and this must have accounted for a lot of its appeal in post–World War II America.

At one time, virtually every major orchestra took this work on tour. This was highly unusual, as new music rarely found a home on the road. There has never been a time when this piece went out of the repertoire. It is essential learning for every conductor.

The publisher of the piece is Boosey & Hawkes, and this edition is now available for study on IMSLP.[1] Be forewarned that the work is still under copyright in the United States.

The instrumentation is surprisingly classic, with only its use of two harps making it even remotely exotic. Here is what is required: three flutes (third = piccolo), three oboes (third = English horn), three clarinets (third = bass clarinet), three bassoons (third = contrabassoon), four horns in F, three trumpets in C, three trombones, tuba, timpani, percussion (bass drum, cymbals, snare drum [without snares], tam-tam, triangle), two harps, and strings. The first published edition notes an optional fourth trumpet part, but it is nowhere to be found in the music. The score is notated so that the conductor has the same information as the musicians.

We also have rehearsal numbers, which correspond with the respective measure numbers in each movement. What is most helpful is that they are always placed at logical phrase points, making it easy for the musicians when it comes to counting.

Performance time is around thirty-five minutes.

First Movement: Introduzione

Bartók was one of the first composers to give us a framework in which to find the tempo. He could have just written *andante non troppo*, and most of us would have found something appropriate. Instead, he chose what he felt were the maximum and minimum metronome marks that the conductor should adopt; in this case it is $\quarternote = 73\text{--}64$. It seems unusual to list these from fast to slow, but at least we have parameters.

Obviously, it is conducted in three. What is also obvious, but often ignored, is the dynamic Bartók gives to the motif in the cellos and basses. Quite often, conductors will pride themselves on how softly those instruments play when, in fact, it is only marked single *piano*. You will also notice that there is no diminuendo for this as well as the next passage. This is important if we are to really adhere to what the composer wrote.

The entries of the divisi violins are *pianissimo*. These divisions are best done on the stand, outside and inside. The sound the violins—as well as the violas—make should be almost inaudible and most certainly less than the lower instruments. Why didn't Bartók call for the violas to use mutes, as he indicates for the violins? Because he wants them to play *sul ponticello*, and it is not possible to have the bow on or near the bridge if the mute is in the way.

The overall feeling should be eerie, and even though we can audibly discern the change of notes, they should produce a chilling effect.

The violas are also supposed to be divided in two parts. What that really means here is that both the upper and lower lines play two notes, which is made clear when you look at **m. 10**. I do not think that the sixteenth note in that bar is meant to be a reattack, but rather a release from the tremolo.

The flute entry is also marked *pianissimo*, but this is not easy to achieve. Even though they are a couple of octaves lower, the cellos and basses might be a tad too loud for the initial flute notes to be heard clearly. So, I try to find a level that is quiet but audible, with the sextuplets well-articulated. The following measure introduces six slurred notes. Some conductors have the final note played somewhat abruptly, but I usually ask the two flutists to sustain it just a little so that the clash between the F♮ and F♯ drives home the feeling of dissonance.

Notice that the strings cut off at different times. The cellos and basses should still be sustaining the note at single *piano*, which makes their presence seem like the most important. I think this is exactly what the composer had in mind.

Since there is no indication to the contrary, the passage that commences at **m. 12** should be played in the same manner as the opening. With everything being a fourth higher in pitch, the tremolos and flutes might sound a little bit louder; try to get them to remain *pianissimo*.

Measure 22 gives me a chance to tell you a little story. The lower strings have the now-expanded version of the tune, but the double basses do not play the first note. Why not? Certainly, either a five-string instrument or one with an extension can play the C♯ and go even lower.

Koussevitzky was a bass player. He wrote what is probably the most popular concerto for that instrument. He understood what could and could not be done. At some point, probably even before one note was written, he insisted that Bartók avoid anything below the E string, saying, "I do not want my Boston Symphony to sound like Stokowski's Philadelphia."

I am not going to point out every instance where this issue comes into play, and it is up to you to decide whether the lower notes should be inserted. My guess is that most of us make these changes and assume that Bartók was not aware of the availability of these extra notes.

However, there is more to this story. It turns out that, as far as I can tell, Bartók never wrote below the E! I looked at almost every one of his orchestral works and could not find any instance of lower notes. But most of the time, he does not need them. In the case of this moment, and a few others in this piece, he did have another option: to include a note an octave higher and then drop back down for the remainder of a phrase. To me, this particular line feels empty without that lower first note in the basses, just as it does at **m. 28**, where the melodic line goes down to a D♯. Again, I find that the basses need to follow the violas and cellos.

Even though Bartók is kind enough to give us metronomic options, as with so many composers, he fails to address certain questions that we need to answer for ourselves. How loud does the crescendo get at the end of **m. 23**? Is the stringendo slight or exaggerated? You will encounter these questions in almost every piece of music; be prepared to have a reasoned response if you are asked by any musician.

I insert very brief spaces between the two D♯s in **mm. 28–29**, just to make sure that these do not sound like tied or slurred notes. The dynamic for the low strings remains at single *piano*, not *pianissimo*. Having given the tempo options at the start of the piece, Bartók just leaves the slower one in place for the solo flutist, who should be allowed to play with rubato. The passage ends with a diminuendo, but only for the flute. The remaining strings hold on to the single *piano*, making the *subito pianissimo* at **m. 35** quite dramatic.

I don't know for certain if Bartók was the first to do it, but every so often, usually at some critical phrase point, he lets us know, down to the second, how much time elapses between sections. Here this must be a guesstimate, since we have an option for the tempo. Later, when there is only one metronomic indication, perhaps it is mathematically accurate. We are close to getting to an area that might be called "quantum musical physics." These timings are interesting but should not be used as a template to be followed literally.

My recommendation for getting some contrast in the introduction is to do the first thirty-four bars with vibrato in the lower strings and then ask them to play without vibrato after that. The timpani is marked a dynamic higher, and one way to accomplish this without overdoing it is to have the musician play softly using a medium or even a hard mallet. The trumpet trio at **m. 44** has sometimes been done *con sordino*, but this is not really the right sound. If it is not quiet enough for you, ask the players to place the instrument a bit closer to the stand and play into it.

While we are speaking of the trumpets, be sure to learn the difference between the rotary valve and the piston instruments. The former was, and still is, a mainstay of many European orchestras. It has a mellower and darker sound than the piston, which was invented before the rotary trumpet. Both types are common in orchestras today, and if you desire a specific sound, you can ask for one or both. But it is possible that the orchestra will have to pay a doubling fee to the musicians to accommodate this request, depending on their contract.

Bartók calls for the trumpets to be in C. Whether he meant that this was how the piece was notated or if he really wanted the instruments pitched this way is debatable. There is a slide on the trumpet that converts the same instrument back and forth from B♭ to C. Unless you really do not care for the sound being produced, it is best to let the musicians decide which instrument to use. I have been asked, prior to rehearsals commencing, which I would prefer. If the option is there, I usually like the rotary trumpet for most music prior to the twentieth century and the piston for works written after that.

The four sixteenth notes in **mm. 44–46** can feel rushed in an effort to avoid sounding like a triplet, but they do have to be different from the appearance of this tune at **m. 51**. Just relax a little, and make sure that the musicians get to the last note of each group before the next beat. The two eighth notes at **m. 47**, also marking the first entry of a trombone, are somewhat weighty, with the crescendo going to no louder than *piano*.

When Bartók gives us a dynamic, we have to observe it. At **m. 51**, single *forte* is more than enough, despite the temptation to exceed this, because the diminuendo in the previous measure ensures plenty of contrast. An interesting feature in this section is how Bartók uses the thirty-second notes. They do not appear in all the instruments playing the melodic line. Does this mean he wants to lessen their impact? Probably not. It is just to vary the color, and he reverses these rhythms between the woodwinds and violins five bars later.

We get our first *fortissimo* at **m. 58**. Hard sticks for the timpani are a must here. The violins should change bows often on the long notes. Make sure they sustain the last note in **m. 60**. The first violins are asked to play the sixteenth notes in **m. 62** on the G string. We know that this is for the sound color, but some orchestras have trouble with the intonation. If your section is struggling, have the inside players play it on the D string; it still isn't easy, but it can help.

A long crescendo and accelerando take place over thirteen bars. Both must be gauged carefully. At some point, you must go into one. The trumpets need to feel secure with the syncopations at **m. 67**, so my suggestion is to make the switch two bars later. Keep the pace moving as you approach a major decision just before the *Allegro vivace*, where Bartók includes a comma. Many conductors choose to think of it as a *luftpause*. For a change, we can at least listen to how it was done at the world premiere, since a recording with Koussevitzky and the Boston Symphony exists. He goes straight into **m. 76** with no pause whatsoever.

How can we be certain that this is what Bartók wanted, and what does that comma really mean? Of the latter, we cannot be sure. What we can do is look for other places in the score where the punctuation mark has been inserted. In my opinion, it is just to ensure that there is the tiniest bit of silence before commencing the next section. To interrupt the carefully paced accelerando only to continue at the tempo at which you have arrived feels awkward. But you will judge these matters for yourself.

As for how to physically conduct this, there is no problem if you go right into the Allegro, but if you add a slight pause, you will have to stop your beat almost in the middle of your body to indicate the pause and then continue, as if a television image were to stop to isolate a detail and then resume right away.

At the Allegro proper, if you just follow what is written, there should be no problems. I make sure that the quarter notes in the 2/8 bars are long and add a little expressive crescendo so that they connect to the next measure. In any passages where a 3/8 bar is followed by a 2/8 bar, make your beat smaller for the latter. I have seen some conductors do the opposite, and it can be confusing for the musicians who are counting rests. Even though it is not indicated, the violas and cellos should play their chords divisi.

The *molto ritenuto* is more like a *meno mosso* and is conducted in three. There is a line over the first note, so perhaps this is more *pesante* than we usually hear. By putting in a 2/8 in **m. 94**, Bartók makes things difficult. To create enough time for an actual silence to occur, some conductors have made a grand pause out of this measure. I would wait just long enough for any reverberation to clear and then commence at a gentle single *forte*. This passage should not get too loud; otherwise, the woodwinds will get swamped a few bars later.

On the page, it seems like the cellos and double basses would sound equal when we arrive at **m. 107**, but it just doesn't work that way. The upper register of the cellos will be more direct than that of the basses, so the latter need to play out a bit more. The first violins at **m. 110** are almost playful but *dolce* as well. As with many conductors, I give a little room between that last note of **m. 121** and the downbeat to allow for a portamento, which I believe creates a nice sentimental moment.

Make sure that the strings are soft enough to allow the woodwind figurations beginning at **m. 123** to come through, especially those that start on low notes. The trombone makes its first appearance at **m. 134**; this is important because it will establish how this phrase is played by all the other instruments as the movement goes on. While I prefer the full-quarter length, some play it more like an eighth.

Do not make a ritard until Bartók says to do so. The slowdown is built into the descending flute line, and the strings relax the tempo in **m. 149**, but it is not as big a shift as you might think. The tempo changes from $\quarternote = 83$ to $\quarternote = 76$, and the marking *Tranquillo* refers to more than the metronome.

The 4/8 is, at this point, conducted in two, making us wonder why the composer didn't write 2/4 in the time signature. Make sure that the oboist does not come in late on the second beat. Also worth noting is the first entry of the harp, with the marking *distinto*; the harp's glissando takes place over the entire bar at **m. 171** and winds up around *mezzo forte*.

The above warning about the oboe entry also applies to the two clarinets at **m. 174**. Meanwhile, be sure to observe the gentle accents in the strings at **mm. 178** and **181**. The harp can be the rhythmic glue to hold all this together.

The wording is slightly cumbersome at **m. 192** for the violins. What Bartók wants is six players in the firsts and four in the seconds. They are divided with one note per stand. He also confuses us by asking for the sixteenths to be played at the tip of the bow, but at the same time, he puts dots over the notes. This is pretty much impossible, so we just play short notes on the string.

Conduct in three for the ritard at **m. 206** and return to one at **m. 208**. The second trombone comes in for the first time, and the indication is that both trombonists use a cardboard mute rather than a metal one. I find it best to conduct **m. 230** in three on account of the slowdown. Pretend that your third beat is like a very short fermata, giving you time for a strong preparatory upbeat to the next section. The tuba joins in for the first time at **m. 233**. Are you sensing a pattern here? The sonic palette of the orchestra is growing as the movement progresses.

Remember that even though you have in front of you what everyone in the orchestra is doing, the musicians only have their individual parts. Unless there are some written cues, no one can see what anyone else is playing and, consequently, **m. 242** is often a mess the first time around. With different groups entering on the first, second, or third beats, players do not yet know how they fit into the mix.

Even the most experienced orchestras can get confused here. I would suggest rehearsing each of the rhythmic groups separately. Start with the violins, then the lower strings, and finally the woodwinds. Placing an accent on the first note of each group of sixteenths can help delineate the entry point. I also suggest altering the bowing to accommodate groups of five notes, rather than four sixteenths followed by a separated eighth, because playing the last note individually creates an unwanted accent that throws off the balance.

Here is something I have never done, but maybe someone else has thought about it and included it. Given that the horns emphasize the string entrances, is it possible that two trumpets, playing *mezzo forte*, could do the same for the woodwinds? There is a certain logic here, but it would be somewhat daring.

The phrase structure varies as we move from **m. 248** to **m. 271**. Often, when bars are beat in one, we can think in terms of a larger pattern to help us feel and convey the phrasing. I envision it this way: six, four, seven, and seven. No, I do not beat that pattern, but I am thinking about it through the passage.

Beginning in **m. 248**, we encounter a dilemma slightly different from the usual "I see a crescendo but do not know what dynamic it goes to" problem that occurs with almost every composer. The second violins begin *forte*. They have a two-bar crescendo in **mm. 252–53**, followed by another single *forte*. The question is whether Bartók wanted that to be a result of the crescendo or a *subito meno forte*. The former makes the most sense, and to do it, you should pull back the dynamic to around *mezzo forte* at **m. 252**. This will apply to most of the entries where a specific dynamic is not printed, including the cello crescendo at **m. 253**. You can easily start every phrase after a crescendo at *mezzo forte*, including at **m. 265**. Beat in three at **m. 271** to observe the slight allargando just before the *Tranquillo*.

A little relaxation also occurs prior to **m. 288**, but staying in one is possible here. When only one instrument is involved—such as at **m. 312**—you can let the soloists determine the ritard on their own.

At **m. 313** the composer introduces a series of contrapuntal entries, very much like fanfares. Keep track of who enters where. At first, they correspond with beginnings of phrases, but starting in **m. 363**, these individual entrances need to be heard equally so that by the time all six voices have come in, the effect is a circus of sound.

In **m. 379**, Bartók omits a dynamic for the first and third horns, but single *forte* is appropriate. However, he is very precise about the shadings of the strings. There are two ways to view the various brass reentries before **m. 396**. The most common is to place accents on each one, but since Bartók does not indicate any, you could also start them just a little bit softer so that the crescendo accumulates more subtly.

At **m. 396**, we arrive at another comma, and again, we don't quite know what to do. I don't think I have heard anyone wait before the violin entrance, but for that to be effective, the downbeat must be as short as possible, and perhaps the violins should begin a touch louder, decreasing their volume just before the entry of the clarinet.

At **m. 425** we can hear the harp's four notes against the woodwinds' three, but sometimes lost are the groupings of five notes in the first violins and cellos. In one of the more unusual instructions, the second harp is asked to play **m. 438** "near the sound board with an appropriately shaped wooden (if possible, metal) stick." Many harpists use spoons, and this creates a very novel effect. The divisi at **m. 456** are clearly laid out—unlike at **m. 192**—and since Bartók does not instruct the violins to use the tip of the bow, they can play all the notes off the string. The harp and three trumpets should be marked *piano*.

We now come to a passage that is usually played without observing what is indicated. Starting in **m. 470**, we are asked to relax the tempo until **m. 476**, when we begin an accelerando. Perhaps because of the contrasting material, many conductors will begin with a *subito poco meno mosso*, picking up the tempo in **m. 472**; this back and forth is repeated in the subsequent two bars. But that is the easy way out of a tricky passage for the conductor.

I believe the contrast is important not only for the musical content but also for the alternating moods. What Bartók seemingly wants is for us to do the first three bars as a continuation of the previous tempo, then to slightly slow down and make a ritard for the remainder. However, a problem presents itself at **m. 477**. If you wish to do the passage as written, I suggest conducting **m. 474** in three, then a bar in four, followed by two measures in three, before finally shifting into one. Getting the first violins to play together on their upbeat to **m. 478** takes a little effort.

However, if you choose the alternating tempos, subdivide the two bars before **m. 476** and then immediately go back into one where the accelerando begins. You have to start a little bit slower to allow room to speed up, arriving at the original Allegro tempo at **m. 488**.

The passage that commences at **m. 494** includes several interesting accents to enjoy, some of which are in the horns. It is tempting to want to push the tempo ahead, but resist. You will see that the double basses have a glissando in **m. 513**. I am not quite sure why, as the orchestra is quite loud at this point, so hearing it is pretty much out of the question. In the last phrase, add a bit of weight to the first note but stay in tempo.

Second Movement: Giuoco delle coppie

Nothing beats a good game. Bartók was playing one with all of us when he gave this movement a subtitle. Originally, there was no name at all, simply *Allegro scherzando*, as listed on the program page at the premiere.

Bartók's original manuscript reveals the words *Presentando le coppie* or "presentation of couples," which he later changed to *Giuoco delle coppie* or "game of the couples" in his blueprint copy sometime before the first printing. This is interesting and gives us a little idea of what the composer had in mind, but it is not the most pressing issue regarding the musical content.

That honor falls to the metronome mark. In Boosey & Hawkes's published score, the tempo was marked as ♩ = 74. While preparing for a recording he made with the Chicago Symphony in 1981, Sir Georg Solti consulted Bartók's original manuscript, which is housed at the Library of Congress, and found that it clearly read "94," a marked difference. As Solti wrote in his *Memoirs*, "Performers must follow Bartók's metronome marks. Those of us who are at home in the Hungarian musical idiom know that one cannot go wrong if one follows these indications."[2]

The principal percussionist of the Chicago Symphony verified that this was indeed the tempo written in his music, and Solti recorded the work with the reinstated metronome. This was a printer's error and has since been corrected by the publisher. Even though the faster pace seems just a bit hurried, it is what Bartók intended.

But what about that "Hungarian idiom" that Sir Georg mentioned? Solti adhered to the older printed metronome mark for his earlier recording of the work in London. As for other great Hungarian maestros, well, Reiner always did it at the quicker tempo. Ormandy stuck to the slower rendition, and both Szell and Dorati landed somewhere in the middle, around ♩ = 84.

Regardless of what tempo you take, within reason, this is one of the cleverest pieces of musical prestidigitation ever penned. It starts with the side drum playing without snares. This is different from, say, a field drum, which usually has a lower timbre. It is up to you to decide what sounds closest to what you have in mind.

Bartók introduces various pairs of instruments, starting with the bassoons. Even though their lines are playful, it is almost equally jocular to hear the underlying chords in the pizzicato strings, especially the slurs between two eighth notes in **m. 17** and **m. 19**. To make this audible, the first note must be played just a little stronger than what came before it, and the finger must move quickly; otherwise the second pitch will not be heard.

Exaggerate the accents and dynamics for the bassoons, and do not let them shortchange the half note at the end of their duet. Next up are the oboes, who are even more playful. Again, the music beneath them is truly delightful. For example, at **m. 28**, the oboes appear to be playing in A minor, but the cellos have pizzicato D♯s—not exactly the height of dissonance, but just enough to be pungent. This type of playfulness will go on through much of the movement, and I do not want to spoil your fun. Nonetheless, I would caution against too much physicality for the duration of the piece. The joy is in hearing the notes as opposed to seeing them.

Bartók creates a novel moment for the first violins at **m. 41**. They play octave B♭s with a trill on the lower note. But the indication is *non divisi*. It does work, so insist on this. The two accents at **m. 45** can be played quite loudly.

Continuing with the woodwinds in pairs, the clarinets take their turn. The bassoons played in sixths, the oboes in thirds, and here the instruments are in sevenths. In **m. 46**, Bartók indicates *pochissimo ritenuto*, which applies to the quintuplet sixteenth notes. The problem is not in the solo instruments but rather the strings. Getting them to play the bounced bows together is not easy.

One possible solution is to establish how much time you will give to the clarinets to make this ritard and then ask them to play it alone. That way the strings have a chance to gauge the speed. Another possibility, and the one I have adopted, is simply to have the clarinets play the five notes equally in the established tempo. Because one note has been added to the mixture, you have automatically slowed enough for the required *poch. rit.*, and it is much easier for the triplet underneath to be performed accurately.

For the first-violin divisi, I would advise doing this by stand because the lower line will need to come out when the pizzicato begins. Although it is not usually a problem, please note that at **m. 57**, all the lower string notes are *forte*, with only the first of each group having the *sforzando*.

The last of the woodwind pairings are the flutes, playing in fifths. Balance here is not a problem. But the viola pizzicato at **m. 69** is best done with hardly any diminuendo. As the line goes downward, there is already a feeling that the dynamic is lessening. The *poco rallentando* for this duo is much more comfortable than the one that the clarinets did. Do not let it get too slow, but going into four for the last bar is fine if you wish. Bring out the double basses' second note in **m. 81**, as no one else is playing here.

A slight touch of jazz comes in with the viola pizzicato at **m. 87**. To highlight that, I start each group with an accent and place a diminuendo on the first phrase. The muted trumpet duet, written in seconds, usually works well, but make sure the strings do not rise above *piano*. The glissandos should start immediately after the first note to fill the entire beat, not played late as we would do in Mahler.

Just before **m. 102**, we have a comma that works. Bartók writes *(breve)*, which could lead you to think that when he does not put this word in, the breaths are long. But if that were the case, why wouldn't he have put in a fermata or even a rest? Everyone comes up a dynamic level at **m. 102** and then back down three bars later. Because the string writing here is a bit dense, they can cover the trumpets. It is nice to observe the isolated *mezzo forte* in the cellos at **m. 111**. Sometimes, depending on how far away they are from the strings, the trumpets might be just a bit late at **m. 116**.

The lovely chorale, answered by the side drum, can be phrased in two possible ways: as six unbroken bars—each followed by a breath—or with tiny lifts after each slur. If you choose the latter, be careful that this does not wind up sounding mannered. **Measure 134** requires a breath at the end of the bar, but the first trombone also changes notes. If the second beat is played like an eighth to allow for the breath and to stay in tempo, it seems abrupt. I sustain that last note just a little bit longer so that the harmony is clear and the musicians have enough time to inhale. The third phrase can also be done with slight separations between the slurred groups or perhaps with a little stress on the first notes of each group.

The horns enter in **m. 147**, followed by the tuba. In **m. 150**, the phrasing in the tuba line differs from that of the horns. I choose to emphasize this and ask the horns to insert a slight separation between the quarters. At **m. 156**, the horns are asked to hold one note for an awfully long time, when you think about it. Of course, some players can do it, but in the interest of safety, the horns can take a little breath after the second bar.

It has become customary to add a slight ritard during the last flute solo. A new wrinkle gets added with the slash marks. Most certainly they indicate a complete break before starting what is now a game of triples, but why didn't Bartók just stick with the commas? We will never know.

Several of us hold back the tempo slightly for the first two notes of the bassoons, resuming *a tempo* right at **m. 165**. But it is, and will be, the additional instruments that make the next few sections so amusing. By now, everyone knows the tune, so we can really bring out the new information. On the isolated eighths (**m. 168**), I have the third bassoon play these notes sustained; if there are two consecutive notes (**m. 170**), then they are short. All the crescendos in the upper lines can be somewhat exaggerated and will hopefully elicit a chuckle or two. Go into four to conduct the ritard in **m. 179** and then back into two with a little accelerando to return to Tempo I. I also insert a crescendo for the third bassoon during the ritard.

Now we have the game of quartets as the oboes and clarinets add more harmonic flavor to the mix. I like to bring out the hint of jazz beginning in **m. 184** by asking for a slight accent on the first note of each slurred group of two sixteenths. Bartók was clever to write *pianissimo* in the first violins at **m. 189**, as the octaves could be attacked too aggressively.

The flutes replace the oboes at **m. 198**, and you can treat the quintuplet with the *poco rit.* at **m. 199** the same way you did at **m. 46**. I bring up the flutes to *mezzo forte*, as the clarinets in their somewhat higher register can be a bit too loud. Be aware that at **m. 208** the flutes have a figure that can get covered up by the clarinets and is important to the harmonic structure. As before, you should go into four at **m. 222**.

Not all accents are created equal, and context is everything. From **m. 228**, the muted violins must drop down just a little after the accent but not so much as to diminish the upcoming *pianissimo*. The harps' glissandos add a great color, so make sure that neither musician lingers on the first note. Violas should play on the string at the tip at **m. 231**, but the accent in the violins is still present. Note the absence of accents from **m. 241** onward.

What looks like a twelve-note group of sixteenths in **m. 243** is really two sextuplets. Ensure that the musicians play this evenly so that the harmonic motion is clear. You might be wondering about that grace note at **m. 244**; Bartók is trying to avoid jumping down a third or more to the next bar.

Have the slurs at **m. 247** played as they appear in the score, starting on an up bow. The final two sixteenths are up bow, down bow. At **m. 249**, each group of two notes starts on an up bow. While not indicated, I find that playing the first eighth note at **m. 251** long and the last one short is quite effective.

The final chord buildup can be done either with or without accents. I like putting them in to make the surprise of the dominant in the first clarinet a bit more pungent. One way to balance this chord properly is to ask all the winds to play together at **m. 254**. Listen to determine if it sounds like a single unit and adjust as needed. This helps the musicians to understand what the intended result of the pyramid should sound like. Once you cut off the winds, just let the side drum play, hold your arms up a bit, and wait a moment before lowering them.

Third Movement: Elegia

Without actually quoting directly, the correlation between this movement and the opening could not be clearer. To begin with, Bartók chose the same metronome marks, again giving us some leeway. The third movement also requires the same contrast between what is *piano* and what is *pianissimo*.

Starting with the opening tune, this time only in the double basses, we can ask them to play expressively and not as if they were providing an accompaniment line. The first three notes in the timpani bolster this tune, with the harp showing us that the two Ds are also reiterated in the basses.

It is essential to sustain the *piano* marking in the low instrument when the other strings enter. The basses can play without vibrato, giving an eerie sensation to the passage. Only in the ninth measure do they join in the general dynamic. Here, the harp glissando should be ethereal, but bring out the quasi-C-major chord, played *non arpeggio*, at the end of the bar. If you wish, the figurations in the clarinet and flute can be somewhat free but must be played in the same way by both musicians. The oboe solo can be done in one breath, but if the player struggles with it, one logical solution is to add a bit of space before the G♯ at **m. 14**.

The three bars before **m. 22** present an interesting problem for the interpreter. Bartók does not employ accents, and each instrument begins *forte*. On paper, it appears that the piccolo and harp simply add to the texture, but since the harp by its very nature cannot enter discreetly, perhaps the piccolo should emphasize this note, which means, in effect, that both musicians play with a slight accent.

At **m. 22** itself, the metronome mark is the same as the slowest tempo indicated at the beginning. If you chose to start at that tempo, theoretically, you should not change the speed. But if you started at a tempo of ♩ = 72, then you will need to make a slight ritard to get to what is essentially a *poco meno mosso*.

There are usually no problems in balance for the violins before **m. 28**. You do have to decide how to split up both the two- and three-part divisi to achieve equality. Warm up the music at the single *piano* in **m. 29**, increasing the volume to around *mezzo forte*. The piccolo player traditionally takes a little breath before **m. 31** to separate this entrance from the two previous bars.

The violin and clarinet articulations seem contradictory in **m. 34**. We see that the clarinets separate the sixteenth notes, but the upper strings have a slur and lines over the first three. What does this mean? Looking at it from a bowing standpoint, the violins' two Es in the first bar are to be separated, and Bartók continues in this manner, even when the notes themselves change.

To me, it is fairly clear, but you have to be clever with the bowing: two down bows, separated, followed by an up bow on the D♯, a down bow on the E, and then a change of bow during the held note so that you can do the same with each subsequent measure. The *non troppo forte* mark for the trumpet is most likely so that the musician will not play too aggressively. As for the timpani, they indeed have sixteenth notes, and two players are required so as not to sound like a tremolo. In other words, do not have one musician play both parts.

Bowing continues to play a key role in the general phrase patterns at **m. 37**. Here, it might be best to separate the two eighth notes, down and up, and ask the violins to change a few times on the B♮. At **m. 39**, a very unusual chord occurs on the third beat. Up until this point, all the previous chords have been consonant. Out of nowhere, and for the only time, a strange B♭ emerges from what is essentially an A-minor chord. Could this be an error? Normally, if it were only in one instrument, we might say yes, but it appears in several, so you can either bring it out or downplay it.

Measure 44 should see the violins ending on an up bow. In a departure from what we have established in the previous two phrases, **m. 45** itself is best played with separate bows to get maximum sound, and I recommend changing bows on the longer notes a couple of times. These two bars are played on the G string. It is worth noting that the last note of **m. 51** is long and does not allow much time before the downbeat.

At **m. 54** the horns have a *forte* with a one-beat diminuendo while the upper strings play a very sudden *forte-piano*, which is played *sul ponticello* and should sound very scary. In case it is not clear, the solo cellos have a glissando between each two-note pizzicato group. This amplifies the oboes and clarinets but can be brought out a bit because it is such an unusual sonority. **Measure 61** starts in four, but it is probably a good idea to subdivide the second half of the bar to coordinate the pizzicato.

The next passage is the most difficult in this movement. We have several instructions from Bartók, including *poco agitato* and *molto rubato*. In some ways, this might be the most Hungarian moment in the entire concerto. Considering the heavy stress on the first syllable of names in the Hungarian language, it is certainly possible to conclude that "rubato" means that the first note of the tune is a little longer than the others. After that, we can move the tempo forward to give the passage the feeling of freedom. This happens three times.

However, following each of these phrases, the harps have a rhythmic figure that must be played rather straightforwardly. In **m. 65**, the violins' accented note may be played long or short but should not sound harsh. A gradual crescendo takes place with the subsequent entries, each one dynamic higher. Because Bartók begins a rallentando at **m. 69**, I don't think it is necessary to lengthen the first note of that bar as I have suggested previously.

Since the violas begin *forte* at **m. 62** and have a crescendo at **m. 69**, we must assume that they go to *fortissimo*. The best way to accomplish the accents on the two G♯s in **mm. 70–71** is to take two bows on the first one and three on the second one.

We have a slight problem to solve in **m. 72**. After a three-bar *poco rallentando*, the next instruction is *tornando al tempo*. If this takes place for the duration of the measure, then there is not much time to spare during the quarter rest. I believe that most conductors ignore the marking and wait for things to settle down.

The same rubato that was heard in the violas now transfers to the woodwinds. The differences are in the underlying material: harp and viola glissandos, strong notes on the third beat, and most importantly, sustained notes in the horns at the end of each bar. Because they are muted, encourage them to bring out these notes, even if it means a slightly brassy tone. To complement what the violas played earlier, it makes sense to have the woodwinds place an accent on the note at **m. 81**.

The arco in the strings at **m. 83** presents a bit of a dilemma because we are not told if this is divisi or if all the notes are played and the top note held. Sustaining the top note really does not work, as it would mean that the cellos would be the only section not playing an A♭. Given that the brass have the full chord, I think that dividing and assigning two notes per player makes the most sense. The woodwinds sustain a beat longer than the strings.

Next Bartók incorporates several references to the first movement. He has interspersed hints of this right from the start of the movement, but from **m. 86** on, he is virtually quoting himself. There are differences, specifically when he fills out the full tune in **mm. 89–91. Measure 92** appears to be a *sforzando* followed by a one-beat diminuendo. Then there is a large two-beat crescendo with a frantic tremolo. At this point, you must trust the composer and the seemingly contradictory dynamics. Of course, the trumpets at *fortississimo* are going to dominate, but the remaining instruments can still make an impact. Keep the violins at *fortissimo*, even as the other instruments begin to diminish their sound levels.

When studying this piece, and even when rehearsing it, you might question how to conduct during the quintuplets in **mm. 97–98**. It is easier than you think. A slight allargando occurs, mostly to accomplish the down bows. This might seem unusual, but if you let the violins play this on their own, they seem to find a natural way of doing it together. You just have to catch the third beat of **m. 98** so that those who cut off, as well as those who play the pizzicato, stay together. Most violin sections will play the G trill on a down bow. The E♯ in **m. 100** has an accent but can be played either long or short.

Harkening back to the opening of the movement, the lower strings play the main theme single *piano* and expressively, sustaining the dynamic so that the various *pianissimo* entrances are distant and ghostly. The downbeat of **m. 111** is long, and the piccolo can make a very slight ritenuto on the final three notes.

At the *calmo* indication, getting the oboes to play a true *pianissimo* is difficult, primarily because the second starts in a somewhat lower register. Balance the chords as best you can so that none of the notes feels melodic; that is left to the first violin section, which I usually ask to crescendo to *mezzo forte* before asking the same of the woodwinds in **mm. 116–17**. Separate the accented tremolos in **mm. 118–19** and perhaps add a diminuendo for the first violins so that the next phrase begins *piano*. But when the cellos crescendo, you might consider increasing to *forte* so that the thirty-second notes are clearly heard during their decrescendo.

As the strings fade out, I ask them to play their last bar without vibrato. Since Bartók just gives the timpani a quarter note at the end, let the piccolo fade out. You do not have to give this cutoff, but it is not a bad idea to hold your arms up for several seconds of silence after the sound has died away.

Fourth Movement: Intermezzo interrotto

This second Scherzo is a marvel of contrasting musical ideas. Some conductors go directly into it following the elegy, but this is not the interruption referred to in the subtitle. In fact, there are two different stories about the meaning—more on this a bit later.

Bartók does not provide a tempo indication, but the metronome marking of ♩ = 110 seems about right. It is certainly possible to choose a slightly slower tempo for the opening bars to create a little more contrast at the Allegretto that follows. You have to start with your right arm up so that what is usually the downbeat is actually the preparation for the first note. I prefer an up bow for everyone and then two bows on the fermata to give the crescendo maximum effect.

At first, the beat patterns are clear in the 5/8 measures. However, as we go along there will be a few contradictions, even within a single bar. The best advice, in general, is to conduct the rhythm relevant to most of the musicians, even when there are rests. Often the composer or editor will try to indicate either the 2 + 3 or 3 + 2 pattern in the notation of those rests.

Should we tell the orchestra in advance how we will conduct these? That could take up an awful lot of rehearsal time. I think it is always best to try to play through the movement, keeping track of where you believe the orchestra might be confused. Once the oboe starts, keep your beat small and refer mostly to the pizzicatos. All the initial 5/8 measures will be 3 + 2.

There is a delicious, almost sexy line in the second violins beginning at **m. 13**, so I insert tiny hairpins between the notes. You will see a notation in **m. 20** regarding what to do if the flute does not have a low B; this is rarely the case today, so you can ignore the remark. We found a vertical line earlier in the piece, and here it is again at **m. 27**. My assumption is that it serves as a break between the notes without a change in tempo. **Measure 29** might require you to tell the cellos and then violas what the horn plays so they can fit in their eighth notes. Just a slight glance at the oboist will be enough to start the *a tempo*.

The violas now have that figure that the second violins had at **m. 13**, so I add the small hairpin here as well. I have my suspicions regarding the indication at **m. 42**. Certainly, *calmo* represents a new tempo, but should it start immediately, or might we take just a little time before the *forte* line in the violas? Well, take a look at the indication: *forte, cantabile*. Why is the comma after the dynamic? Perhaps it was intended to follow the second B, halfway through **m. 42**. To allow some time here, let the violas finish the first half of the bar, not really moving for this, and then resume on the three-note upbeat. The harps normally will play their chords as arpeggios, but another possibility is for just the first harp to play them that way while the second harp plays them unarpeggiated, always lining up with the first harp's top note. The timpani part looks easy to us, but all the pedal changes are challenging. This passage is always on any audition for that instrument. The 7/8 bar is beat as 2 + 3 + 2.

Balance is a problem at **m. 51**. Unless your English horn player has a huge sound, much of this canonical passage gets lost. It may be necessary to ask the first violins to play closer to *mezzo forte* and bring down the violas' volume in the previous bar. You will see that the bars in 5/8 and 7/8 have different phrasings in these instruments. Go with the majority; the English horn player will figure it out. The phrasings coalesce at **m. 59**, and you can make a slight ritard just before the entrance of the oboe at the tempo change in **m. 61**. Stay with the 3 + 2 pattern at **m. 66**.

The introduction to the Trio section can be tricky. I believe that the group of four notes in the cellos and basses must be played legato to avoid feeling it in two-note groupings. Then the vertical line appears in **m. 71** and **m. 73**, giving us the opportunity to take a short breath. Although several conductors lead the 8/8 bars with the phrasing of 3 + 2 + 3 as indicated, I find it more efficient to think of these three bars as a simple 4/4. In the last one, I slip into two for the second half, making the accelerando a bit easier to accomplish.

Various anecdotes have circulated regarding this "interruption." One has Bartók telling Antal Doráti that it is a quote from Lehár's *The Merry Widow*; Ferenc Fricsay said it had something to do with a patriotic Hungarian song. The story that seems to be the truth concerns the composer having heard the

American premiere of Shostakovich's Seventh Symphony on the radio. The incessant melody in the middle of the first movement apparently so enraged Bartók that he decided to parody it here.

What I find most interesting is that the metronome mark at the *più mosso* is the same as the one Solti found at the Library of Congress: ♩ = 94. But none of us perform it at this tempo. We are all closer to 100, at least. This part of the movement cries out for exaggeration. The trills need to be mocking, the descending woodwinds seem to almost fall apart, and of course, the trombone glissandos are as rude as they get. Let those two musicians have their way with them, and do not worry that it is not really in any tempo.

At **m. 92**, notice that this passage is not all that loud. The bassoon line is interesting to bring out here. You can accomplish the violin phrasing at **m. 95** either by asking them to bounce the bow on the slurred notes with dots or to play them with separate strokes. I prefer the former, as it adds to the overall chaotic nature of the sound. The A♭s in the tuba and double basses at **m. 98** and **m. 102** make this moment a favorite of mine.

The glissandos at **m. 105** and **m. 113** should last the entire bar. It is okay if the tam-tam steals focus for a bar, but since we have no indication of when it should stop, just ask the percussionist to lightly dampen it rather than cut off abruptly. Bartók does not indicate a slowdown, and arguably a rallentando has already happened naturally because the distance between the notes has increased.

If you took a bit of time before the first *calmo* indication, you could do so again. I play the downbeat quite short and try to keep the audience guessing as to what is going to happen next. This is in keeping with my philosophy that the audience always includes people who have never heard the piece, and I want them to be surprised.

Muted strings playing *piano* is almost the same as unmuted *pianissimo*. This reiteration of the second theme has much less expression than the first time around. Bartók carefully instructs *non crescendo* in the 7/8 bar, which can be emphasized by making a diminuendo as the line ascends.

The pickups in the English horn at **m. 136** are in the quicker tempo. Despite the dots on the strings' notes at **m. 136**, I ask them to play on the string but at the tip of the bow. Conducting the bar before **m. 140** is not so difficult: stop your beat somewhere in the middle of your body, and then continue downward. This will serve as the preparation for the flute entry.

The fermata cadenza requires you to cut off the first three horns. The flute plays freely, adding a few of the C♯ and F♯ patterns. Wait for the G and F♯, which are usually played a little slower. At this point, signal the first violins to change notes and discreetly cut off the others. Catching the end of the run can seem challenging, especially if you do not have perfect pitch. It is fruitless to think of it in terms of the rhythmic groupings, as this is just a written-out ritardando. The flutist can help you out by indicating to the oboe when to come in. Take your visual cue from that musician, giving a downward preparation to show when the violins stop playing.

The final eight bars are playful, with a nice *pianissimo* touch halfway through. If you were diligent earlier, you will know that the last four notes in the cellos and basses are to be played as one legato phrase rather than two groups of notes. The cutoff is with the last note of the woodwinds and should sound abrupt.

Fifth Movement: Finale

Any composer attempting a five-movement work is always faced with the difficulty of making the last one truly unique. Bartók more than succeeds and, in some ways, summarizes his entire musical life with this Finale. He moves from folk music to virtuosity and hints at his earlier musical styles with such ease that we are apt to forget how coherent the concerto is as a whole.

It begins with a fanfare-like motif that will become the framework for the entire movement. The tempo marking is *pesante* at ♩ = 128. To me, that is a shade fast to really differentiate it from the upcoming Presto. The three trumpets enter *fortissimo* at the fermata, but if this is overplayed, it can almost obliterate the horns.

It is not an accident that these instruments, along with the bassoons and double basses, are only at *forte* when the accelerando begins. We must hear the first notes of the back-and-forth pizzicato, and any dynamic above that will be too loud. Bartók says to "put the bow aside," and the string players involved will usually set them in their laps. The arrows simply tell the players which note will be the last in the arpeggio. Since they start slowly, the initial rolls do not have to be abrupt. Under no circumstances should the violists put their instruments down and play them like a guitar. When they are raised in playing position, the sound projects better to the audience.

For the sake of ensemble, divide the violins in half, with the stands near the back playing the lower line. Try to have an equal number of musicians on each part. Bartók instructs us to have this played *pianissimo* and at the tip. From the conductor's point of view, the upper line will sound stronger if divided as suggested above, so you must encourage everyone who starts any of the four parts to play as softly and clearly as possible.

Once all four groups have entered, we can bring out some subtle inflections. But the violins always tend to get too loud too soon. For that reason, when an extended crescendo appears, it is a good idea to add some dynamics to the parts so that the musicians will know how loud to be as the sound increases. I recommend single *piano* at **m. 28**, *mezzo piano* at **m. 36**, and *mezzo forte* at **m. 41**.

In the meantime, you can make **m. 21** more interesting by bringing out the timpani and bass just a little. There is usually no problem with the woodwinds at **m. 28**, but the horn accents that start in **m. 32** need to be equal in volume and clearly audible. After that, the buildup to **m. 44** works on its own.

Do pay attention to which notes are long and which are short at **m. 44**; these are usually represented with lines and dots. The horn syncopation at **m. 47** might need to start at single *forte*, depending on the acoustic of the stage. More than likely, the bassoons have a misprint here and should duplicate the horn rhythm. **Measure 52** and all the sixteenth notes after are played on the string.

Measure 59 can be made even more interesting if you bring out the changes of pitch in the second and third horns. In that same measure, Bartók includes an indication that he does not use very often in this piece: *più forte*. Prior to the twentieth century, this could either mean louder or crescendo. Here it is clearly the former. Look for interesting rhythmic variants to bring out along the way. At **m. 71**, for instance, the first and third horns have a figure that can start stronger than what they have been playing so far.

Once in a while, a score contains an anomaly that simply cannot be explained. Looking at the viola and cello parts at **m. 74**, we find an arrow that points downward. As we discovered at the beginning of the movement, the direction of the arrow shows which note is played last, usually arriving on the beat. However, the three bars that start at **m. 74** contain what surely must be an error. The lower strings are asked to play a *non divisi* chord arco, from the upper note down to the lower one, with a tenuto line on the top. This is impractical, and it is hard to imagine the composer not wanting the opposite to occur—in other words, start from the low note and then sustain the top one. You can see that these top notes correspond with those in the violins on the second beat of **mm. 74, 75, and 77**.

Musical matters are straightforward until **m. 96**. Other than the flutes, everyone is quite soft. However, getting the bow to the right spot after coming off a crescendo is difficult for the solo strings. The best way to achieve an immediate *pianissimo* is for those who play at **m. 96** to leave out the last four sixteenth notes of the previous bar. This gives them enough time to enter without scrambling. You may wonder why the harps divide what might be possible to play on just one instrument. This is to accommodate the pedal changes, but the two instruments still need to sound similar, as if playing one line of eighth notes.

Measure 112 offers a glimpse of the Finale of Tchaikovsky's Fourth Symphony that amuses me. Bartók's bowing indication makes getting into **m. 119** a bit challenging. Perhaps it is better to start the previous measure up bow, allowing the *subito piano* to come on an up bow, and then separate the next two notes. All the quarters and dotted quarters that are marked as down bows work, but you should ask the strings to hold on to each as long as possible.

It seems obvious, but at **m. 132** the trombones all should sound as if just one were playing the line, even though the first two hold on while the third enters. At **m. 137**, I think that this time, the *più forte* really is a crescendo leading up to **m. 144**. We encounter another anomaly when the bassoon comes in at **m. 148** because there are lines on the first two notes, but the passage is also marked *ben marcato*. This probably means that these initial entries are slightly accented.

With an indication of *Tranquillo* and the metronome mark of ♩ = 114, **m. 161** represents a significant relaxation, like a *molto meno mosso*. Some conductors make a ritardando in the previous measure, trying to ease the eighth notes. My solution is to establish the new tempo at **m. 161** but allow the oboes to finish their phrase at the quicker pace with which they began.

The three-part divisi at **m. 175** can be done stand by stand. Given the dynamic of single *piano*, you might wish to consider breaking up the bowing in the middle of the slur. Bartók marks an eight-bar accelerando, but many conductors get to the new tempo almost four bars too early.

Be sure to distinguish for the listener the *mezzo forte* at **m. 196** and the *forte* at **m. 200**. Articulate the eighth notes in the lower strings, and make sure that the other sections do not go too far above their dynamic or else the second trumpet might need to force the sound.

At **m. 221**, you may detect a balance problem between the horns and trumpets. Keep in mind that the horns play with their bells facing away from you while the trumpets do not. In some venues, this can make a big difference.

Measure 231 is another spot where half of the basses might go down to the low D♭. This puts it more in the territory of the tuba and adds depth to the note. I ask the trombones to add a slight accent every three bars so that the rhythmic pattern of the whole passage is purposely a bit vaguer.

At **m. 245**, even though it is marked at single *forte*, I think it is valid to have the third trumpet and horns play their entries very short and strong to interrupt the activity that is going on. Everyone with sixteenth notes must give as much as possible at **m. 249**. The timpani glissando takes place over the whole bar, and the roll helps us hear the pitch change.

In the lead-up to the quasi-fugato, you must decide about the divisi, but this one seems clear. Each of the string sections, except the double basses, is split in two. One half has the tune while the other half plays an accompanying figure, at least at first. Because of the various moving lines, I recommend assigning the front stands the upper notes. The back of the sections might have to play a bit louder, but this is really the best way to ensure a tight ensemble sound as the motion builds. Do not try to fill in the notes that the harps play but the violins do not.

Each of the melodic entries becomes shorter in length on the half notes. I advise taking two bows in **m. 266**, considering the absence of diminuendos. After that, one bow will work, as long as the *forte* can truly be sustained. All the grace notes are short but need to be heard. You can exaggerate the glissandos between the eighths. Once the triplets commence, the violinists should play them off the string.

Each time a melodic line appears, Bartók adds a bit of spice, whether a pizzicato, a quick figuration, or a rhythmic element. By now, everyone knows the tune, so bringing out these other nuances is always welcome. The *subito mezzo forte* at **m. 314** might have to come down a dynamic level. At **m. 317**, the woodwinds usually play the triplets disconnected. Although it does not feel or sound like it, the string entries at this point are only a half-step away from each other, just as they will be when they appear in the reverse order at **m. 325**.

From **m. 335** onward, each time an instrumental group has a crescendo, the next measure will start at the dynamic of the previous bar. Conduct a tiny ritard at **m. 343** by slightly increasing the size and slowing the speed of your second beat so that the flute and oboe will know when to enter. A very strong pizzicato beginning in **m. 353** can sometimes obscure the continuing harp triplets.

The violin and viola chords in **m. 365** should be divided so that all the notes are short; this can be accomplished with each musician playing two notes. The sixteenths that start in **m. 372** are usually marcato but remain *forte*, as if interrupting the winds. It is not clear to me why Bartók marked the muted trombones *piano*, as they would seem to be continuing the woodwind pattern. At **m. 378** several conductors start the strings at *piano*, but I think it is more proper to continue the *forte* and get as loud as possible at the top of the crescendo. Then return to the single *forte* and remain there for the three bars before Tempo I.

Each successive entry of the strings is at a progressively louder *subito* dynamic. If you wish, you could slightly separate the groups of two eighth notes in the lower strings. Try to bring out the horns a bit at **m. 394** and certainly highlight the trills in the clarinets and flutes. At **m. 411**, the second note of the low brass is short.

Another curious moment occurs at **m. 426**, where the bassoons and horns answer the three-note grouping of the strings; however, only the horn notes are separated. I can understand why Bartók may have marked them separate for the sake of clear articulation, but you may wish to add the slur.

Several pungent accents should be exaggerated from **m. 433**. The music and motion die down, and the lack of rhythmic movement makes it unnecessary to incorporate a ritardando. You can add a subtle downward glissando in the violins at **m. 445** and then perhaps a more pronounced one in the next bar for the cellos and basses. At this point, you should be conducting in one.

Measure 449 is not *pianissimo* and should be played a bit expressively. You can revisit the same phrasing you utilized back at **m. 175**. This passage is a long ritardando, so be sure you are not too slow to begin. The indicated metronome marks are fine, but there is no need to subdivide by conducting in two. The same applies at **m. 482**.

Here we have the strongest reference to some of Bartók's earlier works, with striking dissonances that have not been heard before in this piece. The orchestra might start as softly as possible, but they always seem to increase the dynamic well before the indicated crescendo at **m. 549**. This is partly due to the change from ponticello to normal bowing, but mostly it has to do with the accumulation of textures in the wind instruments.

It is always helpful to rehearse all the instruments other than the strings, just to get a sense of what you would like to bring out. Some of the soloists will need to drop back a little a few bars after their individual entrances. I think the most important lines to hear are the octave leaps that begin various phrases; they provide a reference point to the original theme. Sometimes they occur over two bars, other times as quarter notes in one measure. At times both upward and downward leaps occur simultaneously. During all this, the strings, with all those notes, must maintain the *pianissimo*. It is not about the pitches but rather the color.

You may notice that Bartók occasionally inserts what looks like a double stop in the violins and violas, usually lasting a whole bar. The long note is always on an open string, so it should be played *non divisi*, but this very bizarre sound disappears and is rarely held as long as the composer indicates.

I can suggest a solution for this that requires just a bit of subtlety. Have one stand—I usually pick the third in each section—play just that single note on the open string. That way, it can indeed be held for the full length. They should do the same on subsequent measures that contain the same idea.

Probably unintentional, but interesting, is the fact that when you look at the successive open strings starting at **m. 515**, they correspond to the G, D, A, and E, in order, of the violin tuning notes. These are the same notes that begin the solo part of Berg's Violin Concerto, written ten years earlier.

By the time the ponticello ends at **m. 533**, it is difficult to keep the *pianissimo*, but one possibility is to rehearse the strings at various points in this long passage, asking them to start each one as softly as possible. Maybe, after they have heard the sound, they will remember to sustain this dynamic for the minute or so that it lasts. Determine which notes to bring out as we reach the climactic point of this section.

Measure 556 is marked *Lo stesso tempo, ma pesante* without a metronome indication. If you have perhaps exceeded the speed in the previous buildup, Bartók has given you a way to get back. A slight broadening of the tempo is certainly acceptable. The dynamic is *fortissimo*, but there is a sense of nobility in this brass chorale, so playing it with a rich tone rather than a brassy one makes sense.

The former half note becomes the single beat of the whole bar at **m. 562**. The striking clash of an E♮ and E♭ in the horns and trombones is worth bringing out. And we have one last comma to deal with just before **m. 573**. Traditionally, every conductor takes time before launching into the next measure. But, just for fun, I once edited a recorded version and eliminated the pause, just to see what it would sound like—actually, not bad at all, and we might consider it if there were any evidence that a conductor did it convincingly.

Finally, we come to the ending, or rather, the two endings. When the work premiered, everyone thought that the last bars needed to be fleshed out, feeling that the music concluded too abruptly. We can still listen to the original from the Koussevitzky premiere. I also included it as an option in my own recording. Others have also committed it to disc, but no one actually performs it in concert.

If an orchestra is unfamiliar with the piece, they may be confused as to where this "alternate" ending begins. The score is not exactly clear and would have benefited from a first- and second-ending option. As it is, the players need to cut from the end of **m. 601** to the alternative ending at **m. 602**. If you are inclined to read through the movement at the first rehearsal, it is best to tell the musicians about this before you start, lest all your efforts be thwarted because you have to stop for this spot.

It all amounts to a four-bar crescendo and ritard, followed by a five-bar accelerando back to the main tempo. Many conductors add a bit of *pesante* at the cymbal crash, which can be effective if it is not too slow. Over the last six bars, a decision must be made regarding the brass. Is it an accumulated series of C♯s, or should each have a separate attack? Each of you will have your own thoughts about this. I prefer bringing them out one at a time, right up until the end.

There are two final points to consider. The first regards the timpani. Two measures before the end, we have the F and C. Does the roll hold through the first note or not? My preference is to attack the downbeat strongly and, in a way, give that instrument the last word on the theme. But it is certainly understandable to have the timpani play what is in the tuba part.

Lastly, the trombone glissando is certainly laid out well enough to be heard, but this is not quite the case for the horns. To make the slide audible, ask the horn players to hold the first note just a bit longer and then start the glissando, more like what we would call a "rip."

Make as much crescendo as possible to achieve a feeling of triumph upon the conclusion of this masterpiece.

Conductor's Etiquette

With a piece that is called *Concerto for Orchestra*, you would think that solo bows would be unnecessary. But it is wise to acknowledge the various sections as a whole. The most practical order is the percussion, brass, woodwinds, and strings, including harps. You can single out the flute and piccolo as well as the timpani—any more than that and you might wind up with musicians at your dressing room door wondering why you did not ask them to stand.

> With maturity comes the wish to economize—to be more simple. Maturity is the period when one finds the just measure.
>
> —Bela Bartók

Notes

1. Béla Bartók, *Concerto for Orchestra* (London: Hawkes & Son Ltd., 1946).
2. Georg Solti and Harvey Sachs, *Memoirs* (New York: Alfred A. Knopf, 1997), 227.

Igor Stravinsky: *Le Sacre du Printemps (The Rite of Spring)*

Pictures of Pagan Russia in Two Parts

I have learned throughout my life as a composer chiefly through my mistakes and pursuits of false assumptions, not by my exposure to founts of wisdom and knowledge.

—Igor Stravinsky

Music Division, The New York Public Library. "Igor Stravinsky" New York Public Library Digital Collections. Accessed September 25, 2023. https://digitalcollections.nypl.org/items/1659b9f0-f881-0130-cd2e-58d385a7bbd0

Igor Stravinsky: *Le Sacre du Printemps (The Rite of Spring)*

Even though fifty years had passed since the premiere of this monumental work by the time I first opened the score, I feared the day that I would have to study and lead this piece. Somehow, the complexities of the rhythms, the sheer number of musicians required, and the task of deciphering everything on the page seemed impossible.

But that was back in 1964, when I began my studies at the Juilliard School of Music. Jean Morel, my teacher, was considered one of the masters of conducting technique. He not only knew Stravinsky's music but also had played the percussion part in the first performance of *L'Histoire du soldat*. For the entrance exam, all the conductors auditioning had to prepare the first tableau of *Petrushka*. Yet during the four years that I spent at the school, we never worked on *The Rite of Spring*.

However, I did assist with a class for woodwinds and brass taught by Arthur Weisberg, a bassoonist and expert in new music, in which much of the symphonic repertoire was covered. I served as the string section, playing those parts on the piano. *Sacre* was on the syllabus, providing me with an opportunity to learn the piece in a different way.

During those Juilliard years, I led student performances of *L'Histoire* and the Octet, each containing many of the technical difficulties that characterize the larger-scale work. The first time I conducted *Sacre*—in St. Louis when I was the assistant conductor—occurred when Music Director Walter Susskind asked me to play through it at a rehearsal. He, too, was intimidated by its difficulties. I remember at the first rehearsal, when he got to the *Danse Sacrale*, he said to the orchestra, "I suppose we have to do this sometime."

As the years passed, I began to realize that this piece was not as daunting as I first thought. After all, it is a ballet, and despite all the din and clamor of the tumultuous world premiere, everyone managed. Pierre Monteux conducted that first performance and, as far as I know, he never complained about the difficulties.

Now that the work is so entrenched in the repertoire, the technical hurdles seem less intimidating than the musical ones. How can we make it seem as fresh as it was in 1913? What makes a successful performance of the piece?

Although *The Rite of Spring* has seen a couple of revisions, what we play today is pretty much the same as it has been since the 1940s. Scores are readily available, and the one we will work from is the reprint of the Boosey & Hawkes edition, revised in 1947 and reengraved in 1967.[1] The rehearsal numbers are plentiful and most, but not all, of the errors have been corrected.

The instrumentation is frightening, to say the least: three flutes, the third also playing second piccolo; piccolo; alto flute in G; four oboes, the fourth also playing second English horn; English horn; petite clarinet in D and E♭;

three clarinets in B♭ and A, the third also playing the second bass clarinet; bass clarinet in B♭; four bassoons, the fourth also playing the second contrabassoon; contrabassoon; eight horns in F, the seventh and eighth also playing tenor tubas in B♭; one small trumpet in D; four trumpets in C, the fourth playing bass trumpet in E♭; three trombones; two tubas; timpani with two players (these days, one player does the lion's share of the work, but at least five drums are required); percussion (bass drum, tam-tam, triangle, tambourine, cymbals, and guiro); and strings (14-12-10-10-8 players at minimum). Performance time is usually between thirty-two and thirty-five minutes.

Before we examine the conductor's role in the proceedings, I would like to bring up a related matter, the composer as conductor. Perhaps I will spend a full essay on this topic at some point, but for now, let's focus on Stravinsky. We know he was a decent pianist. But his conducting career did not begin until midway into his life, and almost all his masterpieces were premiered by others. He committed most of his works to disc, although some of the recordings were conducted by Robert Craft.

Stravinsky made three recordings of *Sacre*, not counting pianola versions. His tempos are on the fast side, with performance times ranging from thirty to thirty-two minutes. He does not observe numerous details in the score, both large and small. All three versions feel rushed to me, breathless to the extent that I am not sure if the orchestra will make it through all of it without incident. And indeed, there is a lot of sloppy playing. That said, I cannot discount the energy that crackles off the discs.

Still, these are recorded documents from the composer, admittedly not the greatest conductor of his time. He was always critical of other performances, some of which are considered classics. We can find similar discrepancies between scores and recordings from other more experienced composer/conductors. These differences are certainly due, in part, to the passage of time between when the piece was composed and when it was recorded. We all change.

In the case of *The Rite of Spring* or, indeed, any other work, the best we can do is listen to what the composer thought at different points in time and to recreate what the text and our minds tell us is right. But that will change over the years, as well.

First Part: Adoration of the Earth

Introduction
The score is laid out in such a way that you usually see only the instruments that are playing at a given time. With such large forces, this is surely the best

way to perceive what is happening, although it does force you to study which instruments make entrances after long periods of rest. Even though it is not technically difficult, this opening has an awful lot to untangle.

The tempo marking is Lento, ♩ = 50. But the famous bassoon solo falls under the spell of the *tempo rubato* Stravinsky writes at the beginning. A few times, conductors have tried to get cute by playing Tchaikovsky's Sixth Symphony, with the bassoon beginning in the lower register, as the first half of the program. I do not want to encourage this gimmick because most people in the audience will not get the supposed joke.

Several questions can arise with this first bar. How long are the fermatas? Do we conduct this measure? How scared will the bassoonist be?

As with many works that begin with a solo instrument, it is best to quietly nod to the musician and let them start when they are ready (within reason). Notice the lack of dynamic marking for this introductory gesture. It has become common for the bassoonist to start softly and ease into the second beat with a slight crescendo. Stravinsky gives plenty of opportunities for a breath, but most musicians will not take one until just before the pickup to **reh. 1**.

Let the first bar be as free as possible and then cue in the second horn. If you disagree with the bassoonist's tempo, here is the place to make up the difference. A very small beat will suffice. More than likely, the soloist will take some time before playing the C prior to **reh. 1**, so just wait, and then the moment you hear it, give the cue for the clarinets. All the grace notes are before the beat but performed on the slow and slinky side.

Even at this early stage in his career, Stravinsky was composing with the idea that he might eventually be the conductor, and he includes several instructions regarding what to bring out. For example, he specifies a *poco accelerando* in the second bar of **reh. 1** and asks that the D clarinet be the prominent instrument. As to what should dominate for the rest of the introduction, he provides only a few indications. During the fermata three measures after **reh. 1**, I suggest having the piccolo clarinet and A clarinet hold on a little longer, without a diminuendo. The second A clarinet and first bass clarinet have the same pitches, and it is effective if the listener is unaware of the change of instruments. The same applies at **reh. 2**.

The rubato can continue for the English horn with a slight ritardando on the sixteenths before **reh. 3**. The bassoon and second bass clarinet need some time before the attack at **reh. 3**, so after a gentle cutoff, give them about one beat to breathe. At the *più mosso*, Stravinsky must have intended for the English horn to match or exceed the dynamic of the three bassoons. It is worth rehearsing the bassoons alone so that the various takeovers are smooth. In the fourth bar, there is a slight danger that the English horn notes will sound like three groups of two notes; this rhythm is clarified in the bar before **reh. 4**.

Pay particular attention to the horn entrance at **reh. 4**, which sets up the rhythmic element in the violas and seconds. Usually, I have to explain how these two groups fit in with each other to clear up the problem. Again, the rhythm of the oboe is two groups of triplets. The takeover by the sixth, seventh, and eighth horns should be seamless.

Stravinsky helps us at **reh. 5** by saying that the first horn must be brought out a little, but this seems to go against the various dynamics in play. The oboe usually seems to dominate the proceedings, especially due to the *forte* indication. Much depends on which lines you wish to emphasize and which you decide are secondary.

Here I should stress that just because we see everything on the page, that does not always mean each line will be heard by the audience or even played clearly by the orchestra. A Bach fugue would be meaningless if we were to try to make all lines equal. While navigating the complexities of this piece, be aware of all that is happening but choose the elements you believe are most relevant to the longer line of the music.

On the other hand, you can add a degree of clarity to everything that is occurring in certain passages. At **reh. 6** we have what is marked as an alto flute solo, but the English horn is indicated as the main instrument to bring out, and the bass clarinets also have figurations to consider. The alto flute is a relative newcomer at this point in the score, and from my perspective, must be heard clearly, which may require some dynamic adjustment to the other instruments. For instance, at the end of the fourth bar of **reh. 6**, the second bass clarinet remains *forte*, but only after the second beat. The English horn now becomes a member of the flute section, and unless we take its dynamic down a little, the balance will seem inappropriate. While this changes four before **reh. 7**, I do not bring the English horn back up. Stravinsky does not give us a dynamic for the first-violin trill, but *piano* seems about right.

Just as the conductor must prepare beats to clearly indicate a tempo or rhythm, so must the individual musician always be prepared for what comes next. The flutes' upbeat to **reh. 7** is a very good example. It is meant to sound as if one flute plays all nine notes, but it is trickier than it appears. During the first beat of the bar, the two musicians must already be thinking about the triplets to make a smooth connection. A slight crescendo carries over from the second flute to the first.

At **reh. 7** there are not as many different ideas going on as you might think. The alto flute, A clarinets, bass clarinets, and solo cello are exchanging thoughts on triplets, with the second oboe joining in as well. That leaves the oboe with the figure heard earlier, which turns into a trill. The second horn also sustains a single note. It may be necessary for the solo cello to play the pizzicato almost *forte* while still fitting in as part of the triplet group.

The bar before **reh. 8** is often played as an echo or with a diminuendo, and we should assume that the first horn does the same as the English horn and bassoon. The principal difficulty at **reh. 8** is allowing the alto flute to be heard. There is never a problem with the piccolo clarinet.

The original score marked the oboe solo beginning at **reh. 9** with slurs meant to be played legato. The later editions show not only separated notes but also the word "staccato."

Balancing the double basses at **reh. 10** is important if you wish to bring out the E-major/E-minor element. Stravinsky introduces a new color four measures after **reh. 10** with the indication of flutter tongue in the first flute, second and third oboes, and second clarinet. The dots over the notes cannot be taken seriously, as they must be performed as if they were slurred.

Given all the activity in these pages, you could easily spend hours sorting everything out, and that can be a problem when it comes to rehearsal. Regardless of which other pieces are on the program, time management is crucial to a successful performance. You must not allow yourself to get so bogged down in minute details that you lose precious time as the rehearsals progress. Deciding what will correct itself by natural selection and what you have to say, or show, is the only way. So, for example, that sixth bass part at **reh. 10** might best be brought out by looking at that musician while you are dealing with other matters.

One time, I was rehearsing this piece in St. Louis, and when we got to **reh. 11**, I noticed something. Looking directly at the third clarinet, I said, "You should be playing that on B♭ clarinet." There was stunned silence from the orchestra because at that point, there are more than twenty-five different lines occurring at the same time. Perhaps I just got lucky, but the main point is that rather than having to spend rehearsal time figuring out what was wrong, I knew what the problem was and quickly resolved it. It was a lovely moment to score some points with the orchestra. (All was probably forgotten a few minutes later!)

Once you have taken this introduction apart, it is not a bad idea to go back to the beginning and play it through, just to keep everything in context. You have two options at **reh. 12**. The reappearance of the bassoon melody can either start immediately following the tumult or after a brief pause; this really depends on the acoustics of the room. Of course, if the musician can hold the note for a long time, you can ask for the same quality as earlier, with a soft entrance but this time emerging out of the din. I tend to prefer a clean entry. The grace notes and quintuplets should not be hurried, in effect keeping the rubato in place. You will need to delay giving the second beat for the clarinet trill. Make sure that the resolution note in the bassoon is long enough to be heard.

At the end of the fermata, it is helpful to give two preparatory eighth-note beats prior to the pizzicato to set up the tempo for the next section. Five bars before **reh. 13**, go back to quarter notes for the first two beats, but feel the triplet of the final part of the bar. Subdivide this for the clarinets with a small, clear beat to start. Then return to beating quarters, giving the violas two eighth notes to get them together. Next, just stay in six and then four for the following two measures. The horns, *con sordino*, are marked *piano*, but only so those instruments can be balanced with the clarinets and do not dominate. Sometimes a composer will compensate for the softer dynamic when playing with mutes, and Stravinsky does that here.

The Augurs of Spring: Dances of the Young Girls
Easily the most fun to conduct (but probably not intended to be), this second portion of the ballet starts with those famous down bows and horn syncopations. The latter are aggressive and gruff. Just because the horn line indicates "1 & 2 senza sord.," that does not mean the others have mutes on. Make sure the strings exaggerate the accents along with the horns.

At **reh. 14**, I like to bring out the cellos' G♯ to give the C-major-against-E-major arpeggio added pungency. The second bar of **reh. 15** marks the beginning of a five-bar phrase divided among oboes, trumpet, and violins. The pizzicato diminuendo should be almost nonexistent so the trumpet can make the connection and it all sounds like one continuous line.

The violas play on the string at **reh. 16**, *mezzo forte*. Since the rhythm is steady, you should have little problem being clear for figurations that start either on or off the beat; however, those who have the triplet syncopation just before **reh. 18** must all feel this rhythm together. I usually ask the strings to make a slight crescendo the bar before **reh. 19** to keep the intensity and increase the contrast of the *subito piano*.

Everything is straightforward until the two bars before **reh. 22**. When you arrive at the first fermata, make sure your baton arm is not too high; otherwise, you will not have room for the preparation to the next measure.

Here is something I have never done but have often wondered about: Look at the strings one measure before the double bar. They have four different notes that are virtually always obscured by the timpani and bass drum. We have to find a way to hear them clearly. One possibility is to make sure

88   Igor Stravinsky: *Le Sacre du Printemps (The Rite of Spring)*

that the drums play at a single *forte* or less, but you still need to keep the energy of the moment. What would happen if we were to add the timpani notes into the violas and cellos or . . . wait for it . . . have the timpani play the low F♮ on the second note of the triplet, followed by the G? I am not sure I have the nerve to do this, but it is something to think about.

Stravinsky introduced the four-note motif that dominates this section back at **reh. 14**, and from **reh. 22** onward, he will rarely let up in its use. No matter who is playing, this motif must always come through.

The viola harmonics at **reh. 23** should be played off the string. At **reh. 24**, the solo violin trill should be strong, and a little accent is often added for emphasis. I have found, throughout my career, that string players do not really like to play *col legno*. And at this point, at least for four bars, the dynamic is *forte*. There are musicians who simply will not do it, but one suggestion is to politely ask them to play it near the middle of the bow. If they are too close to the tip, they can potentially damage the tip of the stick. It is also helpful to make sure that they do not come too far off the string.

Leave it up to the two horns to decide how long the first needs to hold on to the note four measures after **reh. 25** to make sure that the second can come in at an equal dynamic. Occasionally, it will be impossible to achieve an ideal match, especially if the musicians have instruments by different manufacturers. This is why some orchestras will purchase, for example, a set of four Wagner tubas from a single maker.

Two measures before **reh. 27**, the clarinets should match the second trumpet's dynamic in the previous bar, and at **reh. 27**, the clarinets can drop down a little to help the alto flute penetrate through the passage. Although we have talked about the constant presence of the four-note motive, it also appears as sixteenth notes in the first violins, so keep that in mind if you are not sure whether it is coming out.

Rehearsal 28 is a good example of how one timpanist can take over both parts and manage most of the difficulties. While a second player can be effective in certain places, this is not one of them. When I first studied this score, I asked several timpani students for their teachers' opinions and found it more than helpful to get information this way.

Whatever syncopation there is, that four-note motive still matters the most. The clarinets look like they should be heard clearly—and they probably will be at the start—but as the instruments start piling up, you risk losing them in the explosion of sound.

Recently, scholars have highlighted the "Russian" element in the folklike melodies and even some of the complex rhythms. For instance, you can take away the second or third trumpet in the fifth bar of **reh. 28** to reveal a simple tune and its harmonies. Adding in the fourth trumpet foreshadows the upcoming Jazz Age. I recommend reading Richard Taruskin's two volumes entitled *Stravinsky and the Russian Traditions* for more insights.[2]

The three solo cellos have a seemingly contradictory marking of *marcatissimo e molto cantabile* here. I suspect that this is to provide the trumpets some support, given that the cellists do not have slurs.

Strangely, Stravinsky clarifies how he wishes the first violins to be divided before **reh. 29** but not the violas. In the case of ten violists, I would ask the outside musicians of the first three desks to play the first line, the inside players of those same stands to take the second line, and the remaining two stands to play the third line when it enters.

Stravinsky adds two colors that provide some real texture as the passage continues. First are the two antique cymbals. You need two players for this, as one hand holds the instrument while the other hand grasps the (usually) metal beater that strikes it. It can be visually and aurally effective if these two musicians are separated from each other a bit. A groan-like sound from the first four horns adds a degree of pain to this accumulated sonority. And this all takes place without a dynamic above single *forte*!

To accommodate the three different simultaneous rhythms at **reh. 30**, this section should feel *pesante* and unrushed. That four-note group is still hanging around, this time in the cellos. *Sforzandos* and crescendos need to be exaggerated, and each time you see the latter marking, the dynamic always returns to *piano*. Interestingly, the reverse applies when there is a diminuendo; each time you see this marking, you return to the dynamic at the start of the section.

Stravinsky adds yet another color to the palette at **reh. 31**. The second violins and violas play pizzicato, but instead of just single strokes in one direction, they move the right-hand fingers back and forth, as if the instruments were guitars placed under the chin. More practical is to have them pluck with just two fingers, since each musician only plays one note at a time. The fourth horn's first note often does not have a great center of pitch, but it can help to ask the player to focus the sound so that it is forceful but not overblown. Aim for equal balance between the horn and the two contrabassoons that answer the phrase, but in most instances, the horn will sound just a bit louder.

The second violins and violas have an interesting scale sequence at **reh. 32**. The best and easiest way to divide this is on the stand. You may need to bring these sixteenths up to *forte* so they can be heard, but with so many things going on, you might prefer to bring another line to the fore. Beginning in the fifth measure, what could be called the main theme of the section should be the dominant idea.

90 Igor Stravinsky: *Le Sacre du Printemps (The Rite of Spring)*

Two measures before **reh. 33**, I cannot help but smile, simply because I can see what Stravinsky is trying to do by writing a flutter-tongue scale for the alto flute at a starting dynamic of *mezzo forte*, but it is not audible. In theory, as layers are added on, these scales will eventually emerge, but this first entry is amusing when taken by itself—except to the alto flute player.

Be very careful not to get carried away in the early stage of the climactic coda at **reh. 33**. The maximum dynamic is *forte* and does not apply to all the instruments. The four-note motive transfers to the first tuba, and this line is demanding because of the somewhat-high register involved as well as the potentially awkward alternation with the second tuba. At **reh. 34** we increase the dynamic level to *fortissimo*, but again, not in all the instruments. This will be the first of the last three declarations of this four-bar phrase, and the syncopations become stronger with each iteration.

All the flutter-tongued instruments create an amazing flurry of sound. Keep in mind that when the lines ascend, they automatically get louder, so you might need to start each one a bit stronger to ensure that the lower notes are heard clearly. Stravinsky adds some tremendous horn rips for the final four measures. Depending on the ability of your musicians, you may have to start the actual glissando just a shade later than indicated, but it is a fantastic color to bring out.

Ritual of Abduction
At first reading, the orchestra will be guessing about the new metronome mark, which you cannot indicate to them in advance. When you go back to start rehearsing this third section, start directly at **reh. 37** so everyone knows what tempo you will utilize. The marking is Presto, $\mathbf{\downarrow}. = 132$. However, if your hall is overly resonant, this may be too fast to get clarity for the sixteenth notes. All the instruments come down from the *molto fortissimo* to a single *forte*. Obviously, you must delineate clearly between those who play in 9/8 and those who are in 3/4. Balancing the timpani and bass drum is important, as no other instruments have this rhythmic material.

In the third bar, Stravinsky is smart to drop the piccolo trumpet down to single *forte* for the sake of the upper woodwinds. It is unclear to me why solo bassoons play the upward figure at **reh. 38**, as the violas' phrase in the other direction usually obscures it. Another challenge is to bring out the instruments that have the grace notes and subsequent strong landing.

Our first truly difficult moment to conduct occurs at **reh. 39**. Almost everyone simply combines these two measures to make one 9/8 bar out of it. A few conductors do it as written, and you are certainly free to be among them, but it can prove frustrating. If you choose the 4 + 5 option, then the pattern is 2 + 2 + 2 + 3. This is viable because those who are not playing in those measures will be able to see the triplet pattern before their entrance in the third bar. The composer could have saved us all a lot of trouble by making it a 4/8 bar followed by a 5/8.

If you go the 9/8 route, the flutter-tongue group finishes after your second beat, and the other woodwinds and four solo violins start on what would be the second eighth of the second beat. The trombones will need to practice this a couple of times on their own. In the second full bar, those instruments that have been trilling need to stop and reattack the third beat, off the string.

Maintain the strictest of tempos at **reh. 40**. All the trumpets and some of the strings have a series of sixteenth notes that never vary, so do not let the horns drag here. One method I have used to hear the violin pizzicato notes better, or at least the accents, is to ask the third and fourth stands to play only the accented notes as strongly as possible, leaving out the other notes.

The two compound bars at **reh. 41** are almost always done in three these days. They are not as complex as the single one found earlier, but the balance between the tubas and horns often needs refinement. The indication *crescendo poco a poco* appears over the next six bars, but the score does not specify dynamics for all the instruments; you can figure it out and adjust as necessary. The goal is to create this often-overlooked crescendo. Hold back the trumpets and have the four solo violins play on the string.

The first of several sections of almost bar-by-bar meter changes begins at this point. The conductor for the world premiere of the ballet, Pierre Monteux, was supposedly comfortable enough with the rhythmic complexities and had enough rehearsal time to get it all worked out. The dancers also had plenty of time to absorb these new-fangled difficulties.

But when Serge Koussevitzky gave the first concert performance, he was so perplexed by the rhythms that he sought the wisdom of musicologist and composer Nicolas Slonimsky, who re-barred the difficult sections so that Koussevitzky only had to deal with simple 2/4 and 3/4 combinations. Presumably, the parts were also edited in this manner. Leonard Bernstein learned the piece from Koussevitzky, his mentor, and since many of us consider Bernstein to be one of the great interpreters of the work, we assumed that he conducted what Stravinsky wrote. He did not.

I believe Bernstein used the Slonimsky edits for all his performances, and to watch him conduct it is quite disconcerting, at least for those of us who know the piece well. Both he and Koussevitzky conducted much more complicated works during their lifetimes but continued conducting *The Rite of Spring* with these almost asymmetrical gestures. You can see Bernstein's score in the New York Philharmonic's online archive.[3]

This first passage at **reh. 43** is relatively easy if you keep in mind that the entire work is a ballet. As such, we must imagine dancers to help us determine where the various stresses should be placed. For example, you can conduct a 7/8 bar in three ways: 3 + 2 + 2, 2 + 3 + 2, or 2 + 2 + 3. Most of the musicians are focusing on their part and only slightly on the conductor. Therefore, no matter how the pattern emerges, the downbeat must be clear. Moreover, you can only help yourself and the musicians by keeping your beat on the small side. Expand a little for the groups of three and contract for the groups of two.

Always remember that some musicians have rests and rely on you to understand when to enter, hence the importance of a clear downbeat. Stravinsky could have made a couple of places easier by writing the 6/8 measures in 3/4, but he certainly wanted the feeling of two main beats to the bar, and we should always conduct them this way. That is what the musicians see in their parts and, unless you have your own edited set, you should stay with what everyone has.

Here is one more piece of advice, and it will apply to almost every spot like **reh. 43**. Rehearse a bit under tempo and when you get it up to speed, have the musicians play the passage without you. (Of course, you have to start them off.) You will be surprised by how well this can work. It shifts the focus to the single most important element for orchestral musicians: listening to each other.

Rehearsal 44 requires some careful adjustment of dynamics. The horns are clearly *forte*, but the trumpets and violins are asked to begin *piano*. The trumpets start a series of sixteenths that increase to an unspecified dynamic, presumably *forte*. Meanwhile, in the fourth and fifth bars, the violins have three indications to get louder and hairpins along the way. Do the dynamics in the violin line coincide with the ongoing crescendo, or do they return to the original dynamic each time? I will leave that one up to you, but my preference is to make each one successively louder than the one before.

Our first triple *forte* occurs at **reh. 45** and is followed by another compound set of measures. This passage is harder than the previous example but should be rehearsed in the same way. The only new decision is what pattern to use within the 5/8 bars. As you can see, those who have rests cannot tell how these bars will be conducted, and the musicians playing only have one beam over all the notes in any given measure.

We can use a guideline here. When possible, make whatever constitutes the end of a group of five match the first part of the next measure. For this passage, we have a 3/8, which is in one, but the next two 5/8 bars should be conducted as 2 + 3 to set up the next 3/8 bar. The 4/8 is in two and the 6/8 is also in two. The bar before **reh. 47** can be done as 3 + 2, again setting up the subsequent 4/8 measure. Stravinsky shows us how the rhythm going forward should be felt and therefore conducted. Note that the eighth bar of **reh. 47** should be played with two down bows.

Throughout this section, do not neglect the hairpins and accents. After you have worked this out, ask the orchestra to play the whole passage from **reh. 45** until the fermata without a conductor, as you did in the previous example. There might be a few slip-ups, but rest assured, the musicians will feel more comfortable and attuned to what their colleagues are doing.

We have not discussed trills in this piece yet. The general rule is that trills go to the next adjacent note within the key signature unless otherwise directed. That is all well and good, but the rule falls apart on the first fermata here. It could be that E♭ goes to either an E♮ or an F. But wait! We are saved from confusion by the change to four flats at the beginning of the next section, so the upper note must be an F.

Spring Rounds
Following the sound and fury, we calm down for a little while. The trills we were talking about change a bit for the first few bars here. Those trills that come to a stop each contain a quarter note with a dot, but certainly, the six bars that start this section must sound continuous. At least during the first five bars, the trill cutoff should be on the same note that the flutist taking over plays.

However, the cutoff pitch could be different at the fermata prior to **reh. 49**. Since we know that the trill goes to an F, the same as the clarinets' last note, it seems best for the flutes to cut off on an F as well.

Before we get to that point, please note that *Tranquillo* is not a tempo but a mood. The metronome mark is ♩ = 108, which is usually quick enough for all those with long trills to be able to get through the whole passage. Although this is a challenge for the first and alto flutes, they must persevere because there is no viable place to take a breath.

As for the two clarinets, I usually have them play the first three bars in one breath, and sometimes they take another breath before the last bar, where I add a slight ritard. Their grace notes should be played slowly and before the beat.

The cutoff also serves to indicate the new tempo at **reh. 49**. Again, Stravinsky gives us a feeling rather than an outright speed, leaving that for the metronome mark. This heavy sonority requires us to follow the indicated bowings, but I recommend telling the strings to sustain as long as possible before lifting. The audience barely hears the pizzicato, so this interesting change of fifths is left primarily to the two bass clarinets. I make just the slightest of crescendos as the three notes progress.

The first violins can be divided by stand. Their part indicates not only a *mezzo forte* dynamic but an accent as well; drop them down after the attack but not so much that it comes as a sudden shock. This occurs each time where the composer has marked *simile*. The *cantabile* line, for some reason, does not have a dynamic but the accompanying one does; I assume that it is the same. Make sure the last note of the phrase is sustained long enough to lead into that low downbeat.

Rehearsal 50 and the passage that follows bring us into the pagan world of Russian folk music. A chant-like melody looms under the surface for a couple of bars before it sings out in full. Stravinsky is careful to mark the horns *mezzo piano*, which is then followed by the *mezzo forte* of the violas and, presumably, the flutes. Because of the singing nature of this melody, many conductors, including me, do not observe the three consecutive down bows, with various options possible. The composer creates a fantastic color when he brings in the flutes with the horns, adding some expression marks for the latter.

At **reh. 51**, the piccolo and E♭ clarinet have a bird-like passage. For this, I recommend relaxing the triplets, so they do not sound overly metronomic.

Now we must deal with a matter that is always complicated. The bar before **reh. 52** is indicated as a 6/4 measure. But when you look at the phrasing, is that really what it is? No. This is clearly a subdivided 3/2. Why would Stravinsky write it this way? We don't know. This subject will come up with many other composers as well.

Having discussed it with numerous composers, I am astonished that some do not believe there is a difference. To them, a bar in six is a bar in six, no matter how it is divided. In this instance, there is no reason to tell the orchestra about your beat pattern, but many other examples require clarification, such as the slow movements of the two Brahms piano concertos. They are both in 6/4, but portions can be phrased as if they were in 3/2. In these pieces, the composer is certainly correct, and it is crucial to tell the members of the orchestra to think this way as they are playing.

In this single measure in *The Rite of Spring*, however, we do not have to say anything, as the way the slurs are written tells us what we need to know. Perhaps Stravinsky did not want the phrasing to be obvious, fearing that we might overdo it. In any event, the crescendo on the final two beats is effective if slightly exaggerated.

We return to the same static music that first appeared. Do not give away what is to come. Sometimes a physical gesture can take away a surprise musical element, and **reh. 53** is one such place. For that reason, I slightly underplay the dynamic two measures before **reh. 53**, almost lulling the listener before unleashing the torrent of sound that comes next.

The composer is toying with us again, defying us to keep things in check by marking the percussion and timpani at single *forte*. Most conductors cannot resist asking the kettledrum musician to play the grace notes slowly but quite loud.

Once again, maestros are divided about the composer's bowings, especially considering the tenuto lines and accents in the winds and brass but no mention of separating the notes. (We encounter the same issue in *The Firebird*.) If you choose to have the strings play "as it comes," then start up bow, which results in a nice crescendo at the end of the fourth bar.

The tremendous yelp from the brass in the fourth bar of **reh. 53** is often slightly or even substantially held back. Some conductors swear they do not slow down at all, but no matter how hard they try, this always feels a bit more *pesante* anyway. Personally, I prefer a somewhat sustained glissando as well as a flowing bow stroke. The three quarter notes that occur six measures before **reh. 54** feel better when separated, so from my perspective, the down bows are appropriate here. The *fortissimo sforzando* marking makes this decision much easier to justify.

For the remainder of this explosive section, you can work out how you wish to handle all the matters above, but you must be consistent. If you held back the brass glissandos the first time, do the same for the next two glissandos as well. One of the remarkable things about the scoring here is how well the strings can cut through the other instruments, allowing the audience to hear the violins and violas clearly just before **reh. 54**. This is such a rich compound chord that I linger on it a while during the fermata.

The cutoff is also the upbeat to the *Vivo* section, even though no one plays on the downbeat. Therefore, you must have the tempo clearly in mind before you give this indication. It is kind of fun to look at the flute line here. Why? Because it never sounds like those notes. The first piccolo's leap of a major seventh feels almost like we are not supposed to know what the pitches are.

We get a reprieve from conducting challenges starting in the second measure of **reh. 54**. The strings play *alla corda*, the quarter notes are mostly short, and the dynamics work well. At **reh. 55** the quarters are again on the short side, apart from those in the horns, at least in my interpretation. I think that the horns serve a melodic function here, so I ask them to sustain the last note of **reh. 55** and the subsequent bar. Not often observed is the return to single *forte* at the third bar of **reh. 55**. This can be quite effective if you really hit the downbeat of **reh. 56** hard.

Now, everything is as it was at the start of this section, with one major difference, and this is another debatable point. The first time around, the final note of the alto flute and piccolo-clarinet trill had a grace note attached, but not here. Was this intentional? What did the composer do on the two recordings and numerous performances he gave as a conductor?

This is one of those mysteries I think you should solve on your own. I can guarantee that you will discover many things about the learning process and how much effort one little note can make in shaping what we do and how we do it.

Ritual of the Rival Tribes

Although there is no fermata before this section begins, most of the time, I wait about as long as I did to begin the previous dance. Be sure to give a strong downbeat for those playing the pizzicato. This is another place where one timpanist can handle both parts, resulting in a more equal balance between the drums. Aside from the first note, the problem often is that the timpanist whacks away *fortissimo*, depriving the low brass of the opportunity to create a wonderful effect.

I see no reason the lower strings and woodwinds cannot make the same crescendo as the horns. When you look carefully at the fifth bar, you can see what the composer clearly intended: The half notes that start the measure are imitated in the low instruments. The first note of the next bar has an accent, but I do not believe it was intended to be short. The strings, however, can play staccato here. These nuances apply at **reh. 58** as well.

This revised edition has removed the original instruction *Ritenuto pesante*, which is unfortunate because it deprives us of an important emphasis. I take the *pesante* instruction to mean hold back the horn and tuba triplet four measures before **reh. 59**, so we can suddenly slow down and dictate each of the notes. But the ritard continues through the bar, and my conclusion is that the whole note should equal the dotted one that comes two bars later. In other words, the note after the triplet lasts six beats. If you feel that your orchestra understands what is occurring, it is not necessary to beat this measure; rather, just count the beats in your head before continuing. The third bar before **reh. 59** resumes *a tempo*.

At **reh. 59**, be careful that the tubas do not stand out above the moving lines in the horns. At single *forte*, the upper woodwinds and pizzicato violins are usually well balanced. It is unclear to me why Stravinsky chose to place the beams as they appear one measure before **reh. 60**. Why not write the grouping as 3 + 2? In any event, it is certainly permissible to go into two at **reh. 60**, but only for four bars. A sudden outburst breaks the momentary calm, and once again, ensure that the moving lines come out.

Rehearsal 61 can also be done in two, but you must establish the rhythmic core in the lower strings; rehearse them on their own so that the basses hear how they fit into the overall scheme. One breath for the trumpets works well here, but again, we have that same dichotomy with a 6/4 measure that is actually a 3/2. If you are conducting half notes, the bars indicated this way should be in three. Stravinsky includes a slur over the entire first-violin passage but breaks it up for the clarinets; I rather like placing a little lift before the upbeat to two measures before **reh. 62**.

We are back in four now, and the growls in the lower instruments are usually differentiated beat by beat. Most conductors will also separate the quarters that occur after the grace notes, but there is something to be said for sustaining those in the strings. The eighth notes that are not slurred can be played somewhat short and off the string. Note the trombone parts, as they are the only instrumental group that has continual accents. You will need to ask the upper strings to retake down bows after each quarter note three measures before **reh. 63**, as this is not indicated in the score or parts.

The trills that appear at the 6/4 bar between **reh. 63** and **reh. 64** go right through the first beat of the following measure, but at the last moment, they must stop so the second beat can be strong. Yes, it is possible to think of this note as a release, but in light of the *sforzando*, I think of it as a reattack. The trumpets have a tremolo indication one measure before **reh. 64**, but this is actually a flutter tongue. I start just loud enough for the first notes to be heard and then make the *molto crescendo* as aggressive as possible.

Enter the tenor tubas, doubled by their larger cousins. Most likely these are played by the seventh and eighth horn players, but I have seen a couple of European orchestras hire two extra musicians for this. At **reh. 64**, you can easily go into two. The strings should use very long strokes for each note, even though they are only single *forte*. Instruments start piling on, and the effect is stunning. At **reh. 65**, the violas are *non divisi*, but the first violins need to divide the two lines; this can be done on the stand, as the rhythm is stable. It is also worth observing that the bass drum starts a chain of events that will culminate at **reh. 70**.

The horn entrances after **reh. 65** are slightly perilous for the musicians playing the high notes. There is nothing the conductor can do about this, and therefore I do not make a fuss over any of them that are inaccurate. The trumpets have an ascending pattern, with other instruments joining in. This automatically creates a crescendo, so it is unnecessary to ask for one as the line moves upward.

98   Igor Stravinsky: Le Sacre du Printemps (The Rite of Spring)

Just before **reh. 66**, the horns drop down to single *forte* and have the indication *ma non tanto*, implying that they are not to stand out too much among the various musical ideas that begin to accumulate. Meanwhile, the bassoons have a Neanderthal motive that establishes the pace of the eighth notes.

Procession of the Sage
Next, the solo cellos and basses join the march, along with the timpani. Also new are the fifth and sixth horns, whose grace notes should be audible and whose quarters should be played for the full length. The first four horns have a melodic line, and it is important to observe the accents as Stravinsky wrote them. At **reh. 68**, the two oboes join the low horns, and the grace notes become sixteenths. I believe that the buildup should be equal once an instrument has entered, so I play these pickups as grace notes and sustain the quarter notes.

With several additional lines at this point, it is simply a matter of choosing how you wish to balance them. Interestingly, the most unusual rhythmic element is in the tam-tam, which basically has three eighth-note rests before each attack. The dynamic is marked *mezzo forte* and *sempre marcato*. A medium mallet is about right, and the percussionist has to dampen the sound so that the next stroke is heard clearly.

We have a truly bold moment at **reh. 70**, where virtually every musician is playing. The time signature is 6/4; however, as several commentators have pointed out, no one is actually doing anything in this meter. It is kind of fun to go through these two pages and look at each instrument group, sorting out how they fit in and what pattern they have—I will leave that to you.

Nevertheless, in terms of what we need to beat, the 6/4 indication makes sense. This has to do with the percussion, who have some subdivision that can be construed as three-beat phrases. The onus is on the timpani, as well as the combination of bass drum and tam-tam, to keep this dance together. Another new instrument has been added to the mixture, the guiro. These days, if the actual gourd does not produce enough sound, percussionists will use a metal scraper of some kind, even a washboard to give it not only aural clarity but an added visual effect as well.

Once all this begins and you have told everyone how you want it balanced, there is not much for the conductor to do. I usually just give a strong downbeat for each measure and let the orchestra do its thing for the remainder of this passage. I keep my left hand up but motionless. When the eight bars have concluded, I freeze my right hand and ask the orchestra to remain in the position they were in when they played the final note before the fermata. We will do this again in a few minutes.

The Sage
This brief interlude has the unusual orchestration of five bassoons, timpani, and solo double bass. Since the preceding silence is so important, the principal bass must put the mute on near the end of the previous dance. Usually, the three instruments playing the eighth notes are separated from each other by many feet. For this reason, I conduct in a very discreet eight, almost invisible to the audience. To help the winds prepare for the long, sustained note, I give a two-beat preparation.

In the fourth bar, I give the cutoff, glance at the solo strings, and then just cue them rather than have them count. Although not specified, I assume that the double-bass note is unmuted; therefore, the two notes on the fermata should be played by the second and third bassists.

Dance of the Earth
Surprisingly, this section and the previous four bars are the only sections in the ballet without a meter change. Marked Prestissimo, it is very brisk, and almost every conductor takes it at a speed around ♩ = 144.

During the fermata before **reh. 72**, establish eye contact with the bass drum player. Some conductors use the rest as the cutoff point, and others give a gesture prior to the downbeat. Either way, everything rests on the orchestra's ability to hear the bass drum clearly. A hard, wooden stick is preferred here. You can also consider continuing to accent the notes that are marked *sforzando*.

The upward swoops all are played with gigantic crescendos, like some primeval force is coming from the ground. Another one of the great debates concerns the length of the isolated quarters versus eighths that dominate from here until **reh. 75**. Some believe they are equal in length, with literally no differentiation, and all played short. We encounter the same dilemma again at the end of the piece.

I personally enjoy the contrast and can easily justify it when we get to the last bar, but not everyone agrees. I prefer full length for the quarters and quite short for the eighths to emphasize the difference. The real glue holding this section together comes in the form of three- and six-note whole-tone scales that appear in the lower instruments throughout the entire dance. It is always important to make these heard throughout.

Three measures before **reh. 73**, Stravinsky has the upper strings play two consecutive down bows, which make sense to observe because they are connected to the rearticulation of the repeated note in the woodwinds and brass. Likewise, at **reh. 73**, the winds and brass need just a bit of space so that the second eighth note can be heard clearly.

A new motive begins at the fourth bar of **reh. 73**: the sixth and eighth horns have a triplet figure that is marked *forte* but also *cuivrez*, or brassy, and the sound that comes from the instruments needs to be assertive; otherwise, it will get lost in the din. We get another example of the difficulty regarding the length of the quarters at **reh. 74** as well; there is nothing to connect them to other material here. At this point, I think that Stravinsky is letting us know that when he puts in the down bows, he means it, and when he does not, we can use our discretion.

He makes his intentions clear in the fourth measure, where he could have just as easily written only quarter notes. Even if, as a conductor, he did not follow his own rules, we can certainly feel justified in selecting the length if we are consistent. This includes the very last quarter before **reh. 75**.

We now have variations on the motives already presented. The violas pick up the missing notes from the horns, eliminating the rests. These are marked *détaché*, played on the string. The cellos take over the scale passage, adding a few more notes after each first beat. The first trumpet brings yet another motive, and this dance is difficult to play at the indicated metronome marking. The sixteenth notes can be double-tongued, but often this produces an uneven dynamic between the trumpets and the violins, and everything must connect smoothly. *Mezzo forte* in the trumpets is always louder than in the fiddles. Balance accordingly.

The violas switch gears at **reh. 76** just as all the horns are beginning to take up the triplet motive. Now there are three groups tossing around the sixteenths. Depending on where the violas in your orchestra are placed, you might need them to be a bit louder than *mezzo forte* to sound at the same level as the first violins and trumpets. Do not let the intensity lag. Through all this, that scale pattern has been building up as well, and the only way to call attention to it is to exaggerate the crescendo and *subito* dynamics that follow.

As the first part concludes, we are again faced with the same problem about the length of the eighths and quarters. Stravinsky further complicates the matter when, at **reh. 78**, he has some of the instruments playing with *staccatissimo* indications and others without. But as I mentioned, you should at least be consistent. I still insist on the quarters being long, and the final reason I can cite is the very last note.

After a tremendous crescendo, which the timpani and bass drum should also observe, what do we see? We have both eighth notes and quarters at the same time, something that has not occurred in this whole final section. You will certainly create drama if you end abruptly, but you will accomplish more if you sustain that last note with those that have the quarter.

Do not move a muscle, just like after those 6/4 bars two sections ago. Try to maintain this position for a couple of seconds before slowly lowering your arms. The same holds true for the orchestra. Imagine what the choreography might look like if the lights stay on for just the briefest moment and then, suddenly, the theater goes dark.

Although I heard one conductor try it, I do not recommend starting the second part of the ballet *attacca*. It must feel as if the piece starts anew.

Second Part: The Sacrifice

Introduction

Take a little time to calm yourself—as well as the orchestra and audience—down before entering a world that is a throwback to a few years before this piece was written. An impressionistic haze will become the background for the next section, with echoes of the past. Although you can exercise some flexibility within the Largo, most of it stays somewhat in tempo at ♩ = 48. You could give two preparatory beats, but with only six instruments playing the moving line, one gesture should suffice if you take the same breath on the upbeat.

Deciding where the woodwinds need to come up for air can be difficult. I usually take some time at the end of the second bar and then continue in a single breath until **reh. 80**. The cellos' F♮, although duplicating one of the horns, is nice to bring out. Think of the third bar as if the Introduction started all over again; this will help you set up the lead-in to the 3/4. We can assume that Stravinsky wanted all the instruments to have a deep sigh here, so the strings can come up to *mezzo forte*.

The roles of the timpani and bass drum are very important at **reh. 80**. In this place, keep in mind that what is written for the timpani is not a tremolo, and if only one musician plays both notes, the overall effect is just not the same. Very soft sticks should be used here. Ask the timpanist to "lean into" the first note, as if there were a tenuto line before the actual rolls start. The string divisi can be done various ways, but I think asking the front half of each section to play the top line and the back half the second staff makes the ensemble and intonation tighter. The use of the word *flautando* in the third bar is not necessary, as these harmonics can only be produced if the bow is just lightly touching the string.

Some conductors ask the flutes to get louder going into **reh. 82**. This is a difficult place for intonation, so make sure to rehearse the eighth-note passage on its own. If you can really get a *pianissimo* from the clarinets in the third bar, the quintet is doing a wonderful job.

Even more spectacular is keeping the oboes, playing in fairly high registers, quiet enough that the alto flute and solo violin are heard clearly at **reh. 83**. Your viola section soloists should be encouraged to rehearse the passage two before **reh. 84** on their own to avoid spending precious minutes adjusting the intonation. But as can happen quite often, one of the musicians may not be up to par or used to playing in such an exposed way; you simply have to play with the cards you are dealt. It was different in the middle of the last century, when autocratic conductors could literally dismiss a member of the orchestra, sometimes on a whim. Be polite but firm when making corrections and focus only on the musical result. The final note before the fermata can be sustained, lest the resolution not be heard properly.

The muted trumpets present an interesting challenge. They are marked *piano* but can sound much softer with the mutes in place. One interesting possibility is to try this with different types of mutes to see if you might like a particular kind of sound.

The five solo cellos play quietly but still expressively at **reh. 85**, while the softness in the rest of the string section counters the warmth of the horns. The first violins have a difficult leap to make, and I have found it helpful to ask them to change bow direction after the harmonic F♯. The trumpets require minimal conducting to indicate each bar as they continue with their lonely wandering. Let them play this duet on their own; they can also take little breaths after each phrase.

The fourth bar of **reh. 86** is about control—not yours, but the bows of the violas, cellos, and violins. Stravinsky expects the triplets to be done in one bounced stroke, and they will have to retake the bow several times to accomplish this. Much depends on how clearly you want this rhythm to project. These notes can also be played with separate bows, on the string, near the tip. Done in that way, the rhythmic element is easier to coordinate.

The same advice applies for the next section, which begins at **reh. 87**. The divisi decisions are straightforward except for the first violins. I usually ask three stands to play the first line, three stands to play the second, and the remaining section members to take the third.

The same ethereal qualities that marked the opening are present here but in different disguises. I know many conductors prioritize rhythmic clarity in this section, but perhaps that is not the only solution; all those tiny flourishes that move upward cannot sound so metronomic as to take away from the atmosphere.

The lower division of cellos plays a very important role at **reh. 87**, so let them sound a bit louder than *pianissimo*. If the violas can be *mezzo piano* two bars later, why not here as well? Balance between the clarinets and muted horn is important, as the latter could become too prominent. I advise against getting fancy in this whole section; the static feeling should last throughout, with no expression whatsoever. End right in tempo.

We have one last elephant in the room: flute harmonics. These are not the same as those that occur in the strings. Nothing sounds an octave higher; it is just a way of playing the note without much air, producing virtually no color. This is also a perilous place for intonation. The flutes can work this out on their own, but you may need to point out where the problems lie.

As a side note, if you find yourself having to fix matters of intonation, I can offer a suggestion. Always have the musicians playing the root of a chord start—in this case, only one flutist. Then add the fifth, or in this case, the fourth of the chord. Once you have this open sound established correctly, insert the note that comes in between, as that musician now has somewhere to drop it in and can adjust as needed. This works in almost any circumstance.

The *più mosso* is just slightly faster; with only three horns, they can home in on your tempo as soon as you give the first beat. If the horn players have multiple mutes, you might want to try out a couple of options to achieve the *très lointain* effect Stravinsky calls for; it should almost seem as if the sound were coming from offstage. Hold on to the flute note a little longer than indicated to emphasize the space between the end of the horn passage and the C-major chord.

At **reh. 90**, the two horns are not muted but still must play softly. Meanwhile, the bass clarinet can make just a little crescendo before arriving at the last note of each bar.

Mystic Circles of the Young Girls

Since **reh. 91** is in the same tempo as **reh. 89**, you need not give a preparatory beat, but if your orchestra has not done the work before, this might require explanation. This old Russian melody is played *espressivo* in the six violas, but more interesting is what is happening below. These instrumentalists need to know how they fit into the pattern. You can ask the section cellists to play, so that everyone hears it. Then rehearse it without those players and have all the other musicians play their various patterns, which form a continuous line of eighth notes. I ask the violas to make a slight crescendo during their final three notes to cover the brass entrance, so the horns and trumpets just emerge after the strings stop playing.

As I have noted several times, whenever possible, always try to show a tempo change in advance. However, at **reh. 93**, you do not need to do so.

Look at the violins so the pizzicato is together, and then just beat in the new tempo since there is no rhythmic element involved. Each little crescendo goes to about *mezzo piano* and then comes back to *pianissimo*. What do we think *meno pianissimo* means at the end of the fourth bar? I presume it is not supposed to be as soft as the dynamic at the start, but this is truly picky. What we can certainly understand is that this sound must be under the dynamic of the alto flute.

The clarinets' major sevenths are intriguing and never sound as dissonant as we would expect; a little lift after the first and third slurs makes a nice phrase. The two notes before **reh. 95** in the first violins and cellos should be *espressivo*, after which they return to their accompanying role. Starting at the bar before **reh. 95**, I like to bring out the second line of the second violins, as they are the only ones who have the harmonization of the melody. The cellos and second violins are marked *mezzo forte*, and both sections can give quite a bit for the crescendo before **reh. 97**.

At **reh. 97**, the Tempo I referred to is the one at **reh. 91**, and you should have little difficulty establishing the speed, even if most people playing have forgotten the first tempo. Be clear with the downbeat and show the space before getting to the second beat. I just repeat the downbeat and treat this measure as a 4/4 preceded by a rest.

In an interesting color combination, the flute and alto flute play in concert with two solo violas. The violas have eighth-note rests after each second beat while the flutes sustain quarter notes. Ask the flutists to avoid a breath until one is absolutely needed, usually just before the 6/4 bar. The arpeggio sign in the lower strings is another way of indicating *non divisi*, but here they can slightly spread out the two notes from low to high, *alla chitarra*.

At **reh. 98**, you can slightly separate the notes that have slurs, both quarters and eighths, but the bass clarinet has sustained notes with tenuto lines. The series of two-bar phrases that follows is quite conservative harmonically in relationship to what has occurred before. The final statement, three before **reh. 101**, involves just six musicians: three oboists and three cellists. One group plays the tune and the other keeps the rhythm intact but moves in the opposite direction, going downward. Turn your attention to the last desks of violas for their strong pizzicato, and at the same time, ensure that the horns do not enter late. You can hold the fermata for quite a while.

The same melodic groups return at **reh. 101**, but the orchestration around them is remarkable. If you have the time, it is worth taking this section apart in rehearsal. Give the musicians who play the eighth notes the opportunity to understand how they connect with each other, then add the various strings who have harmonics like those in the flutes. Add the tune once you think you have achieved a proper balance. The bar before **reh. 102** contains an even stronger pizzicato, with the addition of the second violins; avoid the open string here. The fermata often does not feel long enough, so try to hold it for at least six beats while making a slow diminuendo.

Importantly, a four-bar accelerando—as well as a crescendo—takes place starting at **reh. 102**. Direct your fourth beat at the second horn and try to balance the voices as they enter. As is usual with this type of passage, the composer does not let us know how fast we should be going during the speedup or provide any dynamic indications along the way.

It might be easier to work backward at this juncture. Perhaps we should be at single *forte* when arriving at **reh. 103**. From there, we can figure out the preceding dynamics. Keep in mind that as more instruments enter, the buildup happens naturally, so judge accordingly. Your speed will depend on what you choose to do in the second bar of **reh. 103**. And try to have the tam-tam played with a metal triangle stick, as indicated by the composer.

I surmise that Stravinsky's march-like tempo, $\quarternote = 120$, was dependent on the stage action. Each beat in a steady stream of eleven may have corresponded with a dance gesture, for example. We have come from a speed of $\quarternote = 60$, a twofold increase. But doing a work in concert presents different opportunities, and here we have all manner of interpretations. Some conductors take this measure very solemnly and then explode for the next section, while others get to the 11/4 bar and stick with that tempo for the next section.

Before we move on, let's deal with this famous measure. The strings have all down bows, marked *fortissimo*, but the timpani and bass drum are only playing at single *forte*. What is the reasoning behind Stravinsky's scoring here? Why did he refrain from adding brass or woodwinds to the mix? I suspect he wanted the string sound to emphasize the impact of the eleven crunches, not really the pitches. And again, I think this had a lot to do with the action onstage.

But we do not need to reflect upon that because we can create drama as a visual component in the concert hall. If something looks impactful, it will sound that way, a psychoacoustic phenomenon. For that reason, I make this a very dramatic moment for the audience.

First, the audience sees four timpani being played. I did not say timpanists, because if you think about it, one player performing on two different instruments with the same stroke really looks amazing. Now double that—two players playing on four drums—for an even more impressive visual effect with all the arms moving. Then, I employ another visual aid. Most of you know that a bass drum can be turned on its side and played with the same arm motion as the timpani. I use two of these instruments, with the percussionist between them and playing on both—three musicians, six drums. They do not have to play ultra-*forte* because how it looks makes it seem more forceful. For one last touch, I let the orchestra play this bar on its own once I have given the downbeat. There are other ways to do this bar as well, so have fun.

Glorification of the Chosen One
Even more than the final dance, this section has the most decisions to make about beat patterns. Leaving aside the Koussevitzky/Bernstein emendations, every conductor struggles to solve this puzzle. However, Stravinsky leaves clues about what he might have preferred, at least in a few bars. We do have to look at the unusual marking of ♩♪ = 144. The composer chooses not to set the metronome in terms of the quarter note because he needs to differentiate the threes from the twos. It might have been possible to misconstrue a quarter note as missing the dot, but this way, there is no question.

Look not at the notes but at the rests; they give us the clues we need to decode Stravinsky's wishes. Notice the dotted quarter rest to start off. Some instruments have an eighth rest, but an even better indicator is in the double basses. They have a beamed group of notes that clearly reveal these first two bars as 3 + 2. This means that the loud note in the timpani is part of the first group and not the downbeat of the second. So, the stress in the second half of the measure begins on the sixteenth notes.

Good. We solved that problem. Now, what do we do about the 9/8? Well, many conductors choose to do this as a 3/4 followed by a 3/8. I used to conduct it this way but now find it satisfying doing it as 3 + 3 + 3. It is also clearer for those who are resting the whole bar because what they see is what they get.

The next 5/8 measure is the same as the first ones, but a real problem follows. We have established the phrase structure, so you would think it would hold for the whole movement, regardless of time signature. However, the 7/8 is very misleading. The beam indications for the low instruments show 3 + 2 + 2, while those in the oboes, upper strings, and horns imply 2 + 2 + 3. The logical musical solution is to think of the first part of the bar as tacked onto the 5/8, so if we are to be consistent, we should conduct 2 + 3 + 2. No matter how you decide to do these first five measures, you must stick with that pattern for the entire section.

I advise trying to play this passage without saying anything and, unless it totally falls apart, you will discover that many musicians are not watching you all that closely. Rather, they are tapping their feet, mouthing the rhythm, or just counting like mad. If somehow you get to **reh. 106** without incident, you can stop and explain how you are going to conduct the five-, seven-, and nine-beat bars. I cannot understand why Stravinsky opts for a 3/8 followed by a 4/8 rather than just a 7/8. Perhaps it would look too messy on the page with all those notes.

Lumbering, primitive sounds characterize the writing one measure after **reh. 106**. I try to bring out and connect the lower line of violas and cellos, as they are almost melodic. It does not matter how you lay out the seven beats as long as the last one looks like an upbeat. At **reh. 107**, it is effective to have the trombone and trumpet lines sound like a continuous stream of triplets that projects above the other instruments.

Since I have suggested that the earlier 9/8 should be done in three, the 6/8 at **reh. 109** therefore is in two. Stay with the patterns you established from the outset. Practicing alone is a good exercise, just to get the feeling of this section in your body as well as your head.

A tremendous thwack on the bass drum with an extremely hard wooden mallet starts off **reh. 111**. Amid a lot of loud music in this piece, somehow this seems like the most aggressive sound that occurs. Musicians will sometimes cover their ears or turn away, but of course, they cannot do this while they are playing. Still, if you are not getting the sound you want for fear of a complaint, you have compromised your musical values.

The quarter notes can be on the long side in the brass. Do not let those playing the triplets rush; these can easily become sixteenth notes, which do not occur until two measures before **reh. 113**. The next measure sets up a new, almost melodic pattern that will contrast with the aggressive moments that transpired previously.

With three-part divisi, one of the difficulties is hearing all three parts. Many conductors make the top line appear as if it were a tune. Since the first and second violins have the same material, just having each stand play a line is okay, but try to get the two bottom lines loud enough that a kind of chord emerges.

It is correct, yet also a bit amusing, that the timpanist is asked to play with snare-drum sticks and the bass drum with a timpani mallet.

At **reh. 114**, bringing out the bassoons, lower clarinets, cellos, and basses can prove interesting, especially if you allow the grace notes to be heard and follow the dynamics. The dynamics change for some in the third bar. Through all this, do not let the timpani dominate. One player usually performs this passage and should only emphasize the notes with accents. The layout of the string pizzicato changes, but the original idea remains the same.

Much contrast should take place between the alternating *mezzo forte* and *fortissimo* measures at **reh. 115**. Trumpets and trombones are most likely *fortissimo*. In the second bar of **reh. 116**, some conductors will take a little time for the sixteenth notes in the brass. Whether to do so depends on the tempo you have chosen for the entire section; if it is on the fast side, you might need to hold back just to fit in the four notes. Otherwise, continue in tempo.

At the bar before **reh. 117**, very few conductors follow the *molto allargando* instruction, opting instead for a *subito meno mosso* with a ritard. I suppose if we were to take the marking literally, we would conduct the first two eighths with one beat and then slow down considerably for the last three. But the overwhelming majority of conductors do the whole bar in five and hold back immediately. **Rehearsal 117** is similar to **reh. 107**, and again the triplets should be heard distinctly. Henceforth, almost everything repeats patterns that occurred previously.

After sufficient rehearsal, you can do some of the multi-meter sections without conducting. The more the musicians get used to listening rather than watching, the easier it will be to lead them in the actual performance.

Evocation of the Ancestors

You should refrain from moving during the silence that occurs at **reh. 121**, allowing it to take effect before commencing. Here we encounter a huge difference between the editions. In the early ones, the low strings play with the same dynamic as the bass clarinet (i.e., the cellos and basses hold the long note *fortissimo*, without a *subito piano* marking). I think this makes sense, at least for the wind music that follows.

The metronome marking is ♪ = ♩ here. To me, this always feels too fast for what the music seems to be saying and, like several other conductors, I try to impart a *pesante* feeling. The music indicates a degree of heaviness, as there are no dots over any notes—other than the soft strings after **reh. 122**—to tell us otherwise. However, most conductors do the loud wind passages on the short side.

What should we do about dynamics just after **reh. 122**? Should the low strings remain *fortissimo* here as well? If they do not come down a bit, then the violins and violas will be inaudible. But that pesky bass clarinet is still *fortissimo*! My preference is for the cellos and basses to do the *subito piano* just as the other strings enter.

The crescendo that follows returns us to the aggressive nature of the music. In the loud wind music, be sure to observe the accents, which are in line with the down bows of the strings. All the 3/4 and 2/4 bars are conducted in one. Keep the beats small and you will have very few problems with this section. Continue to adjust the dynamics, as with the earlier passages.

A new variant appears at **reh. 125** and with it a choice. Most conductors have the five bassoons play with the same short notes as the loud passages. But a few conductors, including me, enjoy doing this legato. It sounds more like a lament and can be played quite *espressivo*, with a tiny crescendo two measures after **reh. 126** and a diminuendo in the next bar. Everyone should make the crescendo beginning on the second beat three measures before **reh. 128**.

There is no correlation between the tempo of this evocation and the Lento that begins at **reh. 128**.

Ritual Action of the Ancestors

Here the speed is something close to a preemptive funeral march, quite slow and sultry. The indicated metronome marking of ♩ = 52 seems about right because it allows enough time for the falling bassoon notes to be heard clearly. The tambourine, medium-to-low in timbre, should be played with a light touch. At **reh. 129** we have another decision that can go one of two ways. The horn notes imitate those set up in the pizzicato strings. Almost every conductor has the horns play these short, but considering the absence of tenuto lines or dots, is it possible to hold them for full value? Theoretically, yes, but I think that would throw off the balance by covering the strings.

During the dialogue between the English horn and alto flute, both must agree on how to play the upbeats. One consideration is how they will sound later in the bass trumpet line; that instrument cannot play the upbeats as slowly as the woodwinds, so a bit of a rushed feeling is appropriate here. As the accompanying instruments begin to drop out, we are left with just the timpani and low pizzicatos.

At **reh. 131**, I prefer the English horn to play on the short side, emulating the pizzicato of the violas. This is one of the few places where the alto flute has no problem being heard. We have alternating dynamics that eventually wind up at *mezzo forte*, but at **reh. 132**, we need to continue to hear the alto flute clearly when the muted brass enter. While not specified in this later edition, obviously the brass must play *pianissimo*. It has become common practice to have the two trumpets play the phrase legato, sometimes even slurred. However, many conductors, including me, will ask them to shorten the two eighth notes in the third and fourth bars.

Rehearsal 133 is interesting because the harmonics in the violas should pick up the trilled note in the second violins. The trill indication is probably meant just for those playing the upper line, and the violas should not make a diminuendo. At the 5/4 measure, conductors often ask the violins to put in accents whenever they change notes and ask the same of the violas in the next bar. If you want to do so, fine, but do not exaggerate to the point that it becomes a mannerism.

There is a lot going on at **reh. 134** and you don't hear much of it, but at least make sure that the timpanists do not play too loudly. The piccolo trumpet is supposed to emphasize the higher notes of the phrase without sounding overly soloistic. It does not matter how you beat the 6/4.

We get a change of atmosphere at **reh. 135**, and I advise you to pay careful attention to the dynamics and expression markings. For example, the diminuendo in the oboe and English horns should come down to *piano*, which the strings then match for their two eighth notes. The color of the ponticello is interesting, so try to get your musicians to really do this, with the bow almost on top of the bridge. Three measures after **reh. 135**, a few conductors separate the duplets from the upcoming triplet, but I do not. The triplet itself is played marcato, leading us to the trombone chord on the downbeat followed by a very strong pizzicato.

From **reh. 137**, we encounter a few bars containing crescendos that then start softly in the next measure. This leads to a remarkable sound at **reh. 138**, where seven percussionists, as well as five different timpani, are all playing. Since Stravinsky marks the brass *pesante*, they can really lean into these chords. The horns with the tune are asked to play with the bells in the air. A few orchestras really do this and turn the instrument almost upside down, so the audience sees it and the sound travels upward. I find it effective for the first violins to place an accent on the tremolo after the grace notes. The cymbals are not exactly stopped right away, but they should not ring for too long, either.

Rehearsal 139 should create a sudden jolt after all the sound that has come before. The bass drum plays with a wooden beater. Here is the bass-trumpet problem I spoke about a bit earlier. I have often heard the musician come in a little too soon and arrive at the landing note too early; find out if the trumpeter can relax a little to impart a sexier quality to the upbeat. The English horn picks up the last note from the bass trumpet, and you should rehearse those two instruments alone, so they understand the connection.

Again, with no dynamic to guide us, the second clarinet probably should enter at single *piano* one measure before **reh. 140**. I know that often a solo bass clarinet plays here, but it really is better if you have both do this, especially in the third bar of **reh. 141**, where a different color is intended for the *poco più forte*. Many conductors struggle with how to lead the first bass clarinet into the *Danse Sacrale* during the last bar. Don't sweat it; you are only directing one player, so just give a little nod of your head and then catch the downbeat. The strings only need to know where to place their next note.

Sacrificial Dance (The Chosen One)

Almost all the questions and difficulties we have addressed thus far will come to a head in this final section. Whether it is deciding how to subdivide, distinguishing long from short notes, or making choices about dynamics, we experience it all during this last outburst.

The first detail to remember—and a point I have mentioned a couple of times—is that this work is first and foremost a ballet. As such, you should think of the rhythmically active parts with dancers in mind. When you really look at what appear to be great complexities, you will eventually discover that this boils down to being like a waltz with the occasional extra beat added or subtracted. In the opening section, there are never two bars with just two equal beats but several with three. And every 5/8 measure will automatically be beaten 3 + 2 or vice versa.

For the moment, forget about the pitches and just focus on the rhythm. At a speed of ♪ = 126, it is not exceedingly fast. The bars that contain three sixteenth notes, even if they are part of the 5/8, get a bigger beat, and those with two sixteenths get short strokes. Try it a couple of times, dealing only with the meters, not with the musical content. Remember that if you have a 2/8 bar, both of your beats should be relatively small. Once you are comfortable with that, add in the notes and rests. Do not rehearse this too slowly, as that can complicate matters. And as noted several times earlier, have the orchestra play the passage without your leadership once they appear to know what to do.

The question of long versus short comes up right away in the third bar. This is far more complex than the actual rhythmic aspect of the dance. You see the eighth notes have either dots or hash marks, denoting a short length. But then, what was the point of making them eighths and not sixteenths? In the fourth bar, the winds have a slur into the 2/8, but the strings continue as they were. From my point of view, a lot of the tension gets lost when the eighth note is short, and I much prefer to differentiate the two lengths through virtually the entire Finale. Since this is so important, perhaps it is easier to say that you can either play all the notes short or at the length indicated, regardless of the wedges.

Stravinsky is quite clear about how to subdivide the 5/8 measures, and we should follow his lead. At **reh. 145**, the patterns are different for the first and second bars. I should also point out that the timpanist often has a note to play when none of the other musicians do, frequently as an answer to the bass section, as in the second and third bars of **reh. 142**. At other times, such as **reh. 146**, they play together.

In my opinion, **reh. 149** is the most difficult part of the entire ballet, for both conductor and orchestra. It may not look that complicated, but trust me, a lot can go wrong. I remember all too well a performance at Carnegie Hall with a very well-respected maestro conducting from memory. Everything was exemplary until they reached this point. The conductor's beat became so vague here that the strings and winds simply got off, causing panic on the faces of the musicians and gasps from the audience after a few bars of chaos. Finally, one of the trombonists interjected with the quintuplet, completely out of context, and everyone got back on track.

If you are very confident about your rhythm, the safest way to show everyone where you are is to conduct the 3/8 bars in three and the 2/8 measures in one. Do not appear metronomic, as the rests need to look different from the notes. If you follow this path, then the bars in three should have smaller beats than those you conduct in one, making it a little easier for the orchestra to know where you are at any given point. Just conducting up and down as well as in triangles can often be misconstrued by those who have several bars of rest.

One other benefit of conducting the 2/8 bars in one is that the quintuplets can be played as an actual group of five rather than a combination that sounds closer to 3 + 2. If the trombone and trumpets see only one beat, they are more apt to play the notes equally. At first readings, **reh. 153** might find musicians playing on the rests. This is because once they have heard the five-note motive, they expect it to reappear soon, but it does not. A large gesture at **reh. 154** helps denote a change of sound and shows the musicians that a new phrase has begun.

I should add that the publishers and Stravinsky do not do us any favors by having the beams extend over the bar lines, especially when they include rests. The next time an edition is prepared, I hope that this will be changed to simply show the notes and rests as they occur.

You can make as much noise as you like at **reh. 161**, but try to get the trombone quintuplets to come out as an answer to the piccolo and D trumpet. Continue in the same manner at **reh. 162**, but when you arrive at **reh. 164**, you can now conduct normally in eighths. At this point, the rhythm is so well established that it is difficult to make a mistake. You do not have to make too much of the accelerando and crescendo indications before **reh. 167**.

The earlier editions had the same fermata as the opening of the dance in the first measure of **reh. 167**. Assuming you do not wait, you must direct your attention to the basses and bassoons for their downbeat in the second bar. This often is late and does not have the power of the opening because we have neither an open-string D nor the lower octave. You can add a low C♯ in the basses, but it might muddy the waters.

Igor Stravinsky: *Le Sacre du Printemps* (The Rite of Spring)

More primordial sounds overtake us at **reh. 174**, starting with the three trombone glissandos. Again, looks are deceiving, as it seems like the contrabassoons and basses should be answering this call. Of course, they cannot play in either a brassy way or nearly as loudly, so you have to write this off, just hoping for as much sound as possible. Everyone is too busy paying attention to the percussion anyway. Once again, some timpanists will try to combine all these parts, but it really cannot be done here.

Add the lower line of the horns in the third bar, asking them to play loudly enough that the rhythm is heard. Your beat must be clear as you approach and then conduct the 5/4; this is a place where it is easy for the musicians to get lost. At **reh. 176**, give a sharp beat to coordinate the syncopation in the upper winds and strings. Try to have the clarinets and pizzicato violins play as loudly as possible in the second bar, although you still may not hear it.

Rehearsal 177 presents an interesting choice for the conductor. You could make a case that the upbeat Ds, although not exactly a tune, should connect to the downbeats. This raises the question of whether the quarter notes in the seconds and violas should be long or short. I tend to follow the trumpet line, even though that means different lengths for the quarters. By **reh. 179** when the upper-octave Ds come in, the strong downbeats have disappeared, and there is a crescendo to make at the end.

The bass drum has an important solo at **reh. 180**; no one else is playing on the second sixteenth note, so this cannot be timid. Be aware of the stopped notes in the horns at the fourth measure of **reh. 180**. Even more striking are the *sforzandos* in the tuba and bass lines two bars before **reh. 181**. I like to ask the bass drum and timpani to add these as well. Some editions have a *sforzando* printed and others do not.

The fermata must be just long enough for the audience to wonder what you are going to do next. Several conductors have slowed the next section just a little, adding a *pesante* feeling to it, even though Stravinsky indicates that the tempo is the same. If you can get that heavy feeling without changing speed, great, but if you need to slow the tempo by a couple of clicks, that can be effective as long as you do not distort the sound by making a true *meno mosso*.

What a strange choice of words for the trumpets in the third measure of **reh. 181**: *maestoso*. How do we do this? I think that these notes, at least for a while, are longer and, in general, this section must feel heavier. This is partially achieved through Stravinsky's suggested bowing for the upper strings, always played on the string. Although there is an awful lot going on by **reh. 184**, do not speed up. The horns try to dominate, but the piccolo trumpet gets the better of them. The two trombones decide to step it up and reinforce the eighth notes before the coda.

If you have slowed down, even slightly, **reh. 186** is where you can get back to tempo. Some conductors take this faster than any music that has come before, but to me, this moment must be completely frightening, and you facilitate that feeling by keeping such a steady pace that the tension becomes almost unbearable. Also, if the passage moves too quickly, some harmonic considerations are apt to get lost.

Your job is mostly to keep out of the way. If your beat is too large, it can hamper the clarity that musicians need from you. Let your face and eyes show the anger or energy you wish to impart. Everything we have talked about applies for this final section. It is still a ballet, and you can easily find quasi-waltz-like elements as the coda moves forward.

The first twelve bars are the most difficult, simply because it is challenging for everyone to hear all the downbeats. Bring out the contrabassoon, second tuba, and double basses for a while. A few conductors have the first violins add the G♮ that occurs every other bar in the second violins; I don't think it is necessary, but you might need to encourage the lower voices to embrace those last notes.

The passage at **reh. 189** actually gets a bit easier, if the horns do not rush. From here, the timpani parts are usually done by one player, which makes sense. The brass are only single *forte* in the third bar. Do not let this get too aggressive; there will be time for that later. Now it really is between you and the timpanist. Decide together how much accent you need on those downbeats where they are printed, but this determination is predicated on the crescendo, as well.

At **reh. 193** we are truly in waltz territory. The 2/16 bars are almost like afterthoughts. Dramatic shifts in dynamics begin to occur, and you must make the most of the explosive thwacks, such as the one at **reh. 195**. Here a second timpanist must join in to supplement the first timpani and bass drum. It is helpful for all three of them to hit the downbeats as loud as possible.

All the *meno forte* indications are really *subito piano* marks. Again, please remember that in the 2/8 bars, your beats should be smaller than those in a 3/16 bar.

Stravinsky asks for a gradual crescendo starting around **reh. 198**, but to accomplish that, we also need to find the place that makes sense to drop back. Decrease the dynamic ever so slightly in the third bar, but do not assign an actual marking; it should dip just enough to have room to increase the volume by **reh. 201**.

It is safe to assume that something takes place onstage three bars before the end when the ballet is performed, so the rests, and even the flute run, might be influenced by the action. I start in a slow 3/4, diverging a bit from the metronome mark and tempo. Rather than push through the nine notes, I ask the two musicians to play them just a bit slowly, almost as if they were a set of three triplets. I make the downbeat of the next measure slightly longer so that we can enjoy the G♯ against the G♮. Then I wait and give beats five and six.

Why?

Well, there are several ways to do this ending. Some conductors make it one giant swoop of sound, not differentiating the high notes from the low ones. Others separate them so that the difference is more than apparent. I compromise, keeping in mind that those playing have to know where to come in. In any event, rarely does anyone hear the pitches in the last bar.

I will end with something that Michael Tilson Thomas pointed out to me. If you read the double-bass notes in the last bar from low to high, they spell out DEAD. Clearly not intentional on the part of Stravinsky, but it makes a nice story and provides a good way to conclude.

Conductor's Etiquette

When the piece is over, chances are you will be tired. Nevertheless, you still need to coordinate several well-deserved solo bows for members of the orchestra. I recommend marking them on the last page of the score.

Start with the bassoon. After that, my preferred order is timpani, percussion, bass trumpet, all the brass, bass clarinet, English horn, and alto flute. If you wish to add others, be my guest, but choose wisely.

> The real composer thinks about his work the whole time; he is not always conscious of this, but he is aware of it later when he suddenly knows what he will do.
>
> —Igor Stravinsky

Notes

1. Igor Stravinsky, *The Rite of Spring/Le Sacre du Printemps: Pictures from Pagan Russia in Two Parts* (London: Boosey & Hawkes Music Publishers Ltd, revised 1947, reengraved edition 1967).

2. Richard Taruskin, *Stravinsky and the Russian Traditions: A Biography of the Works through Mavra* (Oxford: Oxford University Press, 1996).

3. "Stravinsky, Igor / *Le Sacre du Printemps*, Score and Parts (ID: 2341)," New York Philharmonic Shelby White & Leon Levy Digital Archives, https://archives.nyphil.org/index.php/artifact/1c7db356-3bd9-4a60-b9ad-3fa94cb07d03-0.1.

George Gershwin:
An American in Paris

True music must repeat the thought and inspirations of the people and the time.

—George Gershwin

Unnamed photographer in employ of Bain News Service, Public domain, via Wikimedia Commons

George Gershwin: *An American in Paris*

Some works are performed so often that even the most studious musicians take them for granted. Along with Ravel's *Bolero* and Mussorgsky's *Pictures at an Exhibition*, *An American in Paris* falls into the category of works that sell tickets and save rehearsal time. Familiarity with the piece carries the day for both the marketing department and the conductor.

However, because of years of ill-prepared performances, a lot of bad habits have found their way into many conductors' interpretations. As we will see, many felicitous passages get neglected or overlooked, leaving us with only a glimpse into this complex and technically thorny piece.

Written and first performed in 1928, it is the only major, purely symphonic work by George Gershwin, whose catalog also includes the pieces for piano and orchestra, the *Cuban Overture*, and a suite derived from *Porgy and Bess*. Gershwin was not really trained in formal composition or orchestration, making this piece a truly impressive accomplishment. Most everything works, especially if you follow what is written in the score and, occasionally, what is not.

Is this piece a symphony, a tone poem, or something else? Gershwin described it as follows in an interview with *Musical America*:

> This new piece, really a rhapsodic ballet, is written very freely and is the most modern music I've yet attempted. The opening part will be developed in typical French style, in the manner of Debussy and the Six [a group of composers comprising Darius Milhaud, Francis Poulenc, Arthur Honegger, Georges Auric, Louis Durey, and Germaine Tailleferre], though the themes are all original. My purpose here is to portray the impressions of an American visitor in Paris as he strolls about the city, listens to the various street noises, and absorbs the French atmosphere. As in my other orchestral compositions, I've not endeavored to present any definite scenes in this music. The rhapsody is programmatic only in a general impressionistic way.[1]

Eminent music critic and composer Deems Taylor provided a rather verbose program note for the work's premiere by the New York Philharmonic in Carnegie Hall under the baton of Walter Damrosch.[2] It is fun to read, but everything you need to know is in the music and not the words.

This brings me to the question of which edition to use. The original published version from 1930 was deemed too complex and unwieldy, specifically in its use of the saxophones.[3] In the 1940s, composer and arranger Frank Campbell-Watson, who had worked on the Concerto in F as well as other Gershwin compositions, made cuts and revisions, most of which were cosmetic, but a few of which had a real impact on the structure and details of the piece.

In 2000, pianist Jack Gibbons, working from the original source material, reconstructed a complete version, eliminating Campbell-Watson's emendations and adding approximately 120 bars of music. He performed this with the City of Oxford Orchestra at Queen Elizabeth Hall.[4]

In 2013, the University of Michigan, in collaboration with the Gershwin estate, undertook the task of creating scholarly editions of all the works in the composer's catalog. Using Gershwin's holograph score and a 1929 Victor recording in which he participated, U of M's Gershwin Initiative, under the direction of editor Mark Clague, published the George and Ira Gershwin Critical Edition to settle the debate over the composer's intentions.[5] Having performed that edition, I see merit in many of the original ideas, but I believe that Campbell-Watson had some very practical solutions that we should continue to employ. We will deal with a few of those as we go through the work. For this analysis, we will primarily utilize the Campbell-Watson revision, as it is more readily available and remains the edition that most orchestras perform today, with occasional references to the others.[6]

What was so cumbersome about the original orchestration? *An American in Paris* was originally scored for three flutes (third doubling on piccolo), two oboes, English horn, two clarinets in B♭, bass clarinet in B♭, two bassoons, contrabassoon (omitted from the Campbell-Watson edition), four horns in F, three trumpets in B♭, three trombones, tuba, timpani, snare drum, bass drum, triangle, wood block, ratchet, cymbals, low and high tom-toms, xylophone, glockenspiel, celesta, four taxi horns labeled as A, B, C, and D with circles around them, alto saxophone, tenor saxophone, baritone saxophone (all doubling soprano and alto saxophones), and strings.

Although most modern audiences have heard the taxi horns sounding the notes A, B, C, and D, Gershwin's intention—as discovered by Mark Clague and the Gershwin Initiative—was to use the pitches A♭, B♭ (above middle C), high D (a third above that) and low A (a third below middle C). In labeling the taxi horns A, B, C, and D with circles around those letters in the score, Gershwin was likely referring to the order in which the four horns play and not the actual pitches that they sound. The composer had hand-selected four taxi horns in Paris, and they can be heard on the first recording of the piece playing the pitches Clague identified.

Still, I find it hard to believe that Gershwin expected to have those pitches played each time the work was performed. I think any four different notes are fine, as long as they are played in the indicated order. You need at least four percussionists (although some orchestras have combined the parts for just three) as well as a timpanist.

Gershwin's original orchestration calls for three musicians to play eight saxophones, which caused a stir among orchestras for being costly and inconvenient. Campbell-Watson reduced the saxophones to just three, one for each musician. In performance, the saxophones are usually placed either to the right of the clarinets or to the left of the bassoons. They are not heard until almost midway through the piece.

The score does not contain measure numbers, unless they have been put in by the orchestra librarian, but does include plenty of well-placed rehearsal numbers. Performance time is roughly seventeen minutes.

One of the first details to notice is the absence of metronome markings. This is most unusual for a twentieth-century work, but it does give the conductor leeway in terms of how fast or slow passages are played. Yes, we have early recordings as reference points, but these are unreliable, as tempos were often determined by how much music could be accommodated on one side of a disc. Still, it is quite surprising how closely most conductors conform to each other's tempos, as if certain speeds have become traditional.

The opening is marked *Allegretto grazioso*, perfect for what has come to be known as the "walking" music. The conductor needs to return to this tempo several times, so establishing the correct speed is quite important—not too fast and not too slow, just an easy jaunt down the street in two. At the fifth bar, I recommend bringing the clarinets up to *mezzo forte* to ensure that this countersubject is heard clearly.

In the fourth bar of **reh. 1**, the six-note group in the flute and oboe gets lost in the clamor of other instruments. I eliminate the diminuendo for these two musicians. Likewise, the solo second violin and viola need to start louder than the indicated *pianissimo* and, as with the flute and bassoon at the beginning, they can take a little breath before the quick triplet.

At **reh. 2**, bring out the clarinets and violas to add a nice bit of spice to the proceedings. The interjections of the trumpets and trombones should be equal in volume, and they should observe the accent on the last note of each group. **Rehearsal 3** has most instruments playing an accent on the first note. I take it just a little farther by asking the trumpets and trombones to make a crescendo to the second note, which should be played very short and clipped. The heading is *Vigoroso*. This is not a tempo, and we will find many descriptive words as we go along.

Our next written clue to the character of this section comes just five bars later. *Giocoso*, usually taken to mean humorous, refers to the first entrance of the taxi horns. Not only is this passage fun to play, but it can also induce some giggles from audience members hearing it for the first time. Also new to the proceedings is the all-important xylophone, here doubling the flutes.

Accents mark the syncopations. A very rarely noticed augmentation of this figure in the bassoons, cellos, and basses happens simultaneously and is worth bringing out. At the same time, the two oboes have something new to offer as well.

Campbell-Watson wisely adds the bassoons and cellos for a downward run in the fourth bar of **reh. 5**. I emphasize this by adding a crescendo to the long note that precedes the run followed by a *forte-piano* in those same instruments. He also adds *Vivo* after **reh. 7**, but we have to take this direction with a grain of salt. The violins' sixteenth notes can sound like a scramble if this new tempo is too fast, so quicken the pace just a little if you wish.

Please notice the trombones at **reh. 8**. They are *forte*, and the lines above and below tell us that these notes are sustained. The ritenuto indication is usually performed by the bass clarinetist as a *meno mosso*. All the instruments that play a short note on the downbeat of the bass clarinet's entrance must really clip this so that the first few notes of the solo are audible. Meanwhile, make sure that the violas are not too loud on their half note.

Which sticks to use and where on the instrument to play the roll are key considerations for the cymbal line at the *a tempo*; different positions provide different sonorities. Additionally, the size of the cymbal can have a significant impact on how this transitional passage is conveyed. As the woodwinds trade off short phrases, their dynamics should be equal and sound as though only one instrument were playing. I have never understood Campbell-Watson's insertion of a ritard in the bar before **reh. 9** and therefore ignore it, as do many other conductors. I suggest thinking of these two bars as a combined measure in 3/4.

The next *Grazioso* applies to the moving lines in the clarinets, second bassoon, and cellos. I probably do not need to tell you that Gershwin's use of the word "bells" refers to a glockenspiel and not a set of chimes. While the composer does not provide a dynamic marking for the tuba entrance, it should be played *forte* because this is the only instrument that has a pickup to the next bar.

As with the suspended cymbal, the use of the wood block presents several possibilities in terms of size and stick technique. Gershwin primarily incorporates it to highlight a particular rhythm that is going on in other instruments. You can decide if this color should be brought out or should mirror other voices.

Two measures before **reh. 10**, the violins need some time to be able to change from arco to pizzicato. The duration of this breath is about the length of a quarter note. It also helps to have the violins play the preceding F♯ up bow.

Gershwin writes a charming but rarely heard interplay between some of the woodwinds at this point. Another oddity is the viola pizzicatos, which contains a rhythm that does not reoccur in the entire piece. Do not be surprised if, after the two bars of reduced forces in the strings, a lot of the violins and violas are unprepared to come in next. It happens so quickly that unless the musicians have played the piece a few times, they have almost no time to take in this *tutti* instruction. There is also a mistake in some sets of material that places the first violins' *tutti* marking three measures before **reh. 11** instead of two before. Do have a look at the cello part four bars before **reh. 11** because the notation can be slightly confusing.

When we arrive at **reh. 11**, the trombones introduce a new tune, "La Sorella," which must have been quite popular in Paris cafés. It seems a bit intrusive, so Gershwin instructs those musicians to play *scherzando*, which here must mean with humor. This can be emphasized by ensuring that the grace notes are clearly audible and not performed particularly quickly.

Rehearsal 12 is often performed as a slight *meno mosso*, with a bit more heaviness. Balance is well considered by the composer because the violas must play with some force to be heard.

Almost all the grace notes in *An American in Paris* are played before the beat. Some are accomplished quickly, but here they are slow and slightly seedy. I ask the cellos and basses to play them in the same manner as the bass trombone. *Mezzo forte* seems too tame, so I suggest a stronger dynamic for this down-and-dirty moment. Conductors are divided over a possible change of tempo directly at the double bar, with some, including me, opting to hold back a bit to achieve the *con umore* effect indicated.

Personally, I think this slight deceleration feels right for the musical content, and you can go back to speed in the bar before **reh. 13** or at that figure itself. Campbell-Watson makes an interesting decision with the horns in the second bar. He writes "closed," another word for stopped, but he also redistributes the part for four musicians as opposed to just the first two players in Gershwin's original. The editor asks the third and fourth horns to play just the chords open, and the resulting new color is appropriate for this section marked *Con umore*.

Three measures before **reh. 15**, the first violins have a spot that is almost unplayable as written. In the previous bar, they are arco and must switch to pizzicato with no pause. This can be done because the first two notes are easily played with the left hand. However, the final note in that bar, a high A, not only makes it impossible to get back to the arco in time but is also nearly inaudible, even when played as loudly as possible. You could try to get it, but if it does not work, I would not spend time rehearsing this because the bells have the same notes. And if someone could explain why the flutes and oboes are written a dynamic softer than the violins, I would love to know.

The positioning of percussion indications on the staff can be confusing. Look at the second line and you find that the person playing the taxi horns appears to be the same one to hit the cymbal. Even using a stick, this musician really has no time to make the switch. The principal percussionist usually divvies up the parts, and in my experience, it is best to leave them to solve these matters.

The manuscript and U of M score have different notes for the first and second trombones in the fourth bar of **reh. 15**. Instead of going down to G♭ and E♭, they go up to high A♭ and E♭. Campbell-Watson probably changed this for safety reasons, but I see no reason contemporary trombonists cannot play the original notes.

A brilliant stroke of genius takes place here upon the entrance of the trumpets. Marked down a degree from all the other instruments, they emerge very gradually from the bustle and, if you judge it just right, create drama through this long, sustained crescendo.

Rehearsal 16 is interesting for the violas. In the original edition, they are divided for four measures starting in the fourth bar, with one half of the section starting on the first beat to play five notes in one bow and the other half starting on the second beat to slur the next five notes. Campbell-Watson has it split up with one group playing the first two bars and the other group the next two bars. Certainly, everyone can play all four without a problem. If you want to bring out this line, split the difference and have everyone play but change bow direction in the middle of each bar.

This next comment is truly picky. In the second bar of **reh. 17**, the triplet figure in the low horns and bass clarinet is never heard, including in my own performances. I can think of no other way to score it effectively, but sometimes I get frustrated seeing something on the page and knowing that it will be lost in the sonority.

Four bars before the *Molto meno mosso* shows the standard doubling of the taxi horns with the French horns. However, there is a problem with the very last bar of this phrase. When it occurs earlier, that last eighth note is played at the same dynamic as the other three. But this time, the score indicates a *subito piano* to correspond with the diminuendo in the woodwinds. I am not sure that this is what Gershwin intended, so I ask the musicians involved to refrain from getting softer.

The double bar is a complete change of tempo, mood, and color, accomplished quite suddenly. And if you are performing in a space that is even slightly resonant, hearing the downbeat of **reh. 19** is difficult. I suggest asking the second and fourth horns to play that final note strongly to finish the phrase. Then, take just a moment before continuing. Technically, to accomplish this, your second beat should veer to the right rather than upward to create room to give the new tempo.

The flute can play these grace notes slower than before, imparting a somewhat sad and lonely tone. Campbell-Watson adds pizzicatos to half of the second violins, and this certainly sets up the other instruments that will follow suit. But the original just calls for them to sustain the F♯, and it might be worth trying it this way to discern its effectiveness.

The two-bar crescendo before **reh. 20** is hard to accomplish, mostly because getting louder on harmonics is not easy. We only increase to *mezzo forte*, but I usually start getting stronger a measure sooner than written. Also, it helps to change to an up bow two bars before **reh. 20**. While I do not know what the violas, cellos, and a few winds are supposed to do with the two diminuendos at **reh. 20**, my instinct is to make a crescendo on the first half of the bar and then come back down for the remainder each time.

The effect of the trombones playing *piano* in the fifth bar is more successful if you exaggerate the crescendo that comes next, but then you have to come back down in the third measure of the phrase. At **reh. 21**, the flutes and piccolo have four bars of sixteenth notes that do not appear in any other instruments. It is not out of the question to ask the two oboes to double this, as their written notes are shared by the trumpets and violins. Also, it is quite fun to have the violas play four down bows in the fifth bar.

Con fuoco is not a tempo, so do not be tempted to get faster here. Likewise, avoid slowing down before the marked ritenuto. However, the horns can feel quite rushed at this point. Along with most of my colleagues, I change this to a hefty *meno mosso*, quite brassy with an exaggerated *forte-piano*. You might need to rehearse this transition with just the horns to solidify what tempo they will play here.

Just a hint of silence can occur before the *Calmato*, where I typically change my speed to ♩ = 84. The crescendo in the strings almost occurs naturally due to the rising figure, but it helps to tell the orchestra which dynamic you would like at the top. Everyone needs to take a breath before starting **reh. 24**. Once again, we find a discrepancy in some printings of the score. The English horn has an *espressivo* hairpin a few bars earlier, and the oboe should have the same.

Here is a little color trick you can try when the cellos jump from C to G for the 5/4 bar. Unless you say something, most of them will play the top note on the D string, requiring a bow crossing, but I have them do an audible portamento and remain on the same string.

Although **reh. 25** is marked *più mosso*, most conductors start the new tempo with the upbeat. A little lift prior to that note helps set the speed, but again, it might be helpful to play a couple of bars, so the orchestra gets an idea of your pulse for this next section. Bringing out the bass clarinet adds another interesting layer of texture. It is difficult to understand what Gershwin intended with the lines over the strings' notes, but they can either be played legato or with little pushes on each.

My best guess as to why the composer only asks for four basses at the *Con moto* is that he imagined it would be too heavy if everyone played. Plus, sometimes with that instrument, the pitches can get obscured during quick lines. But if your whole section can play it in tune, I see no reason not to try it. Another nice, subtle touch is how Gershwin divides the violins here and then, four bars later, does the same with the violas and cellos. Why does he do this? I think it must have to do with the sections removing their mutes to play *senza sordini* at **reh. 27**.

The 1929 recording and U of M edition omit the eight bars between **reh. 26** and **reh. 27**. With due respect to my friends at the university, I think it is simply impractical to leave out these measures. Having performed the critical edition, I can attest that the strings have absolutely no time to take off their mutes, which is why I believe the composer was so clever to write this transition.

At **reh. 27**, try to bring out the accents in the horns and upper strings, as we usually do not hear them. Five bars later at **reh. 28**, Gershwin asks the cymbal player to use drumsticks. The musician should use wooden sticks to play *pianissimo*, somewhere near the bell of the cymbal, with as fast a roll as possible.

The woodwinds can slightly exaggerate their phrasing to clarify the three-note groupings, but do not proceed too slowly, as this is a long time for the two bassoonists to hold their notes.

The *Subito con brio* is usually at the same tempo as the opening of the work. Either a publishing error or a mistake by Gershwin probably accounts for the stick to be mentioned only in the second bar of the cymbal line at **reh. 29**. Surely it should imitate the dynamics of the other instruments, so the cymbals should be played "with stick" from the first bar, playing *forte* for two bars and then *mezzo piano*. The thirty-second notes in the woodwinds are more like grace notes, but keep in mind that the accent is on the last note and not the first.

Campbell-Watson has a good idea at **reh. 30**. The original has no dynamic in the first horn, first trumpet, and first trombone, leading to the assumption that they should remain at *forte*. To allow the woodwinds to cut through, Campbell-Watson drops down the other sections, either via *forte-piano* or *piano* markings. Then he places a two-bar crescendo followed by two bars of diminuendo. This makes perfect sense, but he should have added it for the brass as well. However, to accommodate the moving notes, do not start the crescendo too early. It goes without saying that the repetition of this passage should proceed as before.

The score provides an important instruction for the side drum at **reh. 31**: wire brush. You likely know what it is, but you may not know that it comes in different sizes, each of which can be adjusted to change the sound. In addition, how you use it on the drum can vary significantly. For this passage, it should be tightened so the articulation is clear.

Rehearsing the flutes, oboes, and xylophone two measures before **reh. 33** can help solidify a sense of ensemble. Usually, the percussionist is positioned at a distance from the others, and these five musicians might have difficulty hearing each other.

Four measures before **reh. 34**, the triplet indications in the flute and clarinet line are often misread as slurs, but I think they should be played separately and on the short side. The articulation will be different a few bars later.

We encounter a familiar problem four measures before **reh. 35**, where the upper strings cannot get to the pizzicato without some scrambling and rushing. One solution is to ask half of each section to omit the last note of the previous bar, giving at least some of them a chance to switch to pizzicato on time. Those who play through the previous measure can then enter with pizzicato on the second beat.

I recommend playing without diminuendo during the first two bars of pizzicato to avoid getting too soft at the end. Just follow the horn and trumpet indications. Gershwin gives the horns a four-bar diminuendo four measures before **reh. 36**, but I think the diminuendo should be consistent with the previous passage.

For a short time, everything in the score is straightforward. I suggest that you rehearse the sixteenth-note groups, not only for the pitches but for the ensemble as well. At **reh. 37**, Gershwin indicates a dynamic of *mezzo forte* for the horns in the score's original edition. Campbell-Watson reduces it to *piano*, and I think this works well.

Have the horns take a breath before playing the tune six measures before **reh. 38**. Gershwin calls for everyone to play *fortissimo* at this point in the original score, but Campbell-Watson makes a huge change, and I think the wrong one, by reducing the strings to *piano*. My choice is to stay loud for these measures; they will always sound like a buildup.

Upon arriving at the *Deciso*, encourage the third trumpet to perform as a soloist in the third bar so that the imitations are equal. The 1/4 bars are conducted as if they were the third beat of a 2/4 bar—or at least that is the way they feel. I hope you have noticed that the timpani has a very brief roll on the last note of each bar at **reh. 39**; clearly, it cannot last very long.

One of the more interesting differences between versions occurs at **reh. 40**. The original has no break, whereas Campbell-Watson includes slash marks to indicate a pause. Listening to that first recording, we can ascertain that the size of the orchestra is small, and with early acoustic recordings, the sound is always dry. Contrastingly, today's orchestras are much larger, and we would not be able to hear the first couple of notes, much less the immediate character difference, without a pause. To my ears, the lack of a break makes what should be a nice five-bar interlude sound abrupt.

The *Più moderato, subito scherzando* section is dominated by the English horn, which is marked rubato, one of my least-favorite words in the musical vocabulary. It can mean anything, from tempo to dynamics and phrasings. For this charming moment, I would have chosen *giocoso*, or playful. Let the soloist play freely but keep your eye on the viola syncopations.

Returning to the *a tempo* is tricky. I usually let the violas play the last note on their own and prepare for the quicker pace with the upbeat. I do not particularly like these three bars because they feel tacked on, but Gershwin needs to get back to his main material, so we must make the best of them.

The flute run is fine, but the bassoon entry presents a problem. The flutes, in a higher register, can cut through easily, but the midrange of the deeper instrument gets covered up. Some conductors double the bassoon here, but it is also possible to add the first four notes in the bar before **reh. 41** to the bassoon part and have them played *forte*. This will make the connection much smoother.

Lots of busy work goes on at **reh. 41**—so much that some conductors run through this passage without heeding the *subito mezzo forte* at the fifth bar. In my opinion, you can even drop back more. The original score has only about half of the instrumental forces playing here, so Campbell-Watson wisely pulls everyone back. The snare drum part contains the word "shot" at this point, and it does not mean that the percussionist should have a drink.

You know what "shot" stands for, but did you know that there are different ways of doing it? My preferred method is to lay one stick across the drum, including the rim, and strike it with the other. It is possible to get the same effect with just one stick, but another factor comes into play here. When the work was written, rims of snare drums were usually made of wood, unlike today's rims, which are metal. A snare with wood hoops imparts a very different sound, no matter how you play it. If your percussionist has one, ask to hear what it sounds like and make a choice. Also note that although not explicitly stated, the drummer cannot play the sixteenth notes that follow without returning to normal drum strokes.

We have the instruction *pochissimo rit.* three bars before **reh. 42**. In my view, it should begin two measures earlier because staying in the quick tempo feels a bit impetuous and makes the trombone scale difficult to accomplish. I move the ritard to that measure and essentially arrive at the *Calmato* a bar before it is written. It is nice to hear the bass clarinet just before that, so increasing the dynamic a bit is probably a good idea. Establish an equal dialogue between the clarinet and violas, followed by the second violins, in terms of dynamics.

Four bars after **reh. 42** marks the only appearance of the celeste, which brings me to a side note: The disc label on the first recording lists the "Victor Symphony Orchestra with George Gershwin" (most of the musicians came from the Philadelphia Orchestra) under the "direction of Nathaniel Shilkret."[7] As the story goes, Gershwin was there to "supervise" and apparently became a nuisance, so Shilkret asked him to leave the studio. The problem was that someone forgot to hire a celeste player. Gershwin returned to record this, and he played around with it a bit, starting by performing most of the passage an octave higher than indicated and virtually repeating the second bar.

Although the composer did not write an official "program" for the piece, respected composer and pedagogue Deems Taylor provided a description for the New York Philharmonic's program book, getting a bit carried away with what may or may not be Gershwin's intended storyline. In particular, the violin solo, which Taylor described in quite flowery terms, is supposed to represent a young woman, perhaps under a streetlamp, trying to entice the lonely American out of the cold and out of his money.

The marking for the concertmaster is *poco rubato*. The first recording does not demonstrate much of an attempt to follow the rhythmic proportions in the music, but it does convey a flirtatious quality, and perhaps that is what you should say to the violinist. The second time this occurs, in a much higher register, I think it can be played with a bit more annoyance. The American is represented by the English horn, who dolefully responds, "Thanks, but no thanks."

Next Gershwin presents a series of chords from Stravinsky's *Petrushka* playbook, starting with a clash of C major and F♯ major. This should be performed in as icy a manner as possible. The tempo slows down and two solo violins reprise what the clarinets played back at **reh. 29**. In much the same manner as before, I highlight the three-note groups with slight separations. I also add a portamento before the final eighth notes for both musicians.

The third trombone provides the introduction for a jazzier, blues-like section at **reh. 45**. I usually ask this musician to do a fast glissando to the F and then wait a bit before coming down to the E♭. After the past seven minutes or so of basically introductory material, we get down to business, at least that is what the audience usually thinks at this point. I would need a full book on just this piece to address every decision and conducting trap, but I will share with you here the knowledge every conductor must have, with the understanding that there are several ways to interpret and perform almost everything from this double bar to the end of the piece.

As usual, Gershwin gives no tempo indication, just *Andante ma con ritmo deciso*, referring to the steadiness of the tempo and not the inflections found within. The original edition starts *mezzo forte*, and the Campbell-Watson edition starts *piano*. To create more contrast, I prefer the latter.

First, I should address the grace note in the bassoon. In most cases, all we need to do is decide if a grace note comes before or on the beat. Sometimes, as we have seen earlier, it might be played slowly or quickly, depending on the music that surrounds the note. Here we have something else: a lead-in, and a suggestive one at that. Imagine that the instrument could do a glissando into the F, and that would be the down-and-dirty way to set the mood. Some musicians can come close, but if nothing else, Gershwin must always have a feeling of elegance, as if Fred Astaire were leading the performance.

To me, this section imparts a lonely quality, but it does not take effect until the trumpet entry. We are just establishing the atmosphere here. The early recordings go at a pretty good clip, not what I would normally consider Andante, unless you walk very fast. I stay around ♩ = 72.

Having thought about the wire brushes earlier, in the second measure after the double bar you must consider not only how tight they should be but also how they best convey the rhythm. To decide, a lot will depend on whether you want to emulate the early recordings or move ahead a few years, when orchestras played quite differently.

Up until this point, we have discussed relatively few alterations to what is on the printed page. Starting in this second bar, your choices are several. Let us start by reviewing what we see in the snare drum part: sixteenth notes, no dynamic indicated, hairpins every four notes, and a diminuendo over the whole bar. What to do?

Early renditions played this exactly as written. The brushes were probably tight, striking the drum the same way the sticks did. And with quicker tempos than we hear today, the percussionist certainly used two brushes. As techniques developed, some drummers began swiping them from side to side rather than lifting them off the drumhead. Often, one hand would play all the notes and the other would emphasize either the first or middle of the group.

Then came the idea that this should be sexier. Instead of even notes all the way through, there was a slight delay between the first two notes of the group, almost as if it were a triplet missing its middle. This change certainly made it easier for the player to control the dynamics, and since no one else played this rhythm, the percussionist could exercise a degree of flexibility within the set tempo. This is a choice to discuss with your drummer.

In the fifth bar, the famous solo trumpet holds forth. Some refer to this as a blues, which it is not, at least in terms of its structure. However, in terms of style, so-called blue notes are added, as are slides that do not always land right in tune, and the rhythm is free. But the sound quality is the most important element.

Gershwin wants a "felt crown" to be used. What is it? As described by leading mute manufacturer Tom Crown, "A felt crown is the crown of a fedora hat, usually without the lining or brim. Slits are cut so the hat will stay on and over the bell. This gives the 'jazzy' muted sound that Gershwin must have heard from jazz trumpeters of his time."[8] Sometimes you will see a beret draped over the bell. Some theorize that it should be played open, or even offstage. In any event, the mood to achieve is loneliness, but be careful that this is not done to the point of parody. My advice is to listen to how the trumpeter plays it and, if it is not to your liking, speak to him or her but not in front of the whole orchestra.

Now we come to the saxes. Since this new color has not yet been heard in the piece, we surely want people to know that they have entered. But the star of this part of the piece is the trumpet, so the reeds should not come in too strongly—in fact, Gershwin says *pianissimo*.

Once we establish the new material and sound, we can then play around a little. After instructing the saxes to play the first bar straight and without much vibrato, I ask them to do a Billy May–style lip glissando two bars later. Very few of today's orchestra members are aware of who May was or what this means, so I have to explain. Basically, the glissando is an upward swoop just before the second note that makes it sound just a bit flat at first. Listen to a track like "Lean Baby" featuring May's signature "slurping saxes" and you will understand what I am talking about.

Would it have been utilized in the early performances of this piece? Probably not, but the sound of the three saxes doing this just right is quite something. This is one of two times I employ this effect in the piece.

The *poco rubato* after **reh. 46** is just for the trumpet. Your job is to follow and to place the pizzicatos as accurately as possible. Again, this is a solo moment and as with a concerto, the trumpet player has their own ideas that they have been practicing for years. Any disagreements should be discussed privately.

Everything should be played expressively by the ensemble, even passages that do not appear to be particularly interesting, such as three measures before **reh. 47**. There are many possibilities to add contour, and I will leave it up to you to decide which nuances you prefer. The trombone takes over from the trumpet and may choose to add a glissando here and there. As long as it is in good taste, this is fine, especially between the two last notes.

I never quite understand why, but the string quartet passage two measures before **reh. 48** often poses a problem. If the piece is unfamiliar, then of course, the musicians may not realize that the first violin is playing something different from the others. If necessary, rehearse the others separately, explain what the concertmaster is doing, and then put it together.

What is *Più mosso e meno*? It seems like an oxymoron to me, but maybe the *meno* is just for the last part of the second bar. There certainly are fewer players, but there would be no need to inform the conductor of that. The clarinet lead-in to **reh. 48** usually has a slight ritardando attached, even if it does not say so. Maybe that is what the *meno* is? I usually ask the clarinetist to play the quintuplet as if the last note were just another sixteenth in the pattern. That gives us our slowdown.

Campbell-Watson makes a significant change at the *a tempo*, marking the dynamic down to *piano* from a *subito forte* in Gershwin's original. This is a huge deal. To me, the louder dynamic just feels too harsh for this moment, and we will have plenty of times to perform it at maximum volume. I start it off quite softly, preceding it with a diminuendo on the clarinet run. Then, about halfway through the first measure, I warm it up to around *mezzo forte*.

The crescendo three measures before **reh. 49** goes right to the end of the bar and should be added to all the instruments to sustain the tension, increasing to *forte*. A dramatic *subito piano* comes next, followed by a slight ritard leading into the *poco meno* where the clarinets have a moving line worth bringing out. Gershwin actually writes in a portamento for the upper strings, so it must be observed.

Rehearsal 50 follows a slight accelerando; however, the *a tempo* marking leads us to believe that this is a sudden change. There are also some conflicting dynamics, as the first violins do not have a new one indicated. The consensus seems to be that the conductor should make a gentle ritenuto and diminuendo before this section. If all the instruments drop to *piano*, you can insert an *espressivo* crescendo in the middle of **reh. 50** for the whole orchestra, including the saxes.

A *poco rit.* takes place before the double bar, along with a diminuendo, which does not appear in every instrumental group. At the key change, all the instruments are *mezzo forte*, and in the original, *forte*. The louder dynamic can work, but only if you do not overdo it.

Looking back at the original version, the first note for those with the tune is just an unadorned D, while Campbell-Watson adds a C♯ grace note for the first violins. This gesture gives the entrance poignancy, which can be further amplified by having the trumpet do it as well. You can even put a slide in between the two notes, especially with the felt crown softening the sound.

Two measures before **reh. 52**, Gershwin writes *Deciso ma legato*. Hold back the tempo a bit here. You might also choose to make a ritardando before the *Con moto*, but use this device sparingly, as too many of them can take away from the line in this portion of the piece. The next double-bar dynamic can also be reduced to *piano* effectively.

The lead-in to **reh. 53** presents some options as well. As we have seen, it is not easy to switch from arco to pizzicato quickly. Here, the last note must be short enough to allow the bow arm to adjust to the correct position. Two of the saxes have a moment to shine with solos, and if they are outstanding musicians, you can ask the bass clarinet and bassoons to be tacet. The articulation in the cellos during the ritard often gets ignored, so be sure to observe both the slurs and the dots.

Gershwin includes numerous accents in unexpected places over the course of the work. Study this section carefully, starting just after **reh. 52**, to discern where they are and how they differ as the piece progresses. This is especially important at the *Agitato*. Both the first edition and Campbell-Watson's revision indicate a pause before the *Grandioso*. However, Maestro Shilkret does not observe this in the first recording, barreling straight through without regard to any tempo change or the two-bar ritenuto that follows. I do not recommend being historically informed here. My metronome choice is ♩ = 72, which still gives me lots of space for the *molto rit.* ahead.

We have discussed which sticks might be used for the cymbals, but the larger question is, "When is it one cymbal, and when is it a pair?" The rule of thumb, for most composers, is that they will let us know. Gershwin only does this occasionally. For example, back at the Andante he indicates "with stick," but offers no further instruction to change at the *Grandioso*, a climactic moment calling for crash cymbals.

These omissions or discrepancies are left to the conductor to decide. The same is true for how long the cymbals should ring. Even though the composer has written an eighth note, I do not believe anyone has ever played it short. The bar before **reh. 55** can be conducted in eight, but I prefer to subdivide only the second half of the bar. Because of that *molto rit.*, you can even consider dictating the last sixteenth note. Meanwhile, remember to pay attention to the accents whenever they occur.

Gershwin presents us with an interesting dilemma at **reh. 55**. The score says *a tempo*, but which one? There have been many iterations, but we shall assume that the Andante is the correct reference point. Here is where that first recording comes in handy as a guide, especially because the conductor never slowed down. Common practice for most of the work's performance history has been to play this as fast as all the notes can be heard. However, after a ritard into **reh. 56**, almost every leader does return to the Andante tempo.

The old recording makes a strong case for doing what is written, but it is shocking, probably because I am not used to it. More than likely, I will continue to do this quickly, but maybe someday, as this is still a piece I conduct often, I will give this idea a try. One aspect of my approach that I will not change is to have the cymbals and bass drum start at *mezzo forte* two measures before **reh. 56** and increase the dynamic bit by bit until they are *fortissimo*. And of course, I let the cymbals ring for at least two bars.

Some say the brief chromatic violin solo at the *Calmato* is the lady of the night becoming tired and just wanting to get home. The same could be said of our American. The little woodwind responses are often a tad late, probably because they are unable to hear the solo clearly. A nice touch is to ask the concertmaster to make a glissando between the final B♯ and the long C♯.

The octave leap in the two bassoons is almost impossible because of a natural break due to fingering issues. I can recommend a couple of fixes for this. You can make the case that the slur indication is just telling us that the three notes are a triplet and separate each one. Alternatively, you can break it up into two groups of two slurred eighths, which seems to work, in my experience. A few conductors have had the notes all played short. In the next measure, the horns are in danger of coming in late for their sixteenth triplets and playing them too slowly. I subdivide the fourth beat to resolve this issue.

The clarinet duet is the final remnant of this Andante passage. Here, just before the third beat, I like to put in the Billy May glissando, with the next note a bit under pitch to start. Please be aware that the cellos have lines over the slurred notes. Each can be given a little stress as the phrase fades away.

To swing or not to swing at the Allegro?

Perhaps this is the most discussed moment in the piece after the taxi-horn debate. I should state at the outset that my own view is contrary to what Gershwin seems to desire, judging by his piano roll and the first orchestral recording.

Even though this music is described as "jazzy," it is not jazz but instead closer to ragtime. The main question has to do with evolution: Do we look back or change with the times? We are dealing here with interpretation and not social history, but I would be remiss not to remind you that Prohibition began in 1920 and ended thirteen years later. This is important because it coincides with what is referred to as the Jazz Age.

People sought refuge in illegal clubs where this forbidden music was being played. In France, it was called *Le Jazz Hot*. This was, first and foremost, dance music, straightforward enough to allow people to move around the floor easily. Gershwin can be heard on several recordings, and his pianistic stylings are indeed more classical than improvisatory.

You would think this would be enough evidence to convince us that we must observe the printed rhythms as they are on the page. But along comes Oscar Levant, considered the foremost interpreter of Gershwin's music and his close friend, whose performances over the years begin to resemble the swing style and sound that we associate with jazz. Perhaps it is possible that in his concert works, Gershwin wanted to separate himself from the world of popular culture.

What is this swing style we are talking about and how do we attain it? In the early days of my career, when I performed *An American in Paris* outside of the United States, I found that many orchestras had difficulty understanding how do this. It cannot be easily defined, but I will try. Actually, I will let Louis Armstrong tell us: "Ah, swing, well, we used to call it syncopation—then they called it Ragtime, then blues—then jazz. Now, it's swing. Ha! Ha! White folks, yo'all sho is a mess."[9]

Swing developed in the 1930s, after Gershwin wrote both *Rhapsody in Blue* and *An American in Paris*. In technical terms, swing refers to alternately lengthening the first note and shortening the second in an eighth-note pattern. But trying to describe it goes against the feeling. If you wish to incorporate this style, you will have to sing something to the orchestra, making sure they understand you are not vocalizing triplets. It is subtle, like the earlier-mentioned Fred Astaire.

For our purposes, let us assume that you are going to be more flexible than Gershwin indicates. The first issue is the pickup to **reh. 57**, which is almost always preceded by a ritard in the cellos and a delayed trumpet entry, to come as a surprise. If you choose to play this note in tempo, just make eye contact with the soloist and off you go. But another possibility, and one that I employ, is to have the first trumpet play the pickup note long and with a crescendo.

While I was writing this essay, I decided to ask a couple of prominent first trumpeters this question: "If you are playing the piece and do not know the conductor leading the performance, what do you do when you get to this solo?" The consensus is that a more straightforward style makes sense, and if the conductor wants it played differently, they will say something.

The musicians I asked are longtime veterans of the orchestral workforce and therefore accustomed to playing this and the earlier solo in all manner of styles. But their default stance is to adhere to the rhythm on the page unless the conductor has indicated otherwise. And even though I have played around with it, I am starting to lean toward a more straightforward interpretation myself, as trying to get the whole orchestra to "swing" can sound artificial and forced. This is purely a matter of taste.

No matter which style you choose, the sound should evoke a speakeasy—slightly rough and edgy. If you opt for a later jazz style, the instruments that play the eighth-note rhythm can emulate the swing with added hairpins, while the brushes on the snare, as earlier, follow the same pattern as the other rhythmic instruments. And since the sound is so cool, I like to ask the saxes to play about *mezzo forte*.

Meanwhile, the trumpet can add little touches here and there, never overdoing things, lest it fall into a burlesque. Even the horns can imitate the swing pattern in the fourth bar. The trombone can take over from the trumpet in the same manner, but I prefer for the upper winds and lower strings to play straight eighth notes.

Early swing bands quite often featured violin, but usually just one. If you want the section to continue in the swing style, they have to play on the string, ignoring the dots. Again, the swing rhythm is not a triplet, just a slight elongation of the first note and quickening of the second.

Even though it is not played in the same way, perhaps the best analogy is a Strauss waltz. We know how it is supposed to sound but putting it into words presents a challenge—either you feel it, or you don't. A good general rule is that for continual groups of two eighth notes, you can use the swing pattern, even when it is divided up between instruments, such as in the percussion three measures after **reh. 58**.

The four bars starting at **reh. 59** should be played straight, but the clarinet can embellish a little. Then you can go back to the forbidden style at **reh. 60**. The trumpet may choose to add some slurred notes, such as the first two, but in the swing style. You must, however, revert to the exact rhythm as printed four measures before **reh. 61**. I also find it helpful to go into two here. Coordination between the cellos and bassoon is difficult because of the ritard. One solution is to subdivide the second half of the bar and revert to conducting in two at **reh. 61**.

This next passage is magical, with many interesting things going on. Gershwin presents a straightforward set of quarter notes in the bassoons, timpani, and low strings. Meanwhile, he writes marvelous syncopations in the clarinets and saxes every other bar that need to be brought out. He is surprisingly specific about the snare drum, and my interpretation is that the notes with lines are played with one brush while the continuous eighths are done with the other hand moving from side to side in strict rhythm. The second oboe and English horn have an almost Middle Eastern motif that should be played *forte*.

Regarding the bowing for the violins and violas at **reh. 61**, I ask them to start up bow and follow the crescendo, then change to down bow on the last note of the second bar, but slur this note to exaggerate the glissando. Then I ask them to change to an up bow, independently, somewhere before the triplet. In the fifth bar, I have them take out the slur and change bows frequently on the sustained notes. The printed bowing seven bars before **reh. 62** works very well; however, notice that they will have to retake the down bow five measures before that.

Here is the kicker, which is usually a mess the first time around: The last quarter note before **reh. 62** is correctly indicated as a down bow, but they have to achieve the *subito piano* in the next bar. Ask the violinists to play that quarter short and then quickly reset at the tip of the bow to accomplish the color change on an up bow at **reh. 62**. Insist on it, and make sure everyone has the bow in the correct position. This is one of those places where the bowing looks as good as it sounds.

At **reh. 63** you can return to "swing land" for this section featuring the very big band at its hottest. I have never been convinced by the ritard and simply omit it, returning to a four-to-the-bar beat pattern. Be warned that sometimes the first violin part has a sextuplet upbeat to **reh. 63** resembling the alto sax, while the score just has an eighth note—either works. Nine bars later, get back to the straight rhythm. It would be nice, just once, to hear the oboes and saxes in this place.

Eight bars before **reh. 64** is yet another moment when clearly the cymbals need to be clashed and played loudly with ring. Although it is not loud, a rare trumpet trill with the oboes can come out a bit. All the eighth notes are played off the string here.

Conduct a very tight beat two measures before **reh. 64**. The pattern is almost a 3/8 against the 4/4 bar, but the accent makes all the difference. Exaggerate them.

Yet another place that may be misinterpreted, including in the first recording, begins three bars before **reh. 65**, where both a slur and a dot occur over the same note. In this instance, I think the slur refers to the bowing and that the groups of two notes are separated, not played legato, as is usually the case. The rallentando cannot be too slight, or the transition back to the *Grandioso* is abrupt.

At **reh. 65**, Gershwin provides some useful information. The timpani plays in the center of the drums, producing no pitch but a difference in the range. Finally, he tells us that the cymbal is played with a stick and does not ring. He also offers the suggestion to change the bow in the middle of a sustained note. The horns' accents should sound like bells, and they can back off a little after each attack. Campbell-Watson correctly adds some instruments for the moving lines in the woodwinds; otherwise, they would be inaudible. Keep looking for those offbeat accents.

The tradition at the Largo is to allow the cymbals to clash and vibrate. Another tradition, not always followed, is to ask the trombones to do a glissando in the second bar between the E and B♭.

The *a tempo* at **reh. 67** is difficult to understand. Although it may not be as slow as the preceding Largo, it certainly is not as fast as the Allegro. Even Shilkret stays fairly calm here. In the fourth bar, Gershwin, for whatever reason, allows for the bassoon to play the tuba solo, perhaps if the tuba player were not up to handling it. But on the first recording, we hear a bass clarinet playing the wrong note to start and certainly not playing *espressivo*, as indicated, followed by the strings stopping three beats early and leaving out the E to complete the C-major chord. To top it off, there is no rest before the soloist's last G, although the optional bassoon part has it written that way in the early edition. I have no idea what might have happened here.

A little interlude brings us to the coda. It is a good idea to connect the tuba's note to that of the cellos, as if the instrument has not changed. In terms of tempo, we are back at the very opening of the piece; very few conductors suddenly change speeds at the Allegretto. Various instrumental groups play two slurred quarter notes during this passage and, often, the second one is shortened just a bit. This can help the flute and clarinet project more comfortably.

Interestingly, the first recording eliminates the violins' upbeat to **reh. 70**, but the tempo picks up, and this is common in most performances. The accents in the violins on the last of each group of sixteenths in the fifth bar onward are tough to hear. Meanwhile, we get the last appearance of the taxi horns. Be careful not to let the tempo get away from you. This coda is busy enough. I have never asked them, but I wonder what the violins actually play two bars before the *meno mosso*—it strikes me as far too difficult as written.

Of all the fascinating discoveries made at the University of Michigan, my very favorite is what happens at **reh. 76**. The Campbell-Watson edition shows a timpani roll on the downbeat, with a *forte-piano* as well as a fermata. Guess what? None of those appear in the original! The first beat is empty, the woodwinds and strings have the upbeats, and the timpani does not play until the *Grandioso*. I loved it when I first saw the new score and appreciated it even more when I performed it. But the acoustics demand just a bit of a pause before commencing the scale. This is one nuance that I might keep, even though audiences will gasp. However, should you choose to play the timpani roll, delay the crescendo, lest the upbeat in the other instruments not be audible.

Rehearsal 77 is marked Presto, the fastest tempo indication in the entire work. This is never observed, probably because it sounds too much like a cartoon. This is another moment worth rehearsing slowly so everyone understands how they fit into the picture. I would go so far as to do it one time without conducting, forcing the orchestra to listen to each other carefully.

A couple of false endings make the last page intriguing. The original lacks a fermata at the Largo, but in the early recording, we can hear that this is just too abrupt a transition. There needs to be a slight tenuto on the last chord of the Largo and then a silence before commencing what is marked as a *più mosso*. However, as a concluding device, going faster just does not make sense.

It is unclear why Campbell-Watson changed the dynamic from *piano* to *mezzo forte* here. The final iteration of the blues tune needs to be heard right up until the last note of the phrase, imparting a slightly inconclusive ending to the journey. I have the second saxophonist—who might need to switch to an alto rather than tenor instrument—double the first, starting all those with the tune at the indicated *mezzo forte*. I also embrace one last "Billy May" moment by adding a glissando to the downbeat four measures before the end.

To ensure that the entire phrase is audible, everyone else should start at a *piano* dynamic and refrain from making a crescendo until after the downbeat three measures before the end. Make sure that you know when you want the snare drum to begin for that final upbeat.

My father, Felix Slatkin, recorded this piece with the Hollywood Bowl Symphony Orchestra in the late 1950s.[10] I was shocked when I listened to it recently and discovered that he made a dramatic change to the final saxophone line. Also adding the horns, he changed the note in the third-to-last measure from the printed concert C♮ to the resolution note, F, giving an entirely different meaning to this last phrase. Perhaps other conductors had done this, but honestly, I do not think it works very well.

I will conclude with one last anecdote: In the original, the strings play their last notes pizzicato. Maybe it looked good.

Most performances will continue to use the Campbell-Watson edition since, as of this writing, the University of Michigan version may be out of budget for most orchestras. But they do send along the taxi horns with the parts. I encourage you to listen to that original recording, as there are few better examples of how performance practice of any piece can change over the years.

Conductor's Etiquette

It is fairly clear who gets a solo bow in this piece. The first must go to the trumpet, even if that musician had a bad performance. The next one, for the tuba player, is optional but always appreciated. I usually ask the saxophone players to stand, followed by the concertmaster. Almost all the other solo passages are very short and therefore do not need to be acknowledged.

> The composer does not sit around and wait for an inspiration to walk up and introduce itself. . . . Making music is actually little else than a matter of invention aided and abetted by emotion. In composing we combine what we know of music with what we feel.
>
> —George Gershwin

Notes

1. Hyman Sandow, "Gershwin Presents a New Work," *Musical America* 48, no. 18 (18 August 1928): 5, 12, accessed August 31, 2023, https://archive.org/details/sim_musical-america_1928-08-18_48_18/.

2. Deems Taylor, concert program, December 13, 1928, Program ID 4911, New York Philharmonic Shelby White & Leon Levy Digital Archives, https://archives.nyphil.org/index.php/artifact/f08aa3f0-c460-4f1e-85ec-4dd6d1bc0d09-0.1.

3. George Gershwin, *An American in Paris* (New York: New World Music Corporation, 1930).

4. Margaret Davies, "Review of 'Gershwin Spectacular,'" *Musical Opinion*, December 2000, http://www.jackgibbons.com/reviews.htm.

5. George Gershwin, *An American in Paris: A Tone Poem for Orchestra (1928)*, ed. Mark Clague, based on the George and Ira Gershwin Critical Edition, series 1, vol. 1 (Ann Arbor: The Gershwin Initiative, University of Michigan, 2017).

6. George Gershwin, *An American in Paris for Orchestra (1928)*, revised by Frank Campbell-Watson [c. 1943] (London: Chappell & Co. Ltd., copyright 1930).

7. *Discography of American Historical Recordings*, s.v., "Victor matrix CVE-49711. An American in Paris / Nathaniel Shilkret; Victor Symphony Orchestra," accessed September 7, 2023, https://adp.library.ucsb.edu/index.php/matrix/detail/800023424/CVE-49711-An_American_in_Paris.

8. Tom Crown, "What Is a Mute?" Tom Crown Mutes, accessed September 8, 2023, http://www.tomcrownmutes.com/learn_history.html.

9. Ray Argyle, *Scott Joplin and the Age of Ragtime* (Jefferson, NC: McFarland, 2009), 172.

10. George Gershwin, *Rhapsody in Blue / An American in Paris*, Hollywood Bowl Symphony Orchestra, conducted by Felix Slatkin, Capitol P8343, 1956, LP.

Aaron Copland: *Appalachian Spring* Suite

Inspiration may be a form of super-consciousness, or perhaps of sub-consciousness—I wouldn't know. But I am sure it is the antithesis of self-consciousness.

—Aaron Copland

Aaron Copland by candlelight, Tepoztlán, Mexico, 1944. Photographer: Victor Kraft. Used by permission of Mrs. Victor Kraft, 90 Edgewood Avenue, Cranston, RI 02905-1344.

142   Aaron Copland: *Appalachian Spring* Suite

Aside from Gershwin's *An American in Paris*, this is probably the piece of music from the United States that I have conducted most frequently. It transcends international boundaries and is always appreciated by musicians and public, no matter where it is performed. The work should be in the repertoire of every conductor.

The first consideration and decision that must be made concerns the version. Which to choose depends upon where you are performing the work and the size of the stage. It is first and foremost a ballet, originally written for Martha Graham. The premiere took place in the Coolidge Auditorium at the Library of Congress in Washington, D.C. Having had the opportunity to perform it there myself, I understand why the original version only utilizes thirteen instruments. It is not a big space, and Copland had to find a combination of instruments that would fit into the cramped pit. The original version is scored for four violins, two violas, two cellos, one double bass, a flute, a clarinet, a bassoon, and a piano. The complete ballet takes approximately thirty-five minutes to perform.

Upon its premiere in 1944, the work was a huge success not only for Copland but also for American music. The optimistic storyline about newlyweds building a home together on the frontier harkens back to simpler times, appealing to the mood of a nation engaged in war overseas. Copland originally titled the work *Ballet for Martha* as a tribute to Graham, and it was the great choreographer herself who suggested the name *Appalachian Spring*, inspired by a line in Hart Crane's poem "The Dance." Reviews were ecstatic, and Copland's score won the Pulitzer Prize in Music in 1945.

To help the work reach a wider audience, given the unusual nature of its original orchestration, Copland quickly created a shorter suite from the complete ballet in 1945. He orchestrated the suite for what could be described as a Beethoven-sized ensemble with added piano, harp, and percussion. This is the version that is performed most often today.

In 1954, at the request of Eugene Ormandy, Copland orchestrated a portion of the ballet that comes in the middle of "Simple Gifts" and restored a few other spots that had been cut to make the suite. This expanded version came close to representing the complete work as heard at the premiere, now fleshed out for full orchestra. However, a few passages were still omitted, and in 2016, composer David Newman filled those in.

In 1970, Boosey & Hawkes published a chamber version of the suite utilizing Copland's original instrumentation for thirteen players, giving ensembles today four different choices for performance. In this score-study exercise, we will be looking at the 1945 suite for full orchestra.[1]

This version is scored for woodwinds in pairs, two horns, two trumpets, two trombones, timpani, percussion, piano, harp, and strings. The two percussionists play xylophone, snare drum, bass drum, cymbals, tabor (long drum), wood block, claves, glockenspiel, and triangle. The duration is roughly twenty minutes.

In some ways, this is still a small orchestra. Certainly, it is possible to perform it with a large group, but perhaps the best solution is something in between. In my view, the maximum should be ten first violins, ten second violins, eight violas, six cellos, and four basses. Unless the performance venue is unusually cavernous, that should suffice.

The piano, harp, and percussion should be placed near each other. This makes some of the passages, in particular the final three bars, much easier in terms of ensemble. Everyone else stays in their usual positions. However, since the wind forces are not large, it might be helpful to place the brass instruments closer to the woodwinds than they usually sit.

Keep in mind that the score is transposed. This means that the conductor sees the same notes as the instrumentalist. I am not a big fan of scores in C, as this creates one more step when discussing pitches with those musicians involved. We can blame Prokofiev for that.

The layout of the instruments in the score is conventional. These days, all the notes, dynamics, and phrase indications have been corrected, and the score and parts match. But some glaring omissions and discrepancies remain, which we will discuss here.

The first of these has to do with the string divisi. At no point in this piece are there any moments when a section is divided into three parts, only two, but there are three ways to divvy these up:

"Traditional": The two parts are divided on the stand, with the outside player taking the upper line and the inside player taking the lower line.
"By Stand": The two lines are divided by alternating stands, with the first stand taking the upper part, the second the lower, the third the upper, etc. Since my suggested section size is ten violinists, the last stand then divides the two parts among themselves.
"Front/Back": The front stands all play the top line, and the back stands play the bottom. As with the previous ten-player situation, the first five musicians can play the top line and the other five the bottom line.

Why is this important?

To start with, let's assume that all the violins are massed on the left side of the conductor. Each instrument is facing the same direction, and the sound is going directly out to the audience. In the first scenario above, the lower line might sound equal to the upper, at least to the conductor, but it is not that way for the audience because the bottom line is further away from the listener.

If a page turn falls during a divisi passage, one of the musicians will have to stop playing, leaving a void for perhaps a bar or two. This is a particular problem for symphonies of the classical era when we observe the first movement repeat. In Haydn, for example, you see the violins scramble to either turn back the page for the repeat or turn it ahead.

In the first bar of *Appalachian Spring*, the second violins and violas have the indication "HALF" over their first entrance. What did Copland have in mind? We can go back to Gustav Mahler, who also put in those words occasionally (*die Hälfte*). But Copland specifies that it refers to the front half of the section, not the inside or outside players. How do we know? Looking ahead a few bars, we see the same HALF indication for the other string sections, but the first violins have a divisi within the HALF!

If you were just to look at the individual part, it is easy to understand the potential for confusion among the section members at the initial rehearsal. If we have ten second violins and eight violas, the best way to apply the instruction is for the first five violinists and first four violists to play these passages. For the firsts, we alter the number of musicians in the first half of the section to the first three stands—assign the first three players the top line and the other three the bottom. These divisi indications will be present many times in this score, so it is vitally important for the conductor to establish how he or she wishes to have them performed, preferably prior to playing one note at the first rehearsal.

Moving on to the music itself, we can assume that the metronome marks are legitimate and that there is not much room for leeway in the basic tempos Copland lays out. I find it interesting that the composer will sometimes use English for a tempo indication and other times Italian. For example, four bars before **reh. 6**, which is marked allegro in Italian, Copland writes "as at first" in English.

It is important to show the first two beats of the work rather than just giving the instruments an entry indication on beat three. This helps everyone get a better grasp of the tempo. We do have a bit of a problem with those first two notes, under which appear both a slur and a line. What is it that Copland wants? More than likely, this indicates a very slight separation of these notes, but only enough to retake the bow stroke for articulation purposes.

Please note that in the second measure, the second violins have a diminuendo, but the violas do not. As with so many composers over the ages, Copland does not tell us what dynamic he wants at every point in the score. Here, we do not know how soft the second violins should get. My feeling is that this is an evaporation of sound so that the viola color is dominant. I tell the second violins to go down to *pianissimo* but to start the diminuendo on the third beat instead of the second.

Now the clarinet makes its entrance. The indication *semplice* is clear, but the one in parentheses "(white tone)" is not. You are not going to find a definition in any book, so we must assume that Copland means "colorless." And that is, of course, impossible. More than likely, "white tone" is his way of saying *non espressivo*.

In the fourth bar, the clarinet has a tie into a rest, meaning that the cutoff is indefinite. The time signature 3/2 is correct because that is the way it is phrased (meaning that the last two beats should sound as an upbeat). Although there are six beats in the measure, any subdivision is done within the three pattern. It is worth noting that the violas sustain for two full beats, and the cellos take over from them. Often, conductors let the violas stop just before the cello entrance, but I find that connecting them is quite lovely. Pay attention to the balance when the flute enters. This creates a new color, and no instrument should dominate.

Now we come to one of the most important moments in the work, and the balance established here will apply every time it reoccurs. The bar before **reh. 1** is a mild confluence of two chords that will bloom later in the piece. The juxtaposition of these must sound fully integrated as one. I suggest you ask the strings to play the last three beats of that bar together, holding the chord after everyone has entered. Then balance the chord and ask everyone to take note of the result you have just achieved. Even though it is an arpeggio, no one pitch is meant to stand out. You can even ask the pianist to play the chord so that everyone gets an idea of how their sound fits into the texture. This will happen time and time again throughout the piece.

In fact, this texture becomes the accompaniment that underlies the next group of wind solos. However, before we can tackle the solos, we must address the first entrance of the harp at **reh. 1**. What kind of sound should it be? The dynamic suggests that it is meant to be a little louder than what the other instruments are playing, but it is also possible that this indication is meant to allow for the decay time over the three bars.

For the next few measures, Copland is very careful to note which wind lines are melodic and which are harmonic—more trumpet and bassoon, but less flute and horn. The brass instruments are muted, but what kind of mutes are to be employed? Trumpeters typically use four kinds: straight, Harmon, cup, and occasionally the wah-wah. The go-to mute is the metal straight one, and the players will default to that unless otherwise instructed.

146   Aaron Copland: *Appalachian Spring* Suite

The only mute that really comes into play for the horns is the straight one, but it can be made of different materials. There is also the stop mute, which emulates the sound that occurs when you put your hand in the bell. Trombones have even more choices, but again, the straight mute is what you will get unless you ask for something else.

At **reh. 2**, Copland asks for us to be "Moving forward." Mahler might have written *nicht schleppen*. This is just a gentle push, mostly meant to keep the tempo from slowing down. At this point, it is possible to switch from four beats to two. Personally, I prefer to stay in four for this whole section. I don't want my beat to become too large, as it can go against the way the music sounds.

Interestingly, Copland chooses to have the solo violin play an octave above the flute at this point. The discrepancy in dynamics again is not so much that one instrument should be heard over the other, but simply a matter of balance. Copland neglects to give the two clarinets a dynamic the bar before **reh. 3**, but it is safe to assume that it is *piano*. The alternating chords in the strings need to sound equal.

A two-bar ritard gets us back to the original tempo three bars after **reh. 3**. Everything is pretty much as it has been until just before **reh. 4**. Now the dynamic is *pianissimo*, and it is certainly possible to ask the strings to play without vibrato. I don't do this, as I want to save the effect for other places in the piece. Just a quiet motion, perhaps with a little less bow pressure, will do.

We have a slight dilemma six bars after **reh. 4**. There is a diminuendo following the single *piano* indication, but nothing to tell us how loud or soft we should be in the next bar. Logic dictates that we return to *piano*, so it is a discreet *subito piano*, slightly louder than the final sound of the diminuendo.

At **reh. 5** we have our first decision to make about breathing. I use this word not just for the wind instruments but for the strings as well. The oboe has two-note groupings, but I suspect Copland did not want a separation between these. You can ask for a gentle push on the first note of the group. A lot will depend on your oboist here. It is possible to play the whole phrase in one breath, but instinct will probably have the musician inhale in the middle of the third bar. If that is the case, then the strings can also breathe with the oboe.

It makes sense to insert a little diminuendo for the strings six bars before **reh. 6**, as a *subito pianissimo* five before **reh. 6** seems abrupt. Please note that this is the first entrance of the double basses, and only half of them at that. Show the section that you are aware of this in case they have never played the piece before.

Throughout the entire introduction, keep your beats small and flowing to maintain a calm atmosphere. If you start exaggerating, you not only spoil the mood but also take away some of the flexibility the solo instruments need.

After a long, sustained, and very quiet A in the cellos and basses, we come to a sudden outburst. All the upper strings are playing for the first time at **reh. 6**, which also marks the first entry of a percussion instrument—the xylophone—as well as the piano. How do we prepare for this surprising rush of energy?

Clearly the instruments coming in at this point are not playing in the previous bar. Therefore, we can logically assume that this is a dramatic interruption with no break prior to the downbeat. While some conductors may just give a preparatory upbeat here, I prefer to get the tempo firmly set in my mind and body. I very quietly give two beats before launching into the Allegro. It is important to show the pointed energy in these two gestures but not allow them to appear exaggerated to either orchestra or audience.

Bowing is important at **reh. 6**. You can take it as it comes, which will make the last note of the bar occur on an up bow. However, that will limit the amount of time that you can sustain the fermata. My preference is to retake the down bow on the third beat of the first measure. This will allow for an independent bowing change during the fermata, resulting in two bows on the A. Use your upbeat to serve as a breath before starting the third bar after **reh. 6**.

Interestingly, Copland, along with so many of his American compatriot composers who studied with Nadia Boulanger, chooses to utilize the French word *cuivré* for the horns. This is not a mute, but rather a stopped note with the hand inside the bell of the instrument. The strings play the entire opening section without mutes, so it is not necessary to tell them to remove these devices. By the way, did you notice that the dynamic is single *forte*, not *fortissimo*?

We have, once again, a slight discrepancy between notation and actuality here in the fifth bar after **reh. 6**. The wind parts contain a slur as well as dots. More than likely this is an indication of phrasing rather than a sign to play the notes a bit longer. Short notes prevail, with the winds sounding about the same as the strings' pizzicato.

One of the first danger points in the work comes in the eighth bar after **reh. 6**, when the musicians who are playing enter on the second beat. I cannot tell you how many times, even with professional orchestras, a musician has come in on the downbeat. Usually, I blame myself for giving too big a downbeat, causing the player to mistake that for the entrance. The only thing to do is very quietly conduct the bar of silence before and then keep the gesture small on the first beat of the next measure. The left hand can also help remind the orchestra to refrain from entering.

The strings two bars before **reh. 7** require a strong downbeat and an indication that the first violins do not enter until after an eighth rest. The dynamic is *mezzo forte*, and this works because there is a natural tendency to make a crescendo on upward phrases such as this one. Abruptly stop moving on the third beat of the bar before **reh. 7**, possibly taking just a hint of time before moving on.

The bowing that works well at **reh. 6** can also apply at **reh. 7**, but since there is no fermata to sustain, almost anything will suffice. The fifth bar after **reh. 7** presents an interesting problem to solve. A whole note precedes this measure, but then the first violins have to play pizzicato. When are they supposed to make the physical transition from bowing a note to being ready to pluck the string? Again, our good friend the breath comes into play. Basically, the fourth beat of the bar is a rest, especially if you want to avoid a diminuendo.

Take a close look at these three bars (**mm. 5–7** after **reh. 7**). There are sostenuto lines over some of the notes just prior to a pizzicato. How can this be accomplished without that quarter note being made short? Here is a little trick I use: the outside players in each section play the pizzicato notes and the inside musicians play the arco notes. This is similar to what Copland wants five measures before **reh. 8**, but the musicians at this earlier point are dividing the chores independently. For the last five bars preceding **reh. 8**, you might need to adjust the string dynamic down a bit so the flutes and solo violins can be heard clearly.

Balance is everything at **reh. 8**. You want each moving line to be equally audible. Everyone, including the strings, can crescendo in the bar before **reh. 9**. The chorale in the winds always seems to dominate, and therefore I prefer the strings at *fortissimo* instead of just single *forte*. And you should certainly conduct in two here, possibly doing the bar before in one to set up the visual for the orchestra.

Is it just me, or does anyone else think that the second quarter note at **reh. 9** in the trumpets might be an error? No one else playing the chorale rearticulates the second quarter, and although I have never had the nerve to change it, perhaps one of you will.

The 5/4 bar, seven measures after **reh. 9**, is best conducted with five beats. It is a bit dangerous to go into something that looks like 3 + 2 with just two gestures. More than likely, the winds will get a bit behind the moving eighth notes, so be prepared to correct that. Similarly, the 3/4 bar three measures before **reh. 10** should not be in one. And at **reh. 10**, it is important to note that just one trombone is carrying on the bass line.

Stay in half-note beats until the bar before **reh. 11**.

"What?" you may ask. "No one is playing there. What difference does it make?"

Anything the conductor can do to help the musicians establish strong rhythmic values is always welcome. So, I do this silent bar with four small gestures, indicating the exact tempo of the next section, and then remain in four at **reh. 11**.

Believe it or not, the C at **reh. 11** is the first note played by the timpani in the piece. The choice of mallet for any given passage is usually left to the performer, but you can score some points if you familiarize yourself with the various sticks that are in the percussionist's arsenal. However, judgement should only be made on the sound that comes out, not what you think will work. Clearly a harder mallet will produce a drier effect, which seems appropriate here.

The 7/8 bar two measures after **reh. 11** is a straightforward 2 + 3 + 2. In the fourth measure, make sure to sustain the long note with a bow change, as was the case when this section started. Give the strings room to breathe before jumping to the high F at the eighth bar after **reh. 11**. You can go back into two by the tenth measure.

Rehearsal 12 is a tricky spot for balance. The trumpet and oboes should almost sound as if they were the same instrument. Copland tries to indicate this by doubling the latter, but it is usually not quite enough. Rehearse these instruments without the other winds to achieve parity.

Another section that needs clarifying commences at the fifth bar of **reh. 12**. This is a matter of figuring out what to do regarding the crescendos. Each of the phrases has this indication, so are they continual? Fortunately, Copland lets us know right at **reh. 13** what is supposed to happen. Each crescendo starts at *forte*, followed by an increase in dynamic and then a *subito forte* for the next phrase. This works very well if you pay attention and do it diligently.

Two other points about this last section:

1. Some conductors prefer to stay in three during the 6/8 bars (**mm. 7–8** after **reh. 12**), but my own feeling is that there is something special about this almost Latin syncopation. I prefer it in two.
2. What is a tabor, anyway? Most of the time, this will be played on a low snare with the growly appendage turned off or with a military field drum.

The loudest crescendo possible occurs three and four bars after **reh. 13**, bringing us to the first of only a few triple *fortes* in the entire work. Emphasize the accents, and make sure the eighth notes are clearly heard as they make their way upward. Musicians tend to rush here, and if that occurs, hesitate just a moment before giving the downbeat four measures before **reh. 14**.

At **reh. 14**, most of us slow down a bit to allow a more expressive element to creep in with the flute. The two motifs here must be equal in terms of balance. At first glance, this does not appear to be a problem, but looking ahead a few bars after the entrance, the flute goes down to the middle of the staff, a range in which it can easily be obliterated if the strings are too loud.

Note that Copland writes *espressivo* just for the violas at the upbeat to **reh. 14**. Certainly, he must have intended for the first violins to carry on with the tune, but *espressivo* is not mentioned. I usually keep the first violins at a slightly softer dynamic but insert a few little hairpin crescendos and diminuendos, so they are not just in the background. By two bars before **reh. 15**, *pianissimo* seems appropriate.

Wait a moment for things to settle down before commencing the little coda at **reh. 15**. For this section, I go back to the initial tempo of the Allegro, paying attention to the balance between the glockenspiel and harp harmonics. It is always a good idea to rehearse these two instruments so they can clearly hear each other. Note that the woodwinds have tenuto marks on each of their final notes. I introduce a bit of a ritard for the last iterations of the clarinet and flute.

At **reh. 16**, we come to a serenely beautiful portion of *Appalachian Spring*, beginning with a brief introduction that can best be described as "walking music"—but only if you have three or more feet. It is the only passage in the whole work that reminds me of *Billy the Kid* or *Rodeo*.

Two different moods are tossed back and forth. The first is characterized by the bumptious and simplistic rhythmic figures that have not appeared prior to this moment. The pedal notes have some bite, and the harpist may use a fingernail or a plectrum to achieve a guitar-like sound. This is a wonderful sonority when combined with the muted trombone alternating with the second bassoon.

A trio of instruments—first bassoon, horn, and trumpet—intones the slightly intoxicated and unstable motif. At first, you might think that an equality of sound would achieve the proper balance, but that is not the case here. The bassoon has the top line, with the others filling out the chord. Thus, the bassoon tune must come to the fore a bit.

This is followed by music that has already been heard but will be altered as the work continues (**reh. 17**). A lone clarinet is accompanied by a small group of strings whose numbers are strictly defined by the composer. Pay attention to their slurs, as this will present a puzzle later. Conduct quarter notes, as per Copland's markings.

The give-and-take of these two groups continues until **reh. 19**, when a sudden *sforzando-piano* occurs on the downbeat in the horns, second violins, and cellos. How loud should it be, and how quickly must we get to the softer dynamic? Since the melodic line is *forte*, I usually go for an abrupt accent. This means asking the strings to start at the frog and pull the bow as quickly and loudly as possible to the tip. Keep in mind that they have mutes on, so the effect is almost like a *sul ponticello*.

Many conductors interpret a group of notes with accents as being separated. I don't think that is what the composer intends for the first violins and violas here at **reh. 19**. Instead, they should be long, articulated strokes that are sustained to give a bit more dramatic weight to this sequence. In the subsequent 5/4 bars, I usually ask the second violins and double basses to make a sizable crescendo leading to the next *forte-piano*. In addition, I stretch out their upbeats to allow for growth in the tension and sound.

At the fifth bar after **reh. 19**, the indication "press forward" appears. Why not just *poco accelerando* as it is twelve bars later? And why *più accelerando* in the middle of all that? Is this a gradual increase or sudden? You will have to decide for yourselves and deduce how long they continue.

One of the banes of my musical life has been trying to understand what *meno forte* means. Literally, it would seem to be less loud. But by how much? In this case, I think you can just drop down a dynamic to *mezzo forte*. When there are no dynamics indicated at the peak of a hairpin, just use discretion. More than likely, it is an expression marking and not meant to be exaggerated.

Three bars after **reh. 20**, we have a triple *piano* in the violins. The natural tendency is for the strings to use just a little bow, but I usually ask for more bow with less pressure on the string. This produces a more ethereal sound, and I utilize this technique quite often. Also, just a bit of vibrato gives the sound life.

A few bars later, Copland does it again. Now we get *poco accelerando* with no indication of how long it lasts and how fast it is supposed to wind up. But adding to the complication is the *a tempo* marking that appears three bars before **reh. 21**. Is this a *subito* tempo change, or should we lead into it with an unwritten ritard? And this marking is on the second beat, not the beginning of the bar. Since the upbeat is the same idea as the beginning of the section, I elongate the 5/4 bar as before.

Remember how I told you to pay attention to the slurs earlier? The reason is that four bars after **reh. 21** (and in subsequent bars), the same idea recurs, now with added tenuto lines over the notes. What to do? It is not really a separation but an articulation, with no space in between. But it should have a different sound than its earlier counterparts. Just for the sake of expression, I let the oboe move a bit in the fourth bar of its solo, and then the flute gets to do the same after that. On the final phrase, it is nice if the flutist makes a little diminuendo on the two eighth notes and plays them a bit slower. The strings will need to adjust their dynamics to support the flute.

One of my favorite moments in the entire work takes place in the third bar after **reh. 22**. The bassoon intones a low B on the fourth beat, which is then followed by soft notes in the cellos and basses. I still don't know why this always makes my skin tingle, but it is a remarkable sound. Copland was wise here, letting the bassoon play at single *piano* while the others are triple *pianissimo*. The remaining strings play as they did after **reh. 20**, keeping the simple vibrato going.

Just before the section marked "fast," the flute and clarinet have a moment of repose, and the balance must be perfect. Make sure to give them a discreet cutoff before continuing.

Musicians always need to think about what comes next in any piece of music; it is almost more important to know where you are going than where you are. The next section of *Appalachian Spring* is a perfect example. It is entirely possible to start at **reh. 23** in the manner Copland prescribes. The indication is "fast," and the metronome mark is ♩ = 132. In my opinion, this is a bit too quick, and you must take into consideration the agility of the clarinet in the third bar after **reh. 23**.

Everything is relative. In this case, prior to starting the section at **reh. 23**, you must consider what occurs at **reh. 28**. In turn, you must decide whether you will return to the opening tempo at any point before **reh. 33**. But for the moment, let's just focus on the first part of this segment.

There are two static beats just before **reh. 23**, and the conductor must have the tempo of **reh. 33** in mind well before giving the downbeat. The solo oboe does not have a lot of time to deduce what it will be. Erring on the side of security and safety works best. Following the cutoff of the second clarinet and flute, you should get the tempo quickly into your head and give two preparatory beats, quite small, while checking in with your oboist. This musician sets the tone for the next nine bars.

Copland writes that this section is to be performed "playfully," and that is the perfect word to describe the mood. I remember that when Copland rehearsed this part, his words to the winds were, "Perky, perky." And as mentioned, the clarinet solo in the third bar is not easy, with that very high

A♮ not so easily dispatched. I find that a steady four-beat pattern with the appropriate indications for the short rests that precede most of the entrances is helpful.

When we arrive at the seventh bar after **reh. 23**, it should all sound like the same instrument, as if the individual instruments do not trade off ideas. And it must lead naturally into **reh. 24**. At this point, the horn has a *forte-piano*, but since it is muted, this is more about the color than the dynamic. Two words of caution here: Sometimes the violins rush into the second bar after **reh. 24**, just a little. Make sure the quarter note is held for the full value. On top of that, the second trumpet, usually because of the distance from the podium, tends to be slightly late with the upbeat. Conduct the violins but look at the trumpet. And don't forget about the accents one measure before **reh. 25**.

The two musical ideas that come together at **reh. 25** should sound equal, but as with so many passages like this, the quicker notes tend to dominate. You will find examples of this situation in almost every piece you conduct. It is up to you to listen carefully and adjust by what you hear, not by what you think is occurring. Composers put in dynamics, but conductors are there in the moment. Don't be afraid to change things if need be.

The bar before **reh. 26** can be deceptive. Most everyone has a quarter note, with no indication that it should be short. At the same time, the horns have a diminuendo; the score does not indicate the starting or ending dynamic, but they probably begin *forte*. The effect of the sustained note coming after the shorter one can be heightened by waiting ever so slightly before giving the downbeat for **reh. 26**. The horn dynamic appears to end right at the bar line, probably due to having to fit in a double bar and time signature, but it might continue.

"Snare Drum, Brush on" reads the instruction from Copland at **reh. 26**. What does that mean? There are several ways to interpret this. One unlikely way is to literally brush from side to side on the instrument. This makes no sense, as the notes have dots on them. So, it seems that the musician should play a stroke like that of a stick. But the brush hairs can be adjusted from very tight to loosely spread out, producing different sounds as a result. Here, you want the resonance to be strong enough to be heard but not so loud as to sound like traditional drumsticks. Listen to what the percussionist starts with and alter as needed.

Indicate the syncopation in the strings but keep your eyes on the trumpets so they do not get behind. And don't forget about that delightful crescendo in the third bar after **reh. 26**. At the 2/4 measure five bars after **reh. 26**, I usually wait in a manner similar to the way I conduct at **reh. 24**.

Now we get to another interesting conundrum. The instruction at six measures after **reh. 26** for the snare drum is to play with the "stick (on rim)." This seems simple enough, but when you remember that the drum during the 1940s was made of wood as opposed to today's metal equivalent, that can be a striking change of sonority. It may not be practical to have a second drum out there just for four bars, and perhaps you don't care about this sound. Maybe the percussionist, who has six beats of rest prior, could do it on the side of the bass drum.

The role of the piano in this and the next passage is very important. The material in the first four bars (starting in the sixth bar after **reh. 26**) is different from what anyone else is playing, and the doubling with the brass and strings at **reh. 27** adds a spikiness to the proceedings. In any event, a little exaggeration of the accent on the fourth beat is important for all the instruments.

Now we come to the most awkward transition in the entire ballet. At **reh. 28**, Copland tells us to have a "more deliberate tempo." The metronome mark is just six clicks slower than what has come before, so indeed, not too much. I think this is more about the character of the music than the tempo itself. We are thrust into the world of country fiddling. And this brings up the way the passage is played.

The intuition of most violinists will be to play the passage at **reh. 28** off the string. That is how most recordings sound, and since there are dots on some of the notes, it is a natural reaction. But a dot above a note does not necessarily mean staccato. Copland also indicates *heavy accents*, which would lead one to believe that maybe a better effect can be obtained by playing on the string. There are innumerable solutions for this place. Here is mine:

First, establish a tempo. As mentioned earlier, some of this depends on where you want to be around **reh. 30**. If you slavishly follow the score, that reiteration of the country music will still be at the same speed, but the faster tempo of what came before can get bogged down. Some conductors do a slight *più mosso* at **reh. 30**, but then they get stuck five bars later with the now faster-than-deliberate speed.

In my earliest performances I used to do as above. It never felt right, but it was all I could imagine. Now, I only differentiate slightly between the two tempos, trying to make the heavy accents give the impression of a much slower speed. There has never been a question in my mind about how to play it: on the string. If it were possible, and not silly, it might have been fun to have the violins play it like the fiddlers in the South, with the instrument placed on the hip.

Aaron Copland: *Appalachian Spring* Suite 155

As far as the bowings go, simpler is better. Now that I have my own set of parts that I send out in advance, there is no quarreling about it. But most of you will not have that luxury. More than likely, the concertmaster will have based their thoughts on the bowings that are in the score. Presumably they were entered by the composer after some consultation with a violinist. For me to accomplish the slightly crude playing I am after, I just tell everyone to play it "as it comes," without retakes on down bows, and whenever they come to an up bow on the last beat of a measure, I ask them to sustain it, make a little crescendo, and connect it to the next bar. You may not agree, but it does give this whole passage a real sense of character.

Copland provides a puzzling instruction at **reh. 29**. He indicates that the clarinets and horns should play "*non legato*, relaxed." The first part I understand—the second, not so much. Although I spent some time with Copland and we discussed this piece, I never asked him about this direction. Maybe someone out there has more insight. *Non legato* in this case clearly means short, yet I have no idea how to do this relaxed. *Mezzo forte*, as written, is the best we can do here. But we can also make it more interesting by exaggerating the accent in the brass and percussion and not placing an unwanted one on the quarter note. It should sound just a bit jazzy.

If you have chosen to do the previous passage on the slower side, **reh. 30** is the place to catch up. As noted, it is possible to keep this at the more restrained tempo, but it really can sound sluggish this way. And because Copland instructs the upper strings to play marcato, we can abandon the "as it comes" bowing from the earlier incarnation.

All proceeds in orderly fashion until **reh. 31**. The alternating beat pattern is clear. As in almost all cases with any time-signature changes, the beat that has two eighths in it is small, and those with three eighths are spread out a bit. Do not try to get fancy with subdivisions, but do pay attention to the bassoon, left hand of the piano, and lower strings. Notice that none of the instruments playing the second note in the 5/8 measures has an accent. It is crucial to the rhythmic structure to hear this note clearly and distinctly. One way of clarifying this passage is to make sure the pianist does not use the pedal. A dry sound is needed, and there are dots on all the notes as well as lines. The trombones and horns must not play more than single *forte*, maybe less, depending on how many lower strings you have.

I truly do not understand why Copland did not have the cellos play the last note of the 5/8 bar two measures after **reh. 31** (and corresponding measures until one bar before **reh. 32**) with the other instruments. Usually when something like this occurs, it is because it does not fit with the up or down motion of the entire line. But the bassoons play the note, and they go up, while the basses go down. We know the cello does not have a low A, but they can do as their colleagues in the winds do, so I add the notes. I also have them play arco instead of pizzicato if I can't hear the rhythm clearly.

The conclusion of this section is straightforward, but please pay attention to the suspended cymbals for the final four bars before **reh. 33**. The roll should be fast and with an exaggerated crescendo each time. This is followed by an abrupt stopping of the sound, and it is perfectly fine if the cymbal covers up the orchestra at the end.

Don't move a muscle at the conclusion and keep your arms up. The orchestra also needs to hold their position until the next notes sound. Sometimes a visual can be as dramatic as the music, and this is one of those places that might elicit premature applause.

A brief transition leads to one of the more technically difficult parts of the piece. Having maintained an appropriate silence, you give the first two beats, very clearly, of the measure at **reh. 33**, but not so large as to make it appear as though there were music going on. A rich *fortissimo*, noble rather than aggressive, holds sway for five measures. In that last bar, there is a notational discrepancy in some editions that you must correct. You might find in your edition that the trombones have A–C♯–D♯–E, but the cellos and bass are different, with A–B–C♯–E. In my experience, if you do not have your own set of parts, this inconsistency is also in the players' music.

In the next portion of the ballet, the trouble begins immediately. At **reh. 35**, we are at least aided by a rest on the first beat. But how do we give the cutoff from the bar before? We don't; it is taken care of by the downbeat itself. Remember when I wrote about trying to give two-beat preparations whenever possible for any new tempo? It can be done here, but not easily.

Silence might be the best friend of the conductor. In this spot, I give a very quiet upbeat and have the musicians release the sustained note. Then I give a larger beat for the rest, followed by a sharp indication for that *sforzando*. The right hand shows the pattern as clearly as possible, and the left indicates how loud, and then soft, these two notes will be.

Don't get fancy. Just let the beats flow naturally. Remember, this is a ballet, and the dance-like qualities must always be evident. Lay down the patterns so everyone knows when the next bar occurs. What happens in between usually works out, and we are primarily conducting for those who only play a few notes in this passage; 3/8 measures are conducted in one (not too big). You will need to give a strong downbeat in the bar before **reh. 36**, which should prevent the brass from entering too soon.

What comes next is almost always a problem, and a lot of conductors have trouble making the transition to the Presto while dealing with the slight accelerando. But don't worry; I have a really good solution for this. Four before **reh. 37**, these two bars are still beat in three. I think it is because of the speeding up that many of my colleagues stay in four right up to the tempo change. But what works best—and is easiest for the violists to grasp—is going into two at two bars before the Presto. Depending on how much, if any, accelerando you make, it is much easier for the violas to start together and speed up as needed. Try it. You'll like it.

The Presto itself is about character. I am somewhat amused that Copland writes *non legato* for the first violins and staccato for the seconds. But of course, he includes nothing for the same material in the flute. Go figure. As far as the tempo goes, 92 bpm is not out of the question, but do not let anything go so fast as to prevent the basses from being able to play the pizzicato clearly at **reh. 39**.

Pay attention to the notes that have lines over them. The composer is just trying to make sure we understand that the quarter notes are not played the same as the eighths. It is nice if you can get the layered crescendo, in which one group reaches the top dynamic before the other, just before **reh. 39**, especially the *fortissimo* in the violas and cellos.

At **reh. 40**, I can understand why Copland puts in the suggested bowing based on the assumption that accents can only be done on down bows. Of course, that is not true, and by following the bowings he has written, undesirable spaces between the notes are created. I take the whole passage as it comes right up until **reh. 41**. But after each *sforzando*, I ask for a slight drop in dynamic to make sure that the winds come through. The same applies to the brass after each accent.

What is it that we are supposed to hear at **reh. 41**? The rhythmic pattern is certainly important, but there are these moving lines as well—scale-like notes going down in some of the instruments as well as harmonic, single-note alterations in every bar for some of the musicians. I think it is important to emphasize these, as the rhythm is always clear. Since Copland calls for divisi in the upper strings but does not tell us how to divide it, perhaps we have more musicians play the lower two notes than the higher notes. And the single brass instruments that change each bar can bring out those notes.

But what about that crescendo two measures before **reh. 42**? If you look back at **reh. 40**, you find that this is just single *forte*. Keeping this dynamic in place until the indication to get louder can work. But it is also effective, if slightly out of character, to drop down a bit two bars before **reh. 42** and then really nail the accents on the final two notes.

There are two ways to begin the section starting at **reh. 42**. You can either remain in two and give a strong second beat to set the wheels in motion again, or you can conduct this bar in four, just in case you feel that the tempo was derailed earlier. My teacher, Jean Morel, had an elegant way of accomplishing this. He would give the first two beats as quarter notes and then the next one as a half note. His rationale was that by the time the orchestra starts playing, they are not watching you anyway. Works for me. It is also possible to do this five measures before **reh. 43**.

I recommend going into four at **reh. 43** and alternating between quarters and 3/8 beats until **reh. 44**. It is too much trouble to get this together conducting in half notes. The 6/8 bar presents a slight dilemma. The rhythm is clearer if you do it in two beats, but conducting in three can be easier for the musicians to follow—your choice. I do it in two.

I break one of my cardinal rules one bar before **reh. 44**. Usually during silent measures, I either beat very discreetly or, sometimes, not at all. Here, however, you must show the players those three beats of rest so they can set themselves up for what comes next. The 2/4 bar is best done in one, and that should not be a problem if you have been very clear the bar before.

No difficulties leading into **reh. 46** except deciding what you want to bring out prior to the solo entrances. Obviously, the audience needs to hear the piccolo at this point, so the second violins underneath must remain *piano*. Here is something I do, just because I think it adds a little tension. The violin harmonic in the second bar after **reh. 46** gets a *forte-piano*. I know, Copland had nothing of the sort in mind, but it is such a great sound that using it has now become second nature to me. Some orchestra musicians have called my slight alterations to the text "Slatkinisms." I don't know if that is complimentary, commentary, or an insult.

For some reason, even veteran flute players can have a little bit of trouble with the 3/4 bar four measures before **reh. 47** and the subsequent measure as well. It usually just takes a second run of the passage to correct it. Isn't it interesting that Copland gives us an indication of a softer dynamic after the *sforzandos* at **reh. 47**, but he did not do that back at **reh. 40**?

Now we come to what is possibly the most technically complicated spot in the whole piece. At **reh. 48**, the violins have what seems like an innocuous passage. But if not played correctly, it can throw off the whole climax of this section. The reason it is often a mess is because the section plays the first note with a little accent, completely unintentionally. Instead, it works better to put an emphasis on the second note, the one that occurs on the beat. So instead of sounding, Da-da-da, it is da-Da-da. This needs to carry through in almost every measure so that the focal point is always the G and not the lower notes.

Then there is that pesky first trumpet part that begins five bars after **reh. 48**. This is the only instrument that has anything resembling this syncopation, and unless it is solid, it always sounds like a mistake. I try to bring out that line. The trumpeter needs a very distinct beat from the conductor, as it is impossible to sort out what else is going on. However, you will notice that the violins match the trumpet, despite playing their flurry of eighths. It is not worth trying to get them to sync up, so just bring out that single trumpet line. When all else fails, remember that the xylophone will probably cover it up anyway.

At **reh. 49**, stay in two, then conduct in three for the next bar, then conduct quarter notes. This sets up the last difficult rhythmic section of alternating meters and is clear for the orchestra. Pay attention to the two 5/8 bars; they are beat differently (first as 2 + 3 and then as 3 + 2). The earlier instruction for the 6/8 applies at one bar before **reh. 50**, but preparing for what occurs next can be complex. The instruction "more deliberate tempo" appears to be on the bar line one measure after **reh. 50**. Even though the three pickup notes echo the material that has just been played, I believe that the upbeat is really a lead-in to the weightier character of the next bar, so I do it a bit slower. To make that work, I also hold back the prior rests, making the entire 5/4 bar slightly ponderous. I continue to slow down for the 3/8 bar and subsequent measures.

If you do this while thinking about the tempo of **reh. 51**, the lead-in should appear quite natural. On occasion, the concertmaster has asked for a little more time before commencing with the solo. To this day, I don't know why they want it that way.

Rehearsal 51 is quite straightforward. The indication for the harp, "brittle," can be misleading due to the dynamic being only *mezzo forte*. I think it is to be played *non arpeggio* and have a slightly rough sound. Stay in quarter notes the whole time, right up to **reh. 55**.

Because of the note leap and the divisi, I take just a short breath before **reh. 52**. Don't forget to bring out the double basses, as no other instruments have these two notes. As far as the bassoon fermata two bars before **reh. 53**, the note does not need to be overly long.

Sometimes I think that a different sonority aids a particular passage. Such is the case at **reh. 54**. With a relatively large string section, I prefer a rich tone to start, something closer to *forte*. Copland has the diminuendo going down to *piano*, but then increases it a bit with the next *mezzo piano*. To keep consistent with my alteration, I take a breath before a change to *mezzo forte*. Then we diminish to *piano*, but again, I insert a very slight pause before commencing with what can be considered an "amen."

At **reh. 55** we arrive at the portion of the score that all the listeners have been waiting for: *Simple Gifts*. It became so popular that Copland created a separate version of these variations as a stand-alone set. In our edition, it may be a gift, but it is hardly simple.

Okay, it starts off easy enough, but already at **reh. 56**, we encounter a problem. I don't know why, but the upper woodwinds are somewhat reluctant to really do the *sforzando* and play loudly for a measure and a half. One tactic that can help is to ask the triangle player to use a slightly larger instrument to avoid a tinkly sound. The takeover of the melody by the two clarinets must be seamless and sound as if a single performer were playing.

Four bars before **reh. 57**, if they have not already done it, make sure that those playing the two eighths and quarter notes agree as to how long or short the notes should be. Rehearsing them as a unit is an efficient way to resolve any discrepancies.

We can assume that Copland wants the upbeat to **reh. 57** to be in the new, "trifle faster" tempo. So, that pickup note must start just a fraction later in the old tempo; this is not as hard as it sounds. If neither the oboe nor the bassoon has played the piece before, you can expect that an accidental or two might be misread in the G♭ section. The same dynamics problem that occurs at **reh. 56** happens again at **reh. 58**. There must be a true change of dynamic, almost forceful here, before the retreat to the calmer nature of the tune.

Copland gives us a wonderful color, one that has not yet been heard in the piece, in the measure before **reh. 59**. To get a proper balance, rehearse the glockenspiel, harp, and piano together before adding the other instruments. Since the harp is the only one with sixteenth notes, this must be clearly audible. The remaining instruments usually balance well, but you might need to elevate the dynamic in the second violins.

The melody is first stated by the trombone and violas at **reh. 59**. The former is just a shadow for the string instrument and should not be prominent. The same applies at **reh. 60** with the horn and first violins. Again, if the orchestra is unfamiliar with the piece, I can almost guarantee that one of the cellists or bassists will come in a bar early, as they hear the pattern of previous entries. Keep an eye on them and see if you can prevent this.

At **reh. 61**, the basses' pizzicatos can be tricky to pull off in terms of ensemble. It helps for you to have the cellos play alone so that the basses can see how they fit in. Two measures before **reh. 62**, Copland includes a couple of traps. The first is for the violins. Many times, they want to play the eighth notes off the string, but we have no indication that it should be done this way. The other is the potential for an unwanted accelerando when just a crescendo will do. However, some scores will say "Move forward." If you do increase your speed, be very careful that your tempo can accommodate the many sixteenth notes coming up in the next variation.

Rehearsal 62 is in one. In the eighth bar, remember that if a breath is needed, it must come after the first note and not at the end of the bar. The string flurries should sound quite virtuosic. I play the quarter note at the end long, but certainly it can be done otherwise. Do not rush headlong into **reh. 63**. The brass need a moment to breathe.

The transition into **reh. 64** is more or less the same idea as the one at **reh. 57**, with the upbeat being in the new tempo. It is for that reason that I conduct this bar and the subsequent variation in two. Most conductors stay in one, but what often happens is that the note prior to **reh. 64** seems rushed.

Take a little time before starting the final triple *forte* variation at **reh. 65**. It must be loud, of course, but noble, not aggressive. It is possible, if the timpanist can be discreet about it, to have that musician add a low D in the measure before **reh. 66**, just to keep the same rhythm as the other bass notes. You can take a bit of time three bars before **reh. 67**, but make sure you conduct the bar before the fermata so that those who cut off know when to do so. I don't think the isolated timpani note one bar before **reh. 67** is meant to be reattacked but rather just used as a release point. How long should the fermata be? You should allow enough time for the strings to remove their mutes but not so much time that the brass might run out of breath.

We have finally arrived at one of the most sublime codas in all of music. Mood is everything here, and there are many ways of performing these last two minutes. The triple *piano* at **reh. 67** might be a bit too soft and lack warmth, but perhaps you want a colder sound here. Copland's own recordings are certainly not at that extreme dynamic. Pay attention to the horn cutoff in the second bar. They can certainly do this by themselves, but the first time around, it is a good idea to let them know you are watching.

Often, singing a passage can help you understand how to phrase it. We have the instruction "like a prayer," which lends credence to the singing idea. The slurs, which seem to work against the long phrase, do not help matters. It is almost impossible to vocalize the line all the way up to **reh. 68**, so you will have to take a breath somewhere. I do it every two bars after the downbeat. The real conundrum is two bars before **reh. 68**. We have what appear to be two notes tied, but they both have tenuto lines, indicating a rearticulation. My solution is to slightly separate them as if they were a series of "amens." This occurs three more times. For some reason, the double basses don't like doing it for their entrance, but you should insist that it be consistent with the other instruments.

The same breathing structure works for the woodwinds at **reh. 69**. Encourage very warm and rich playing at **reh. 70**, with the same breaths and separations. Some conductors have the basses play a low C two bars before **reh. 71**. This really depends on the acoustic of the hall; the added resonance can be effective if played softly. It is important that all the strings play with vibrato until the very end. You will see why in a moment.

Copland indicates that only half of the group should play from **reh. 71** onward, but my preference is to use everyone. More people performing at very soft dynamics is a marvelous sound; nothing gets covered up, and the last eight bars will benefit. Try to get the flutes to blend with the first violins.

I do something a bit different at **reh. 72**. The solo violin performs a bit stronger than the other instruments, and then the flute comes to the fore, with the violin going back into the section sonority.

The clarinet gives its last "white tone" incantation, and the strings start the final pyramid chord. Each entrance raises the dynamic and must be sustained, even though others are still very soft. It is a gradual increase, in its way. You can rehearse this in the same manner as the start of the work, establishing the desired result so everyone knows where to wind up.

The last three bars are exactly why the glockenspiel and harp need to be close to each other. Obtaining the ideal balance will have a lot to do with the choice of mallet, something soft but with a little heft to match the harmonics. I play it safe and before each of the three entrances, I give them beats three and four. And the last entrance is slightly softer than the two that come before.

Now comes the "Slatkinism," but more than likely others have done it. You may have been wondering why I keep asking for vibrato. Here is the rationale: This ending is one of the most moving moments in the whole repertoire. Copland has written the perfect example of cautious optimism, with the two chords leaving just a slight feeling of doubt as to the meaning of the ending.

For me, a new sound is needed here and therefore a different way of conducting. Time must stand still. Once the orchestra has learned the music, starting at **reh. 73**, there is no reason to beat time. Let the clarinetist play the solo without a conductor. Then, starting with the cellos in the fourth bar, just indicate the note changes to each section, possibly with a very *dolce* accent. Make sure that they increase their dynamic as indicated. When all the instruments are settled at the first fermata, turn your attention to the harp and glockenspiel. Keep your left hand raised, palm up, as it will have a lot to do.

Sustain the single *piano* in the strings for two bars. If the players are on your left and in the back, you can indicate the two preparatory beats with the left hand and then gently give them the cues. Two measures before the end, after the note sounds, start to bring the left hand to a straight line, very slowly. Give the final note to the two instruments, and when your hand comes to rest on the horizontal plane, the strings should gradually stop their vibrato. I can assure you that this will be one of the most memorable diminuendos and *pianissimos* imaginable. Wait a bit and don't even give a true cutoff. Just close the hand. Hold this position until you feel that the length of silence has been appropriate.

While several other details in the work need a conductor's loving care, hopefully some of these tips will aid you in learning and conducting this true masterpiece.

Conductor's Etiquette

When the work ends and the applause begins, always have the orchestra stand before you to take a bow. Upon your return to the stage, I suggest you acknowledge the woodwinds as a group rather than single out any one musician.

> The whole problem can be stated quite simply by asking, "Is there a meaning to music?" My answer would be, "Yes." And "Can you state in so many words what the meaning is?" My answer to that would be, "No."
>
> —Aaron Copland

Note

1. Aaron Copland, *Appalachian Spring: Suite for Full Orchestra* (New York: Boosey & Hawkes Inc., 1945).

Samuel Barber: *Adagio for Strings*

I can only say that I myself wrote always as I wished, without a tremendous desire to find the latest thing possible.

—Samuel Barber

Library of Congress, Prints & Photographs Division, Carl Van Vechten Collection, [reproduction number, e.g., LC-USZ62-54231]

166 Samuel Barber: *Adagio for Strings*

Deemed "the saddest music ever written," Barber's *Adagio for Strings* is often played on very solemn occasions. At just five pages long, the work has been performed by every major orchestra and almost all others.

Given its frequent appearance on programs throughout the world, you would think that Barber's *Adagio* is not particularly difficult to conduct. You would be wrong. Deceptively simple at first glance and upon first hearing, it presents numerous technical and musical traps requiring a great deal of thought and advanced planning.

Barber wrote this music in 1936 as the slow movement of a string quartet and soon realized that it would make a good piece for a larger ensemble. Keeping most of the music from the original version intact, he filled out some of the chords with supplemental notes and added a bass part. He sent it, unsolicited, to Arturo Toscanini, who returned it a few months later without comment. The composer was upset until he learned that the maestro had scheduled it for performances in 1938 and had already memorized the piece.

Because of its origins, the *Adagio* can be played by string ensembles of almost any size, making it very easy to program. On a concert with three pieces on the first half, it perhaps best follows a slightly noisy and fast-paced work. It can also serve as an opener, and the somber tone may come as a surprise to an audience accustomed to rousing overtures. The *Adagio* is also sometimes played as an encore, usually in tribute to fallen heroes.

Barber's *Adagio* has very personal connections for me. It was the one and only work I conducted in my first year as a student at the Aspen Music Festival and School back in 1964. I chose it rather than a flashy piece because I believed I would learn more about how to sustain a long line, probably the most difficult thing for a conductor to do.

The piece appeared frequently on many of my programs, and I recorded it commercially twice. Four days after the 9/11 attacks, I led a performance of it in London at the Last Night of the Proms, by far the most emotional musical experience of my life.

Setting the mood and establishing the basic tempo are the paramount matters to consider at the beginning of the work. These factors will affect the overall timing of the entire piece. Barber did not provide metronome marks, so all we see are the words *Adagio molto* followed by *espress. cantando*. To illustrate how significantly tempos have varied from performance to performance, table 7.1 provides timing examples from five commercial and concert recordings.

My initial exposure to the work was from the recording my father made with the Hollywood Bowl Symphony Orchestra when I was in high school.[1] In the 1980s, I recorded two versions with the St. Louis Symphony

Table 7.1.

Conductor	Orchestra	Year	Label	Timing
Felix Slatkin	Hollywood Bowl Symphony Orchestra	1959	Capitol	7:44
Leonard Slatkin	St. Louis Symphony Orchestra	1983	Telarc	7:37
Leonard Slatkin	St. Louis Symphony Orchestra	1989	EMI	9:09
Leonard Slatkin	BBC Symphony Orchestra	2001	BBC	10:14
Leonard Slatkin	Detroit Symphony Orchestra	2016	Live from Orchestra Hall	8:28

Orchestra, and videos of my live performances with the BBC Symphony Orchestra at the Proms (2001)[2] and Detroit Symphony Orchestra (2016) can still be viewed on YouTube.[3]

The main point is that despite the two-and-a-half-minute difference between some of my interpretations, the *Adagio* always casts its emotional spell very powerfully. If you can sustain the tension through the buildup to the climax, the tempo seems not to matter.

This work remains in copyright, so it is unavailable for free. However, for study purposes, you can go to the New York Philharmonic digital archive and find a copy of it there, slightly marked by Bernstein.[4] His score, probably the first published version, only cost one dollar and fifty cents.

Several editions are available at various prices. The most reliable, and the one used by most orchestras, is published by G. Schirmer.[5] Even if you are not planning to conduct this piece soon, it is nevertheless valuable to study it, as the *Adagio* is one of those works that might need to be dropped into a program quickly should the occasion warrant it.

Another important decision to make is whether to use a baton. Most conductors these days use a stick, but occasionally, a piece comes along for which the actual beating of time is unwarranted. I think works such as this one are better served without the angularity that the baton tends to show. In many ways this is psychological, as you can certainly get an exquisite result with the stick.

The next question has to do with how to beat the first few bars. Should they be conducted in four or eight? Although meter signatures are used throughout the piece, the beginning should not convey a feeling of pulse. It is unnecessary to give the usual preparation. In fact, the sound should emerge from nowhere. In the first bar, use your left hand to bring in the first violins on the B♭ on an up bow and just slowly bring up your arm, but only a little. For once, it is okay to be vague about the landing point of the downbeat as the violins enter at the softest possible dynamic level. It does not matter if the actual attack is not uniform.

My own practice is to ask the first violins to start with no vibrato. I use my left hand to show a very slight crescendo while the section begins to warm up the sound with a little vibrato. The right arm then cues in the other instruments, all starting at *pianissimo*. Getting the desired sound is a function of the right hand as well.

Bowing is an especially complicated matter in this piece. For example, in the Schirmer edition, you will notice a long slur over the first three bars in the first violins. Of course, this is impossible to play in one bow, especially at a very slow tempo. We must decide where bow changes should occur in this line, and virtually all the other long phrases, so as not to interrupt the flow. Be aware that changing bow direction at a bar line can possibly result in an undesirable stress on the downbeat.

To create a more seamless sound, I adopt an approach to divisi where the outside players use one bowing and the inside players another. For example, when the work begins, all the first violins start on an up bow. Then, on the downbeat of the second measure, the inside musicians reiterate the B♭ on a down bow. They play four more slurred quarter notes and change to an up bow on the B♭ in the third beat of the second measure for the next four notes. They switch to a down bow on the D♭ in the first beat of the third bar, then to an up bow four notes later on the C in the third beat of the third measure, followed by a down bow on the downbeat of the fourth bar.

Meanwhile, the outside players also start on an up bow, but they do not change to a down bow until the first A♮ in the second measure. After that, they switch to an up bow for the next A♮ on the third beat of that bar, then to a down bow for the C on the downbeat of the third measure. Four notes later, on the third beat of that measure, they change to up bow on the D♭ and end with a down bow for the C on the downbeat of the fourth measure.

These divisi bowings must, of course, be put in the parts in advance. Although I will not give you each of the changes I make, I will point out a few key instances as we go along. Keep in mind that you do not have to do it this way and may prefer one of many alternatives in which everyone changes bow direction together.

The first measure is almost free in terms of the beat. I give two slight fermatas, one for the first violins and then another for the remainder of the strings, before establishing a tempo in the second measure. Now we come to the question of beating four half notes or eight quarter notes. Certainly, some of this depends on the tempo. I usually use my left arm to give the first few notes for the first violins in eight. Once they understand the tempo, I change to conducting in four with some subdivisions along the way.

The crescendo in the non-melodic instruments in the first measure should be very gentle, but in the third bar, the level can increase to an understated *mezzo forte*. As with the second measure, even though we see this crescendo going through the bar line, it really seems to suggest no decrease in the dynamic on the downbeat of the next bar rather than a loudening.

Now we come to perhaps the most complicated decision to make, one that will occur several times throughout the work. After the dotted half note in the fourth measure, Barber includes a comma. What does this mean?

Usually, it connotes a breath, but here it seems to mean more than that. You can find some performances in which conductors do not take much time between the end of the third beat and the first-violin reentry. This seems rushed to me and not in keeping with the solemn nature of what the music implies.

Again, think of this first note as a fermata that lasts more or less the indicated three beats. Then, cut off the orchestra with the right arm. Wait a little bit and cue in the firsts with the left hand to prevent the remainder of the strings from playing on the fourth beat. Then bring those musicians in with the right arm on the fifth beat.

It sounds complicated, but if you practice it a few times at home, working on the independence of your two arms, it becomes easier and more natural. By the way, the dynamic of the fourth measure should be perhaps *mezzo piano*, as there are several of these moments to go, and we do not want anything to sound too strong this early. When the first violins reiterate the C, they should do so at the same level as the cutoff, *mezzo piano*.

Sometimes, with the divisi bowing, everyone starts off the same and the split occurs a few notes into the phrase. This is the case for the second phrase in the first violins. In the fifth measure, after the long B♭, which should be on a down bow, the section starts the quarter-note group on an up bow. Then, on the first beat of the sixth measure, the outer players change to a down bow on the B♭, while the inner players change on the A♭. After that, each group plays four notes in one bow until the F in the eight bar.

By this time, those in the audience used to seeing all the strings bowing together may be confused, but that is not your problem. Of course, it is certainly possible, if not likely, that your preference will be to employ a unanimous bowing style for the whole piece. I am sharing my approach to the bowings, but they are not the norm.

There are a couple of moments where you can go "old school" and introduce some subtle portamentos. These must be done discreetly, or they will sound out of place within the general tone of the work, which favors simplicity. One such spot is the bar before **reh. 1**, where you could ask the first violins to gently slide up from the C to the G♭.

At **reh. 1**, the violas get their turn with the tune. But their line starts *pianissimo*, and the listener cannot easily recognize that the initial long note is the beginning of this melody. It emerges in the second bar of the phrase, where you must bring up the volume of the section enough to overtake the first violins. My solution is to increase the violas to *mezzo forte* at the end of the crescendo. Then I ask the violas to join in the divisi bowing. Starting on the indicated *pianissimo* at **reh. 1**, everyone changes to an up bow in the next bar. The outside musicians play three notes before changing to a down bow on the third beat of the bar, while the inside musicians play four notes before changing bow direction.

As I mentioned, the second bar after **reh. 1** presents a tricky balance issue. The first violins sustain a *mezzo forte* B♭ followed by a *subito piano*. Meanwhile, the violas are just beginning their moving melodic notes, which can be easily covered up. There are two options to resolve the problem. One is to add a diminuendo on the B♭, but to my ears, that takes away the first dissonance we have in the piece. The other choice, as mentioned above, and the one I prefer, is to make sure that the violas match the *mezzo forte* dynamic at the beginning of that bar.

The 6/2 bar (four measures after **reh. 1**) is not two groups of three notes but rather four beats followed by two. The violas have a comma in their part, but because the first violins have moving quarters, we cannot take the same amount of time that we did at the beginning of the piece. You can think of this comma as a quarter-note rest so that the attack of the repeated F is clear.

Two measures before **reh. 2**, I add a small crescendo to the cellos and basses to emphasize the low D♭. However, I do not put this increase in dynamic in the other string parts. I ask all the strings to make a diminuendo the bar before **reh. 2**. The first violins can add a further nuance by gently sliding down between the B♭ and A♭. A slight ritardando can be introduced as well.

At **reh. 2**, think of the whole note as if it had a fermata over it. There is no need to beat time; just indicate the cutoff when you feel the length is right. The rest on the third beat for the violins, cellos, and basses is the equivalent of the previous comma, after which the violas start the theme again.

No matter where the violas are seated onstage, I can almost guarantee that one or more musicians from another section will come in early here. You can try to give the cutoff with both arms, look intently at the violas, and attempt to lead just them. Still, you may need to stop and explain what is going to happen to avoid "premature articulation," as Glenn Dicterow, the former concertmaster of the New York Philharmonic, put it.

The 6/2 bar before **reh. 3** introduces a marking we have not yet seen. Barber places tenuto lines over four of the viola notes as well as a slur. Some conductors will do this legato, as I used to prefer. These days, I have taken to giving a little push on each of the notes in keeping with the true meaning of tenuto (held). The first violins interrupt with a *subito mezzo forte*. A few conductors have them make a crescendo to this dynamic.

Now it is the cellos' turn to play the tune. If the pace has slowed, **reh. 3** is a good place to either get back to your original tempo or, as I do, start moving ahead slightly. Often, the first violins, seeing the end of their phrase in the bars before **reh. 3**, will slow down instinctively. Nonetheless, you need to ensure that they do not.

Since we have moving notes at **reh. 3**, the cellos do not have a comma or even much of a pause between notes. I recommend using the same type of alternate divisi bowing described above at the beginning of the work in the first violins and violas. The cellos should start on the D string and move to the A string a few notes before the 5/2 bar. Why?

This is a personal matter for me, a nuance my mother suggested that I have incorporated ever since I began conducting the piece. The note that starts the 5/2 bar is a C, and the musicians are on the A string. Instead of a comma before the next C, I ask the cellists to do what is best referred to as a "shift slide" from the A string to the D without any break. The repeated C is played a little more softly than the one that begins the bar.

Getting the slide to sound graceful is not easy the first couple of times you try it. The idea is to modify the color, and the string change gives you the possibility of doing something interesting with the other musicians who enter on the fifth beat. Just after the cellos play the second note, I ask the second violins, followed by the others, to make a diminuendo to *pianississimo* by the end of the fifth beat. This creates a feeling of time being suspended.

Three bars before **reh. 4**, the music is similar to the second phrase in the first violins at the beginning of the piece. Everyone cuts off, then you wait a moment to give the cellos their cue before bringing in the rest of the musicians on the fourth beat.

Here is where the almost painful buildup begins, and for maximum effect, it pays to save some energy through nuanced dynamics. Because the textures are now thick, a couple of the entries might otherwise get lost. Putting an accent on the third beat in the seventh bar of **reh. 4** helps the seconds, but they must sustain all the quarter notes that occur after this note. The same holds true for the cellos two bars later. At this point, and perhaps before, we can go back to a unison bowing.

As the intensity grows, the number of bow strokes needed increases. Four measures before the fermata, those playing quarter notes can now play two groups of two followed by single strokes on the last four. Most conductors hold back before the *fortissimo*. At this point, you can take as many bows as necessary but observe the *sforzando* by having everyone play a strong accent. Give the strings an idea of how long you are going to hold the fermata so they can prepare to end on an up bow.

Don't move! The same holds true for the orchestra. This silence must be dramatic and clear to those in the audience who might otherwise think the piece has concluded. When you are ready to continue, move slowly so that the strings have time to get into position for an up bow.

Barber gives us another matter to address beginning seven bars after **reh. 4**, where he writes *sul* G in the second violins. He clearly wants a dark color, but this can come at a cost, possibly creating an intonation problem at the end of the quarter-note group where the notes are quite high.

My solution, if you can call it that, is to have the violins play on the D string but without vibrato. In fact, I apply this effect to all the instruments. I also separate the groups of two notes at **reh. 5**, starting with the pickups. To me, these seem like a series of "amens." I also take them out of tempo and only beat the notes rather than the whole bars. It is certainly also permissible to connect them.

At the Tempo Primo, we must make a decision about the mutes that Barber indicates (*sord. ad lib.*). The only place to put them on is during the two beats of silence that precede the Tempo Primo, which disrupts the tension created during the silence no matter which model of mute is used.

Orchestras typically ignore this instruction, although in my second recording, we observed it because we could easily stop to put on the mutes and edit the result. I wound up preferring the darker sound with the mutes off.

For the first time, we have two groups of instruments playing the tune at the Tempo Primo, and I ask them to resume playing with vibrato. Since the violas do not sit next to the first violins, the only way to even try to avoid a false entry from the other instruments is to use your left hand for the firsts while looking at the violas and giving the cue. If you are successful at preventing the other instruments from coming in, you are one of the few to accomplish this feat. Once everyone understands what is occurring and has marked it in their parts, the false entrance usually does not happen again.

As for the melody, the written dynamic is *mezzo forte*. Keep in mind that this is probably intended for performances with mutes, which of course automatically make the sound softer. The volume level is therefore more likely to be *mezzo piano* without them. As you did at the start of the piece, begin the tune in eight and switch to four when you think everyone understands your tempo.

I reintroduce the divisi bowings for the first violins in the second bar of the Tempo Primo, with the outside players moving on the A♮ and the inside players changing bow direction on the B♭. One bar before **reh. 6**, the crescendo leads all the strings to *mezzo forte*, which they sustain for three beats. The first violins repeat the C at that dynamic while the other instruments come in *piano*. Everyone makes a diminuendo, as indicated, which can be stretched out a little. It is fine if you are already *pianissimo* at **reh. 6**.

We have a little conundrum four bars before the end. Barber must have forgotten about his commas and has the first violins cutting off before the rest of the instruments. Most conductors will release everyone at the same time. We can indulge in a bit of conductorial legerdemain for the next entrance. Give the B♭ of the first violins with the left hand, indicating a bit of heft to the sound. Then show them a little diminuendo while bringing in the other instruments with your right hand, *pianissimo*. Make it clear that there are still three bars to go before arriving at the final *pianissimo*, which is really a *niente*.

When you feel that the harmony has settled to the dynamic you want, use your left hand to indicate the next three notes in the first violins. These have slight stresses, as indicated by tenuto lines. However, they are under the spell of a diminuendo, so the color changes for each note. The best bowing here is to play the A♮ on an up bow and the next two notes on down bows.

When the first violins arrive at the A♮ two bars before the end, there is no line and, therefore, no accent. Everyone holds on to this F-major chord. Keep using the left hand only for the first violins to show that their note sustains while cutting off the others with the right hand. Then give the final chord.

Here is a lovely effect that you can try for the final four bars. In my experience, it results in the best possible fadeout and ending, as the sound literally disappears. Your hands should be somewhat separated, with the left hand sustaining the first violins. Slowly bring your hands together while at the same time turning over your left hand so that the palm faces downward to indicate to the musicians that they should stop their vibrato. Instead of a traditional cutoff, simply close your hands.

When done this way, the effect can be magical. Of course, try to maintain a proper amount of silence for both musicians and audience, although the occasional cough is difficult to avoid.

Conductor's Etiquette

The ability to prevent applause is difficult to master. For this piece, as well as, for example, Tchaikovsky's Sixth Symphony or Mahler's Ninth, I often wish that the lights would fade and no clapping would occur. But that never happens. Try to avoid letting the audience see the final cutoff, should you choose to give one. Hold the position you are in without dropping your arms. Finally, when you feel enough time has elapsed, slowly relax your shoulders and gradually bring down your arms. When the applause starts, wait a bit before asking the strings to rise. Do not turn around to the public before the musicians are standing, and never take a solo bow when you return to the stage.

> There's no reason music should be difficult for an audience to understand.
>
> —Samuel Barber

Notes

1. Hollywood Bowl Symphony Orchestra, *Strings by Starlight*, conducted by Felix Slatkin, Capitol SP8444, 1959, LP.

2. Proms-Music-Vault, "BBC Proms 2001—Last Night of the Proms," September 11, 2022, https://youtu.be/YxRymFqy3E4?si=2Stt70H0wPDBigNM.

3. Detroit Symphony Orchestra, "Barber Adagio for Strings," November 28, 2016, https://youtu.be/N3MHeNt6Yjs?si=gPwz9DfC9aJ4d4ps.

4. "Barber, Samuel / Adagio for Strings (ID: 1604)," New York Philharmonic Shelby White & Leon Levy Digital Archives, https://archives.nyphil.org/index.php/artifact/e06a857a-1bfd-4d92-80a1-06acd103d0d2-0.1/.

5. Samuel Barber, *Adagio for Strings* (New York: G. Schirmer, Inc., 1939).

Benjamin Britten:
The Young Person's Guide to the Orchestra

Music does not excite until it is performed.

—Benjamin Britten

Szalay Zoltán, CC BY-SA 3.0 https://creativecommons.org/licenses/by-sa/3.0, via Wikimedia Commons

It occurred to me that this particular essay could be called "The Young Conductor's Guide to *The Young Person's Guide*."

Fledgling podium minders will more than likely encounter *The Young Person's Guide to the Orchestra*, along with Prokofiev's *Peter and the Wolf* and Saint-Saëns's *The Carnival of the Animals*, very early in their careers. Frequently programmed on children's concerts, this work has also been used as a showpiece for orchestras ever since its premiere in 1946.

Its pedigree does not trace back to the concert hall, originally. Rather, the British Ministry of Education commissioned and presented it as a short film called *Instruments of the Orchestra*, directed by distinguished film composer Muir Mathieson and featuring the London Symphony Orchestra under the direction of Sir Malcolm Sargent.[1]

Eric Crozier, who directed and produced Britten's 1945 opera *Peter Grimes*, wrote the spoken commentary to supplement the music. Because of the very Englishness of the words, various versions have been presented, replacing terms like penny-whistle and side drum with recorder and snare drum. And over the years, several authors and speakers have rewritten the full narration.

Sargent realized from the moment he saw the score that this would be an ideal work on its own, without narration. He gave the first concert performance in Liverpool a month before the film was released.

The work is subtitled "Variations and Fugue on a Theme of Henry Purcell," the name by which it is known when performed without narration. The aforementioned theme is taken from "Rondeau," the second movement of Purcell's incidental music to the play *Abdelazer*, composed in 1695.[2]

Performing the work with narrator is quite different from a straight-out orchestral performance, and each presentation method poses different challenges. This piece is not as easy to conduct as it sounds. As we go through the work, I will try to point out the differences and the skills needed to bring it to life, regardless of how it is executed.

For a work written in the middle of the twentieth century, it is surprisingly sparse in its orchestration, aside from the percussion—no English horn, bass clarinet, or contrabassoon, and only two trumpets. Of course, this makes the work easier to perform with smaller forces, but the degree of difficulty is high for many in the orchestra.

The instrumentation is as follows: two flutes and piccolo, two oboes, two clarinets in B♭ and A, two bassoons, four horns in F, two trumpets in C, three trombones, tuba, timpani, percussion (the score calls for five players, but it can be done with four), harp, and strings (my minimum size is 10-8-6-6-4 players).

Now comes the bad news: This work is still in copyright and therefore not available on IMSLP. However, its publisher, Boosey & Hawkes, offers a relatively low-cost edition.[3] It should be in every conductor's library.

Britten devises a clever way to handle rehearsal indications. For the opening portions, he simply assigns a letter to each of the sections, calling them **Theme A**, **Theme B**, etc. Each instrumental group corresponds with a letter as they appear. Thus, the flutes are **Variation A**, oboes **Variation B**, and so forth. For the fugue, he returns to the beginning of the alphabet, marking a new rehearsal letter when each instrumental group joins in.

Before we start, please look at how Britten has indicated the way to play the piece both with and without narration. It can be confusing and, sometimes, in the heat of the moment, you might forget which ending corresponds with the version you are actually doing.

The general rule is to utilize the first endings when performing it with the spoken commentary and the second endings when playing it without narration. Sometimes the words are long enough to take up several bars and cross over the pages of the score. Some conductors will tape in pieces of paper to cover up the sections that do not apply to the version they are performing. Until you have done the work several times, I suggest something along this line, cumbersome as it is.

Assuming you are mostly sticking to what Crozier wrote, the coordination between the music and text is clear. If the occasional word or phrase will be altered, I recommend penciling in the changes; otherwise, you risk confusion between what you see and what you hear.

The composer does not provide metronome marks, and this is understandable. A few of the variations are somewhat virtuosic, and the speed can vary wildly between the soloists in different orchestras. Britten, himself an excellent conductor, must have sensed a need for flexibility. The opening is marked *Allegro maestoso e largamente*. This seems contradictory until you go back to Elgar, who also used *largamente* as a feeling rather than a speed. The piece starts at single *forte*, imparting a truly noble English sensibility to this section.

The staccatos on the eighth notes in the upper strings, woodwinds, and trumpets should be played a bit heavier, not overly short. You will find crescendos, starting in the third bar, that tell you neither how loud to get nor the dynamic at which to start. You will be able to figure this out quickly. Interestingly, the only instruments to play a *forte-piano* are the first trumpet and bass drum here in the third bar.

Let's deal with the narrated version first. The speaker enters somewhere between the fourth and fifth bars of the first ending, depending on the speed at which the words are recited, as well as what text is used. Britten has placed these entrances based on the Crozier version.

Where does the narrator stand onstage? Unless they are conversant with the score, they need to see you clearly. The speaker is usually placed to the conductor's left, receiving cues from the left hand. Try to give these entrances discreetly to keep the audience's attention on the words rather than the visual aspect.

Often, the narrator does not read music. You are fortunate if they do and even more lucky if they can decipher a score, in which case you have no cues to give. But let's say that our star is not only unable to understand what is on the page but also insecure about how to present the text.

I recommend meeting with the narrator, just as you would a soloist, prior to their first rehearsal, to answer any questions and make them feel comfortable, especially if this is their first time performing with an orchestra. Encourage them to focus on engaging the listeners and enhancing the experience by reciting the text slowly and clearly.

Hopefully you will get a sense of your narrator's pacing and capabilities during the meeting and can start to make judgements about the timing of your cues. It is better if they end their commentary early rather than right at the last moment, or worse, during the next section. On the other hand, bringing in the speaker too soon can result in an undesirable lull in the action.

Britten lends a helping hand by inserting fermatas, most of the time, in the last bar of a section. This allows us to wait if the speaker is behind the orchestra. But if the opposite is true, then simply conduct through the measure.

For the orchestra-only version, go directly from the second ending into the next section, in this case, **Theme B**. Since the orchestra is alone, ignore the fermata. The final crescendo can be very pronounced since it leads into the next theme.

Theme C calls for a rich single *forte* for all the brass. Pay particular attention to ensure that the two trumpets match each other in sound and color. Sometimes, if it feels like the speaker is slow, conductors will hold back the tempo a bit at this first ending to avoid the fermata.

Theme D is played on the string and marcato. This includes the quarter notes in the fourth bar and onward. If narrated, just wait until the speaker is finished. When played without a narrator, just one bar of bass-drum roll will suffice.

Theme E presents the first problem regarding the number of percussionists needed. The final bar of this theme indicates a trill in all the instruments, and five players are required to do that as written. But wait! If the cymbal has a roll, what happens in the second and fourth bars? Indeed, those must be clashed with two plates, and the player then has two bars to put them down and get to the suspended cymbal.

Okay. If we have just four percussionists, what do we do? Certainly, we need the bass drum and cymbal. The tambourine is an effective color, so by process of elimination, the triangle is the instrument to go. The tune is divided between the timpani and snare drum. You have a couple of choices for the fermata: Since there is no narration, you can ignore it, making a stark *forte-piano* and starting the crescendo immediately. Alternatively, you can stretch it out, holding on to the soft dynamic a bit longer before getting louder.

Theme F begins without a narrated introduction. Sometimes, conductors will be a bit *pesante* one bar before the first Presto. In some ways, this section is the trickiest to coordinate with the text because you must guess how long each of the fermatas should last. To eliminate this uncertainty, consider only observing the fermata in the final bar. When performing without the words, go straight through and have the flutes play the figures that are indicated by smaller-than-usual notes in the score.

If you are using the original commentary, these days it may not be proper to refer to the piccolo as "the shrill little brother" of the flute.

I should mention the marking of *près de la table sempre* in the harp line, which asks the musician to pluck near the soundboard. This produces a dry and distinct sonority. Here it makes a nice harmonic difference between the flutes and the tremolo D in the second violins.

Variation A stays in the previous tempo. Follow the dynamics scrupulously, observing the difference between *mezzo forte-pianissimo* and *forte-piano*, in particular. Although marked Presto, this is more in the category of an Allegro. As before, when you have a narrator, just wait on the final fermata as needed. If leading the orchestra alone, most conductors will make a ritard before commencing the next variation.

Conducted in eight, **Variation B** features the oboe. Pay attention to the slight separation between the dotted eighths and sixteenths in the violas and cellos. Britten tells us when to allow for rubato and when to stay in tempo. Give the first oboe as much time as they would like to shape the *espressivo* passages. Without the speaker, I make a slight ritard in the last bar.

The speed of the eighth note becomes that of the dotted quarter for the next section, **Variation C**. I tend to choose a Moderato tempo, ♩. = 64, just relaxed enough to allow the clarinets to fit in all the notes without rushing. The open E string in the third bar is a nice touch, but the composer seems to want the sound to be stopped, as he wrote a wedge over the note. Most conductors let it ring a bit to allow the listener to hear this unusual sound.

The first clarinet will follow your lead coming out of the first fermata—just hold the second beat and start up again in the tempo. The fermata that occurs five bars later works differently because you have to wait until the run starts before giving the gesture for the next measure. It is quite nice if the clarinet almost disappears at the end of this scale. Usually, conductors allow some freedom two measures before the 4/4.

The march at **Variation D** has a bit of a pompous character, and a tempo of around ♩ = 112 seems about right. The sixteenths in the strings should be played on the quick side. You must set the speed for the rubato bars to keep the basses together. In fact, you should focus most of your attention in this variation on the steady rhythm, allowing the bassoons to play on their own.

The score is missing a return to *a tempo* in the measures following these somewhat free ones. I have seen conductors completely forget to give the fourth beat of the *molto rall.* (this happened to me). Do not make that mistake. The bar before the two endings usually contains a ritard for the second bassoon.

No matter which ending you are doing, it is effective if the clarinets can enter underneath the horns and then emerge with their trill. I don't really know why Britten put in a *molto rit.* in the version without narration.

Variation E virtually explodes with the violins' entrance. Beginning in the ninth measure, we can imagine the stunning visual effect of the dialogue between the firsts and seconds if they are split on opposite sides of the stage, hurling these phrases back and forth. However, I do not recommend changing your setup just for the sake of this one variation.

This section is played on the string, using as full a bow as possible. You might be tempted to slightly exaggerate the mazurka rhythm, but I think playing it straightforward is more in character with the piece.

Four measures before the repeated bar, the horns have some accents to observe. The pizzicatos are played *non divisi*, but when the scale appears, I ask at least one stand to play only the lower notes so they can be heard more clearly. How many times do we play the last bar if performing without a narrator? I usually opt for three times total, which seems like more than enough. I also add a diminuendo and a ritard the last time.

Since other pieces utilize this same sort of *ad lib.* repetition, I should mention how to convey the transition to the next measure. Hold your left hand up just a bit while beating time with only the right hand. When you are ready to continue, indicate this by moving the left hand as if giving the upbeat for the next bar.

Variation F allows the violas a chance to shine. All we are told is *Meno mosso*; the tempo itself is determined by the speed of the cello variation that comes next. I prefer a speed around ♩ = 72, not too slow. The violas will manage most of the dynamics well enough on their own. Meanwhile, your job is to coordinate all those punctuated eighth notes.

The transition into the next variation presents an example of the narration working against the overall line. If you get stuck having to make a ritard and hold a fermata, you lose the sense of connection to the next section, whereas without the text, you simply stay in tempo.

In **Variation G**, Britten writes a series of slight diminuendos for the viola. We can lean on the first notes of those figures a bit each time they occur for a lovely effect.

As for the cellos, a discreet portamento lends a nice expressive touch in a couple of places, the first of which happens at the end of the third bar when they ascend from an F♯ to an E♮. The other requires more explanation. Six measures before the end of **Variation G**, the cellists play the D♮ on the A string. Then, they can shift over to the D string, with a touch of a portamento, for the C♮, resulting in a slightly darker sound.

If you employ a speaker, try to time the bassoon's last bar so that you do not have to make a fermata on the final note. Without the narrator, a slight ritard will help establish the tempo that starts off the basses.

Beginning **Variation H** is not easy. Believe it or not, the basses will mostly go their own way. They know how fast—or slow—this begins. Your job is to get the woodwinds and tambourine together. Follow the lead of the lower instruments, arriving at the Allegro with a speed around ♩ = 132. They might get a little behind your beat for the legato moment.

At the *rall. molto*, go into three for the triplet and then transition into two for the next bar. Sometimes conductors will separate the two notes here, but I like to connect them in reference to what I think is an unintentional quote from the opening bassoon passage of Tchaikovsky's "Pathétique" Symphony. I doubt that even seasoned concertgoers will think of it this way, so I am just throwing it out there for your consideration.

Stay in tempo for the woodwinds' five-bar passage before the double bar and do not slow down. Then, beat twice as slowly at the 2/2. It can help to go into one for the last measure to show what your beat will be for the next three or four bars. With narration, this is a four-measure phrase, and without, it is a three-measure phrase with a change of harmony in each bar. It is quite easy to overlook the excluded bar the way it is printed.

Interestingly, Britten instructs the violins to play tremolos during this transition, but they have two notes. Probably no one has ever misconstrued this, but it raises a question: what is a tremolo versus a trill? Normally, we see the indication for the former over just one note. The violins move the bow quickly to produce the desired effect. And a trill is between two notes, but stepwise. Here Britten combines the two.

Variation I can present balance issues. If you are doing it for an audience of actual young people, I recommend placing the harp somewhere that will enable the listeners to see the instrument, probably near the edge of the stage, for a striking visual effect.

Just when we resolved the trill/tremolo matter, now we find a true misnomer. Britten asks for a gong, but that is incorrect. Perhaps in Great Britain this terminology is acceptable, but the gong is a pitched instrument, whereas the tam-tam does not produce an audible note. This variation benefits from the rich, resonant, dark sound of the tam-tam.

Going into the seventh bar, you have to be really accurate with your upbeat to get the most precise attack from the brass. This note is played with mutes, but somewhat aggressively, quite the opposite of the featured instrument.

The tempo remains the same for **Variation J**, but here we beat in three. The low strings play an exaggerated ponticello, almost on top of the bridge. The sixteenth notes in the horns should be performed quickly but very audibly. It is impossible for the basses to get to the pizzicato in the fourth bar as written. They have to stop the tremolo somewhere and more than likely will do this on your third beat. You can also opt for half the section to drop out on beat three to play the pizzicato, with the others joining in after them.

In the fourth measure, the solo violas and cellos should blend into the sonority of the horns. I don't really have the horns play a short quarter note in this measure, instead waiting until they fade out and the strings emerge. The harp's low notes are barely audible when the instrument is in the distance, another argument for placing it on the outside.

Throughout this variation, the timpanist is asked to play with snare-drum sticks, but some musicians who use calfskin heads might prefer wooden mallets instead. No matter where the harp is placed, it needs to be quite a bit louder than marked for the last four bars.

The tempo of **Variation K** entirely depends on how fast the two trumpeters can play it. For the reading, take it in two, around ♩ = 152, but be prepared to do it faster if the musicians ask for this later, in which case you might want to consider conducting it in one.

As with the previous *ad lib.* repetition, just keep beating time with the right arm, moving the left only when you are ready to continue. I suggest that you conduct in two for these final two bars.

Most conductors take **Variation L** at what we would consider a less-than-allegro tempo, a noble and almost Elgarian speed along the lines of ♩ = 92. Britten tells us that the featured trombone and tuba are to play sostenuto, while the woodwind and other brass play short eighth notes. The climax, when the low brass increase their volume to just single *forte*, has short quarters for the accompanying instruments. We can interpret the *più forte* to mean crescendo, getting us to the *fortissimo*. If you are using the original text, the narrator should begin speaking a bar earlier than indicated.

Next, the percussion section shines in the wonderful **Variation M**, which showcases a few of the individual instruments. Let the players decide which mallets and sticks to use; should you disagree with a particular choice, you can let them know later. The cues for the speaker are listed clearly and all work well.

I find it helpful to rehearse this variation one time without percussion to illuminate some of the finer details taking place elsewhere in the orchestra. Suddenly, you hear harmonies that might otherwise go unnoticed and can highlight the sound effects that emulate what is going on with the solo instruments.

The strings bounce their bows for the triplets, giving a somewhat Spanish flavor to this variation. Little felicitous details make **Variation M**, in some ways, the most interesting of all. But Britten does not provide supplemental rehearsal numbers or letters to help us, should we need to stop and start somewhere other than the beginning. It can be helpful for the librarian to put a few in to mark where the different percussion instruments enter.

It is more fun to let you discover the hidden gems, so I am not going to give too many of them away. However, I will point out the nuances in the strings that occur every so often. For example, the violas and cellos have a marvelous dissonance in the final triangle bar, and the basses have a stunning sudden *forte* at the end of the xylophone phrase.

Please take time to peruse this section carefully and savor the inventive way the composer writes for percussion. He does allow for fewer players near the end and tells us which instruments to omit if need be.

The final spoken section shows the violins playing triple *piano* but also calls for a diminuendo. Just let the sound fade out at the end, not bothering to work on getting down to quadruple *piano*.

Now we come to the magnificent Fugue, one of the finest twentieth-century examples of the form. Here Britten shows off his contrapuntal chops while sticking to the same game plan that he has established over the previous fifteen minutes to introduce the individual instruments.

Tempos for the Fugue can vary significantly, and the conductor's choice will be based on the ability of the musicians to negotiate the speed. I find it helpful to think ahead to the time when the Purcell tune reappears. If the Fugue starts too slow, this can feel lugubrious rather than triumphant. And if it begins too fast, the notes will blur as more instruments pile on. I suggest a speed around ♩ = 152. Occasionally, a conductor will try to conduct this in one—it does not work.

Pay close attention to the number of bars between the entrances of each instrumental group. Fortunately, the score includes rehearsal letters, should we need to stop and start. Meanwhile, be equally mindful of the dynamics, as Britten is very specific about how to achieve the balances he envisions.

Many years ago, I was shown a clever bowing for the violins when they enter, both firsts and seconds: They use a down bow as indicated at **Letter E** and then play the next six separated eighth notes all on up bows. This only occurs for the first two appearances of this phrase in each section. In my experience, the violinists wind up really enjoying this bowing. You cannot do it with the violas, as they are playing *forte*.

Letter H through **Letter I** is a transitional passage, and you must make a very big diminuendo to help the harp get through at that entrance. Five measures before **Letter J** represents another transitional moment that requires a decisive crescendo in the last bar to set up the stentorian horns. Some conductors and horn sections will try to play the complete tune rather than dividing it up as written—more power to them if it works. The same holds true for the trumpets. It is a bit tougher for the trombones to play the complete tune coming off the glissando, so it is best to let them play this as written. You can ask the tuba to play all the notes as well.

Letter M brings back the percussion, and I have heard many performances in which they are banging away *fortissimo*, obscuring the music going on underneath. Only the snare drum and tambourine have what amounts to the melody, and their dynamic is single *forte*.

I am always puzzled by Britten's indications for the brass just before the time-signature change to 3/4. They have some interesting material, especially the triplets that almost seem out of place. Try rehearsing this lead-in without the percussion one time and see what you think.

The grand moment arrives and, of course, the question of "how do I beat this?" arises along with it. In my early days as a conductor, I used to get quite fancy, conducting the bars without the duple rhythm in three and the others in one. This worked fine until I got to the *fortissimo*, where I would pray that somehow, we would all be together three measures before the *Animato*.

I finally realized that everybody knows the tune inside out, including not only the notes but also the steady pulse. They are only looking for the occasional downbeat; they understand how to fit in everything else. So now, like most of my colleagues, I just stay in three for the whole passage.

The *Animato* is just a tad faster. Strive to emphasize the accents in the timpani and snare drum. I usually slow down a bit three bars before the end, kind of a *subito poco meno mosso*. Go into six for the eighth notes two measures before the end, closing on a sonorous D-major chord. It is possible to consider asking the double basses to play the low D here, but the composer has written below the E elsewhere and more than likely did not want that effect.

Thus ends one of the most remarkable pieces in the literature, one we often take for granted. Reappraisal and study show us that there is so much more to the work than the title suggests. Perhaps we can add our own moniker and call the piece "The Musician's Guide to the Wonders of the Orchestra."

Conductor's Etiquette

Solo bows are unnecessary for members of the orchestra, but if you wish, you might want to have the different sections rise as a group. Treat the narrator in the same manner as any soloist, except without giving them a moment alone when reentering the stage. And of course, no encore.

> The old idea of a composer suddenly having a terrific idea and sitting up all night to write it is nonsense. Nighttime is for sleeping.
>
> —Benjamin Britten

Notes

1. *Instruments of the Orchestra*, directed by Muir Mathieson (London: BFI National Archive on behalf of the National Archives, 1946).

2. Henry Purcell, *Abdelazer* Suite, ed. Hilmar Höckner (New York: E. F. Kalmus, n.d.).

3. Benjamin Britten, *The Young Person's Guide to the Orchestra Op. 34: Variations and Fugue on a Theme of Purcell* (London: Boosey & Hawkes Ltd., 1946).

Bibliography

Argyle, Ray. *Scott Joplin and the Age of Ragtime*. Jefferson, NC: McFarland, 2009.
Barber, Samuel. *Adagio for Strings*. New York: G. Schirmer, Inc., 1939.
"Barber, Samuel / Adagio for Strings (ID: 1604)." New York Philharmonic Shelby White & Leon Levy Digital Archives. https://archives.nyphil.org/index.php/artifact/e06a857a-1bfd-4d92-80a1-06acd103d0d2-0.1/.
Bartók, Béla. *Concerto for Orchestra*. London: Hawkes & Son Ltd., 1946.
Britten, Benjamin. *The Young Person's Guide to the Orchestra Op. 34: Variations and Fugue on a Theme of Purcell*. London: Boosey & Hawkes Ltd., 1946.
"A Conductor's No-Nonsense Response to a Tempo Dilemma." *Classical Source*, February 10, 2023. https://www.classicalsource.com/article/a-conductors-no-nonsense-response-to-a-tempo-dilemma/.
Copland, Aaron. *Appalachian Spring: Suite for Full Orchestra*. New York: Boosey & Hawkes Inc., 1945.
Crown, Tom. "What Is a Mute?" Tom Crown Mutes. Accessed September 8, 2023. http://www.tomcrownmutes.com/learn_history.html.
Davies, Margaret. "Review of 'Gershwin Spectacular.'" *Musical Opinion* (December 2000). http://www.jackgibbons.com/reviews.htm.
Debussy, Claude. *La Mer*. Edited by Marie Rolf. *Oeuvres complètes*, vol. 5. Paris: Durand, 1997.
Debussy, Claude. *La Mer: Three Symphonic Sketches*. Edited by Douglas Woodfull-Harris. Kassel, Germany: Bärenreiter-Verlag Urtext, 2014.
Debussy, Claude. *Three Great Orchestral Works in Full Score: Prélude à l'après-midi d'un faune, Nocturnes, La Mer*. New York: Dover Publications, 1983.
Detroit Symphony Orchestra. "Barber Adagio for Strings." November 28, 2016. https://youtu.be/N3MHeNt6Yjs?si=gPwz9DfC9aJ4d4ps.

Bibliography

Discography of American Historical Recordings, s.v. "Victor matrix CVE-49711. An American in Paris / Nathaniel Shilkret; Victor Symphony Orchestra." Accessed September 7, 2023. https://adp.library.ucsb.edu/index.php/matrix/detail/800023424/CVE-49711-An_American_in_Paris.

"Evgeny Mravinsky Conducts Shostakovich Symphony no. 5—video 1973." You Tube video. https://youtu.be/eQOMsLmzJ8c.

Gershwin, George. *An American in Paris*. New York: New World Music Corporation, 1930.

Gershwin, George. *An American in Paris for Orchestra (1928)*, revised by Frank Campbell-Watson [c. 1943]. London: Chappell & Co. Ltd., copyright 1930.

Gershwin, George. *An American in Paris: A Tone Poem for Orchestra (1928)*. Edited by Mark Clague. Based on the George and Ira Gershwin Critical Edition, series 1, vol. 1. Ann Arbor: The Gershwin Initiative, University of Michigan, 2017.

Gershwin, George. *Rhapsody in Blue / An American in Paris*. Hollywood Bowl Symphony Orchestra. Conducted by Felix Slatkin. Capitol P8343, 1956, LP.

"Glossary of Musical Terms." Boosey & Hawkes. https://www.boosey.com/cr/musicalterms.

Hollywood Bowl Symphony Orchestra. *Strings by Starlight*. Conducted by Felix Slatkin. Capitol SP8444, 1959, LP.

Instruments of the Orchestra. Directed by Muir Mathieson. London: BFI National Archive on behalf of the National Archives, 1946.

International Music Score Library Project (IMSLP)/Petrucci Music Library. https://imslp.org.

New York Philharmonic Shelby White & Leon Levy Digital Archives. https://archives.nyphil.org.

Proms-Music-Vault. "BBC Proms 2001—Last Night of the Proms." September 11, 2022. https://youtu.be/YxRymFqy3E4?si=2Stt70H0wPDBigNM.

Purcell, Henry. *Abdelazer* Suite. Edited by Hilmar Höckner. New York: E. F. Kalmus, n.d.

Sandow, Hyman. "Gershwin Presents a New Work." *Musical America* 48, no. 18 (18 August 1928): 5, 12. Accessed August 31, 2023. https://archive.org/details/sim_musical-america_1928-08-18_48_18/.

Shostakovich, Dmitri. *Symphony No. 5 in D Minor, Op. 47*. Berlin: Sikorski, 2002.

"Shostakovich, Dmitri / Symphony No. 5, D Minor, op. 47 (ID: 1590)." New York Philharmonic Shelby White & Leon Levy Digital Archives. https://archives.nyphil.org/index.php/artifact/8e3fcd6c-4881-4794-9e6e-1501e7da7036-0.1/fullview#page/160/mode/2up.

Shostakovich, Dmitri Dmitrievich, Solomon Volkov, and Buis Antonina. *Testimony: The Memoirs of Dmitri Shostakovich*. New York: Harper & Row, 1979.

Solti, Georg, and Harvey Sachs. *Memoirs*. New York: Alfred A. Knopf, 1997.

"A Soviet Artist's Practical Creative Reply to Just Criticism." Oxford Reference. https://www.oxfordreference.com/view/10.1093/oi/authority.20110803100520427.

Stravinsky, Igor. *The Rite of Spring/Le Sacre du Printemps: Pictures from Pagan Russia in Two Parts*. London: Boosey & Hawkes Music Publishers Ltd., revised 1947, reengraved edition 1967.

"Stravinsky, Igor / *Le Sacre du Printemps*, Score and Parts (ID: 2341)." New York Philharmonic Shelby White & Leon Levy Digital Archives. https://archives.nyphil.org/index.php/artifact/1c7db356-3bd9-4a60-b9ad-3fa94cb07d03-0.1.

Taruskin, Richard. *Stravinsky and the Russian Traditions: A Biography of the Works through Mavra*. Oxford: Oxford University Press, 1996.

Taylor, Deems. Concert program, December 13, 1928, Program ID 4911. New York Philharmonic Shelby White & Leon Levy Digital Archives. https://archives.nyphil.org/index.php/artifact/f08aa3f0-c460-4f1e-85ec-4dd6d1bc0d09-0.1.

About the Author

Internationally acclaimed conductor **Leonard Slatkin** is Music Director Laureate of the Detroit Symphony Orchestra, Directeur Musical Honoraire of the Orchestre National de Lyon, Conductor Laureate of the St. Louis Symphony Orchestra, and Principal Guest Conductor of the Orquesta Filarmónica de Gran Canaria. He maintains a rigorous schedule of guest conducting throughout the world and is active as a composer, author, and educator.

A recipient of the prestigious National Medal of Arts, Slatkin also holds the rank of Chevalier in the French Legion of Honor. He has received the Prix Charbonnier from the Federation of Alliances Françaises, Austria's Decoration of Honor in Silver, the League of American Orchestras' Gold Baton Award, and the 2013 ASCAP Deems Taylor Special Recognition Award for his debut book, *Conducting Business*. His second book, *Leading Tones: Reflections on Music, Musicians, and the Music Industry*, was published in 2017, followed by *Classical Crossroads: The Path Forward for Music in the 21st Century* (2021).

Slatkin has also held posts as Music Director of the New Orleans, St. Louis, and National symphony orchestras, and he was Chief Conductor of the BBC Symphony Orchestra. He has served as Principal Guest Conductor of London's Philharmonia and Royal Philharmonic, the Pittsburgh Symphony Orchestra, the Los Angeles Philharmonic at the Hollywood Bowl, and the Minnesota Orchestra. He makes his home in St. Louis with his wife, composer Cindy McTee.

www.ingramcontent.com/pod-product-compliance
Lightning Source LLC
Chambersburg PA
CBHW020737230426
43665CB00009B/470